SAVING YELLOWSTONE

Center Point
Large Print

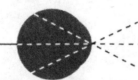

**This Large Print Book carries the
Seal of Approval of N.A.V.H.**

SAVING YELLOWSTONE

Exploration and Preservation in Reconstruction America

MEGAN KATE NELSON

CENTER POINT LARGE PRINT
THORNDIKE, MAINE

For Anne Moore and Marlys Ferrill

CONTENTS

SAVING YELLOWSTONE

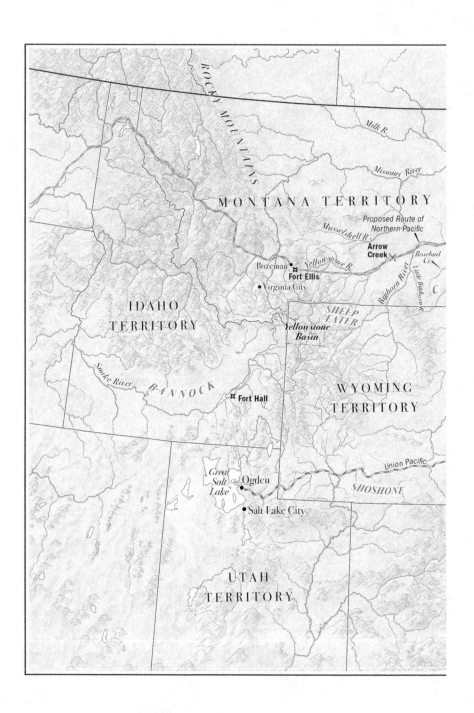

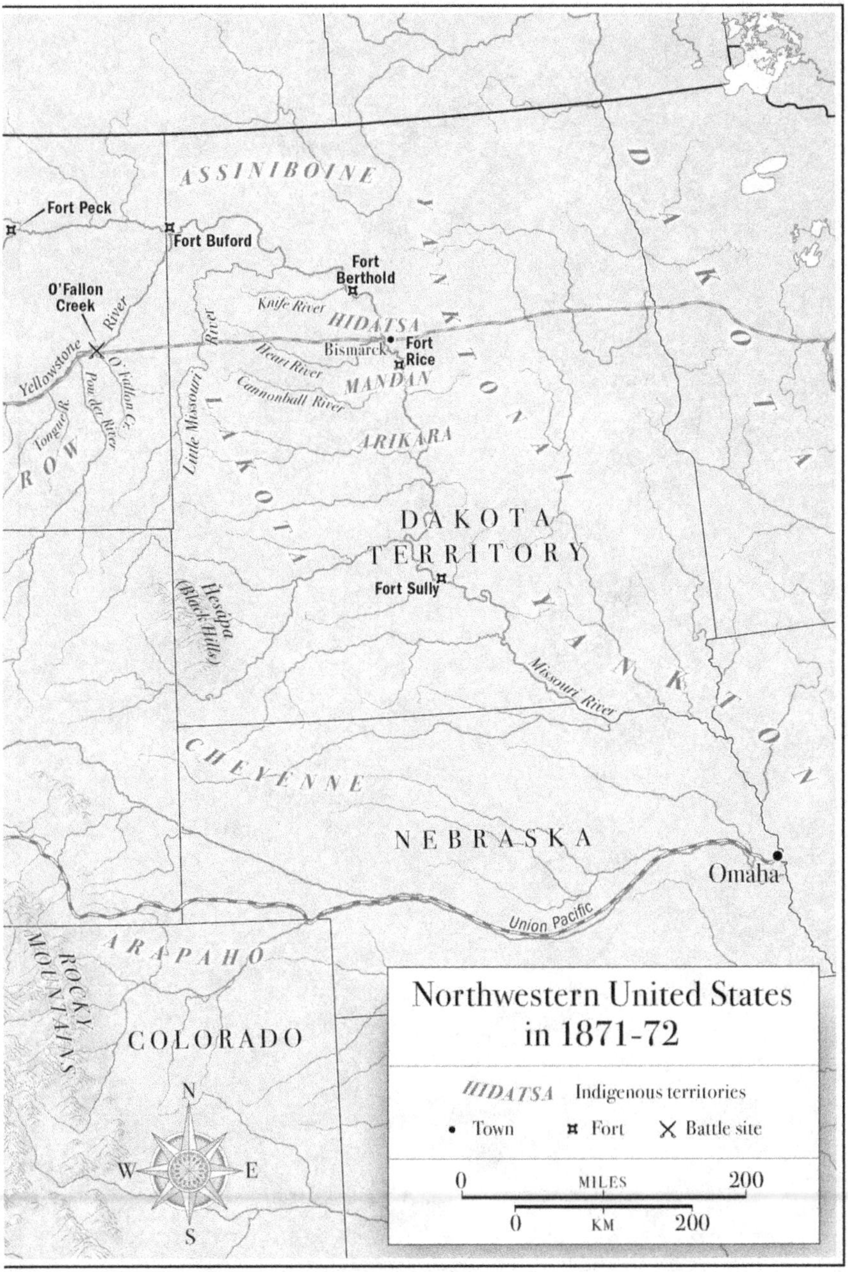

Northwestern United States in 1871-72
HIDATSA Indigenous territories
Town
Fort
Battle site
0 MILES 200
0 KM 200
ASSINIBOINE
Fort Peck
Fort Buford
Fort Berthold
O'Fallon Creek
Knife River
HIDATSA
Yellowstone River
Bismarck
Fort Rice
Heart River
MANDAN
Cannonball River
O'Fallon Cr.
Powder River
Tongue R.
ROW
Little Missouri River
LAKOTA
ARIKARA
YANKTONAI
DAKOTA
DAKOTA TERRITORY
Fort Sully
Hesapa (Black Hills)
Missouri River
YANKTON
CHEYENNE
NEBRASKA
Omaha
Union Pacific
ARAPAHO
ROCKY MOUNTAINS
COLORADO
N
W
E
S

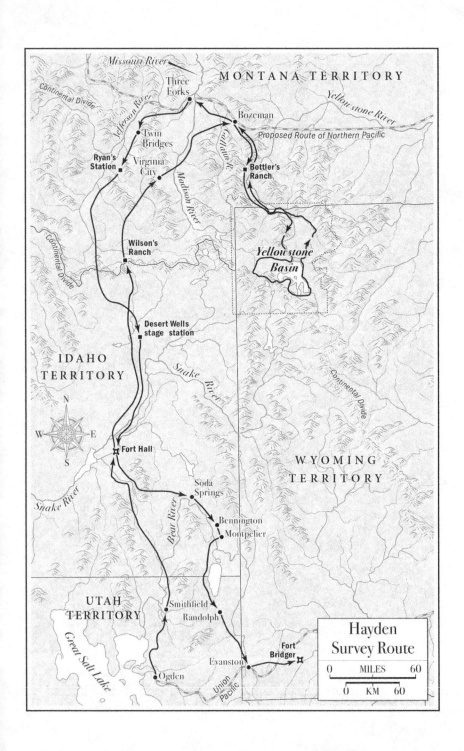

Missouri River

MONTANA TERRITORY

Continental Divide

Three Forks

Jefferson River

Yellowstone River

Bozeman

Proposed Route of Northern Pacific

Twin Bridges

Gallatin R.

Ryan's Station

Virginia City

Bottler's Ranch

Madison River

Continental Divide

Wilson's Ranch

Yellowstone Basin

Desert Wells stage station

IDAHO TERRITORY

Snake River

Continental Divide

N
W   E
S

Fort Hall

WYOMING TERRITORY

Soda Springs

Bear River

Snake River

Bennington

Montpelier

UTAH TERRITORY

Smithfield

Randolph

Great Salt Lake

Fort Bridger

Evanston

Ogden

Union Pacific

Hayden Survey Route

0   MILES   60

0   KM   60

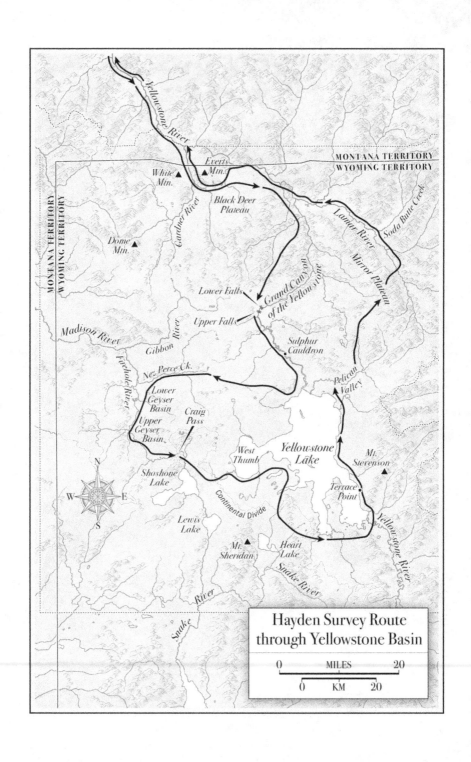

Hayden Survey Route
through Yellowstone Basin

MILES
0   20

KM
0   20

PROLOGUE

Lost

The Cut, Montana Territory. October 1870.

T he dog stopped along the trail ahead of him, growling. Yellowstone Jack Baronett reined in his horse and dismounted, taking his gun from the saddle. He soon saw what had captured the dog's attention: an animal was dragging itself slowly up the side of the Cut, a narrow canyon through the Gallatin Mountains leading to the Yellowstone Basin beyond. A black bear, Jack thought, possibly wounded. He approached warily, his feet crunching on the hard crust of three-day snow. Drawing closer, he could see that it was not a bear. It was a man.

He was crawling on his knees and elbows and making a low, groaning noise. His clothes were in tatters, his long beard matted. His fingers curled into claws. The skin on his face and arms was thin and translucent, clinging to his bones like wet paper.

This could be the man Yellowstone Jack had been looking for. The explorer whose friends had put up a bounty for his return. The man who had been given up for lost.

"Are you Truman Everts?" he asked.

The man looked up at Jack through half-closed eyes.

"Yes," he croaked. "All that is left of him."

Jack smiled.

"We have come for you," he said.

"I am saved!" Everts whispered, and collapsed on the trail, unconscious.

Six weeks before Jack found him in the Cut, Truman Everts said goodbye to his nineteen-year-old daughter, Bessie, and left the small mining town of Helena, Montana, to join an expedition to Yellowstone Basin. He was an unlikely candidate for an adventure in the wilderness. A fifty-four-year-old widower who was terribly nearsighted, Everts had served as Assessor of Internal Revenue for Montana Territory for several years until his term ended in February 1870. He was preparing to return to the East Coast with Bessie in July when a few friends suggested a scout of the Yellowstone country. Everts was no mountain man, but he could ride a horse and shoot a gun. He was reasonably sure he could handle himself on the roughest of mountain trails, or in a fight with Crow or Shoshone warriors they might run across.

And Everts was curious. In 1870, despite the arrival of thousands of Americans and European immigrants in the Great Northwest—

an area extending from the western edge of the Great Lakes to the Pacific coast—Yellowstone remained beyond the reach of the territorial or the federal government. The Basin was hemmed in by four mountain ranges; on maps of the region made in the 1870s, they looked like the rim of a giant crater. Slicing through them were narrow canyons like the Cut, created by rivers clawing their way from the Basin through the mountains and into the broad valleys of Montana and Wyoming.

The largest of these waterways was the Yellowstone, which rushed through the Gallatin Mountains before arcing to the north and east toward the Missouri River. Crow and Lakota peoples called the river Heȟáka (Elk), but French traders working at forts along the Missouri in the eighteenth century recorded the name that the Gros Ventre gave it: Mi-tse-a-daz-i (Yellow Rock River), after the rocks that lined its banks downstream.

Along the Yellowstone River and the Basin's other waterways were paths cut into the soil by the hooves of horses and the edges of the travois (sledges) they pulled. For thousands of years, Blackfoot, Nez Perce, Crow, Shoshone, and Bannock bands crossed Yellowstone Basin in all seasons, on their way to hunt buffalo and elk in the Great Plains. One band of Shoshones, known as the Tududeka (Sheepeaters) for the animals they raised, lived most of the year in the mountain ranges encircling the Basin.

In the early nineteenth century, French, English, and American trappers followed the trails that these Indigenous peoples had made. Most returned. The stories they told, of thundering waterfalls and cliffs made of glass, of mud volcanoes and geysers that exploded out of the ground in huge clouds of steam and boiling water, seemed absurd. Everyone knew that trappers were inveterate liars who loved a good story. It seemed foolhardy to believe them. And yet. What if these stories were true?

In 1860 a U.S. military expedition came close to entering Yellowstone country from the southeast side, but the Wind River Range, with its saw-toothed peaks still covered in snow in midsummer, made it a physical impossibility. Local miners made plans to explore Yellowstone during the Civil War and the years after, but they had failed to raise funding or secure military escorts to protect them from Indigenous bands who saw them as trespassers. In 1869, a three-man team set out on their own and returned after more than a month in the Yellowstone, confirming many of the details of the trappers' tales. When these men tried to publish their stories in national newspapers, editors refused, believing that they were lying. Within Montana Territory, however, these amateur explorations gave new credence to reports of the trappers and spurred men like Truman Everts to seriously consider, and then commit to, striking out for this purported land of natural wonders.

The 1870 expedition had come together under the leadership of Nathaniel Langford, who arrived in Montana in 1864 after prospectors discovered gold in the northern reaches of the Rocky Mountains. Langford did not have much luck in the mines, so he turned to politics. After Andrew Johnson took office in the wake of Abraham Lincoln's assassination, the president chose Langford as Montana's territorial governor. But Johnson's subsequent battles with the Republican Congress over Reconstruction policies had delayed and then scuttled Langford's appointment. He decided he liked Montana, however, and that he did not need to take office to lobby for future investment in and migration to his new home territory. A successful expedition to Yellowstone could be just the thing to bring national attention and investment capital to the Territory.

Langford recruited Everts and several of Helena's other leading citizens, including Henry Washburn, a U.S. Army veteran and the surveyor-general of Montana Territory, to join him on this summer adventure. He hired packers to load more than forty animals carrying provisions and equipment, and two Black men to cook for the party. Nute and Johnny were part of a small community of two hundred "free colored persons" living in Montana in 1870, in a territory whose non-Native population was 90 percent white. These residents, in addition to 2,000 Chinese immigrants who had been drawn to the mining camps of the northern Rockies in the 1860s, were slightly outnumbered by the more than 20,000 Indigenous peoples living in many communities across Montana.

After a one-hundred-mile journey southeast to Bozeman, Langford's party secured a protective detail of five U.S. Army soldiers from Fort Ellis, under the command of a young officer named Gustavus C. Doane. After leaving the fort, the expedition made its way along Indigenous trails and followed the Yellowstone River into the Basin.

At first, the expedition proceeded without a hitch. Everts, Langford, and the others rose every day at 8:00 a.m. and rode through the country until early afternoon, coming upon natural wonders at every turn. Devil's Slide, with its towering, parallel walls of dark rock. Tower Falls, its waters crashing down into a chasm surrounded by spires of light brown shale, "some resembl[ing] towers, others the spires of churches, and others . . . as lithe and slender as the minarets of a mosque." Springs whose hot waters bubbled up in constant agitation, their banks encrusted with a white substance, thin and delicate, like porcelain.

The lower and upper Yellowstone Falls, which they viewed from above, dove into a sink of foam and spray at the bottom of a deep canyon. At first they shrank back from the edge in terror, but then they were drawn toward it by the sparkle of the sunlight on the waterfalls, and the canyon walls glowing yellow and pink. Delighted, they laughed and sang and dashed along the rim.

From there they made their way past mud springs shading from yellow to pink to dark brown, then through a dense green forest, before emerging onto the shores of Yellowstone Lake. Here, in the first week of September 1870, the expedition ran into trouble. The woods that edged the western side of the lake were full of fallen timber. As they moved into the thicket the packhorses stumbled at almost every step, and the expedition members lost the trail. The men argued about the way forward.

Everts, who was known in Helena for his hot temper, went off by himself in a huff. When darkness closed in around him that night, he was not particularly concerned. Throughout the trip, team members had wandered off and always found their way back. Perhaps the experience of being completely turned around would bring Everts a greater understanding of himself, like Henry David Thoreau suggested in *Walden*.

"Not till we are lost," Thoreau wrote in 1854, "not till we have lost the world, do we begin to find ourselves, and realize where we are and the infinite extent of our relations."

Everts settled in, hitching his horse to a tree branch. He built a fire, wrapped himself in a blanket, and went to sleep. The next day, he made slow progress through the fallen trees, searching for the trail that would take him back to the lakeside camp. When Everts dismounted to inspect a fork in the trail, his horse bolted. The animal carried away all Everts's food, his gun and pistols, fishing tackle, matches, blankets, and extra clothing. Taking an inventory of his pockets, Everts found only two knives and a small opera glass.

It took another few days for Everts to realize that he was really, truly lost and that this experience would not be surprising and valuable, as Thoreau promised, but terrifying. With that epiphany came an almost debilitating sense of destitution. He was alone and without any resources. How would he survive long enough to find his way back to the expedition team?

For the next month, Everts wandered through Yellowstone Basin, subsisting on handfuls of thistle roots and small animals he was able to catch with his hands. When he thought about being captured by Crow or Shoshone warriors, the possibility no longer seemed like a threat but a possible salvation. These peoples never came. They were far away from the Basin that time of year, hunting buffalo in the Plains to ensure their survival in the winter to come. Everts thought he was moving northward, toward the Gallatin Mountains and home, but he could not be sure. In early October, a snowstorm set in and Everts, soaked to the skin and his feet frostbitten, sought out a group of steaming hot springs. The heat radiating up through the ground warmed his system, but while shifting in his sleep he broke through the fragile white crust along the spring's edge and scalded his hip.

Everts's mental state deteriorated. He began to hallucinate, lapsing into strange reveries. He imagined other people into being, friends and loved ones who helped guide him through Yellowstone's forests and canyons. He lost all sense of time and had no interest in his surroundings. When Everts found himself at Yellowstone Falls once again after weeks of wandering, he turned away, embittered. The region's marvels had lured him to his destruction, and he could not bear to see them.

Everts had almost given up and delivered himself to fate when Yellowstone Jack found him in the Cut. It was clear that he could not ride a horse, so Jack sent the packer he had brought with him back more than one hundred miles to Fort Ellis to find a wagon to transport Everts out of the Yellowstone Valley. In the meantime, the two men found shelter in a miner's cabin, where Everts rested for ten days.

By the time Everts returned to Bozeman, the news of his survival had spread across Montana, causing a sensation.

"At last the lost man is found," declared the *Helena Weekly Herald*. "The discovery of Mr. Everts, after such a lapse of time, and under the extraordinary circumstances . . . is simply miraculous."

One month later, several of Everts's friends threw a lavish dinner party for him in Helena. The tables in the town's most popular restaurant sagged with the weight of elk, venison, and antelope, six different vegetables, and a huge spread of pies, puddings, cakes, and other confections. It was the kind of meal that Everts had dreamed about during his trials in Yellowstone. He gazed upon the table but found he could not eat. He walked slowly through the party, leaning on a walking stick. Everyone wanted to hear his story.

Truman Everts related his tale of suffering and salvation to family, friends, and newspaper reporters, and then to a larger American public in an article he wrote for the new illustrated magazine *Scribner's Monthly*, whose inaugural issue had been published just a few months before. His story of survival was one of hundreds in a genre that had become well established by 1870, stories that valorized white men who went out into the wilderness and lost their way, their minds, and their humanity. Everything about them was laid bare, but they endured. These narratives erased Native peoples from the wilderness while emphasizing natural resources there for the taking. Everts's story helped to bring Yellowstone into the American imagination as a place of both wonder and terror.

Accounts like Everts's, of men surviving the direst of circumstances while displaying internal strength, ingenuity, and determination, were alluring for white Americans searching for unity in the years after the Civil War. Four years of unimaginable bloodshed—more than 600,000 dead men, their bodies strewn across the fields and swamps of the eastern states and the high desert passes of the Southwest—had torn America apart.

By 1870, the nation was in the midst of a national Reconstruction, both economic and political. During the Civil War, the U.S. government had increased tariff rates, released hundreds of millions of dollars' worth of greenbacks (paper money) into the market, instituted income taxes, and took on a huge national debt in order to boost industrial production and pay for the U.S. war effort. As the nation transitioned to peacetime after 1865 and politicians bickered about which wartime measures to continue or abandon, the northern economy slumped. The southern economy, meanwhile, was in ruins. After four years of war that destroyed croplands, railroads, and factories, and after the Emancipation Proclamation (1863) and then the Thirteenth Amendment (1865) freed men and women who had previously been assessed as property, most of the wealth across the South had disappeared, and the prospects for its development were grim.

The nation's political situation was just as turbulent. After the assassination of Abraham Lincoln, Andrew Johnson announced his plan for the Reconstruction. It was an appeasement rather than a reckoning. The states of the former Confederacy would have to pass the Thirteenth Amendment to reenter the Union, but former Confederates could apply for pardons and the return of any property that the U.S. Army had confiscated during the war.

Encouraged by Johnson's leniency, white southerners almost immediately reasserted power in their communities, trying to return emancipated men and women to their previous states of servitude. State legislatures across the South passed Black Codes, establishing fines and other punishments for formerly enslaved people who dared gather with one another, engage in interracial sex, or purchase firearms.

In 1866, enraged at Johnson's disinterest in protecting Black southerners, the Republican-dominated Thirty-Ninth Congress passed a Civil Rights Act along with an extension and expansion of the 1865 Freedman's Bureau Bill, both over President Johnson's veto. They began to draft the Fourteenth Amendment, which declared that all persons born or naturalized in the United States were citizens, and that no state could pass any law that would abridge their rights.

In the Reconstruction Act of 1867, Congress established five military districts in the South and required former Confederate states to provide for universal manhood suffrage regardless of race in their constitutions. Southern communities erupted in violence. In 1868, the Ku Klux Klan, a white supremacist terrorist group founded in Pulaski, Tennessee, in 1865–66, began to spread rapidly throughout the South. Disguised in sheets and wearing elaborate headdresses, the Klan rampaged through the countryside, whipping, raping, and killing Black men and women and white Republicans, and burning down their homes.

During this early period of Reconstruction, Congress was constantly at odds with President Johnson. Ulysses S. Grant, who served as General of the Armies during the Johnson administration, saw the president's vetoes as a betrayal of

Abraham Lincoln's vision for the country. Lincoln's Reconstruction plan had been somewhat moderate, but he had been dedicated to helping formerly enslaved people transition to lives of freedom. In 1868, voters elected Grant to replace Johnson. They also sent a contingent of radical Republicans to Washington, D.C., politicians intent on using the full authority of the federal government to ensure Black Americans could exercise their newly acquired rights. During his first administration, Grant and his cabinet supported these congressional actions, and Grant sent U.S. Army soldiers to enforce the Fourteenth and Fifteenth Amendments across the South. It was an extraordinary—if short-lived— demonstration of the government's willingness to intervene when states refused to protect their own citizens.

The Grant administration also funded projects and promoted development schemes to bring the West more firmly into the Union, wresting control of it from Indigenous nations to settle it with white farmers, ranchers, and miners. To understand the extent of the West's natural resources and its suitability for agriculture, mining, and other forms of production, Congress appropriated money for several geological surveys in the years after the war. These dovetailed with the Homestead Act (passed in 1862 and meant to provide land for white and Black

Americans loyal to the U.S. government during the Civil War) and the construction of the first transcontinental railroad (completed in 1869) to promote settler colonialism: a process through which white Americans took Indigenous territory, removed Natives to reservations, and replaced them as settlers on stolen land.

Also integral to this process was visual and literary culture—particularly photographs, magazines, and government survey reports—that helped to connect the goals of settler colonialism with the widespread belief among white Americans that the country's natural wonders were proof of national greatness. Large and vivid landscape paintings of grand scenery in the mountain West became popular in this moment. If these images depicted Native peoples at all, they were always on the cusp of vanishing, making way for the oncoming flood of white migrants into the heart of the continent.

Government surveys, settlement policies, literature, and visual art worked together to argue that the United States was "nature's nation," blessed by God with features that made the country exceptional. They portrayed the American West as a land to be explored, mapped, and claimed for the American people.

In 1871, the Grant administration's projects in the South and in the West were connected by the Republican Party's belief in the power of the federal government to protect its white and Black citizens on the one hand, and force the assimilation of Native peoples on the other. These actions were not uncontested. Across the nation, white Americans argued about whether the federal government should interfere in state decisions regarding the rights and the protections of citizenship. In the Indigenous homelands of the West, large numbers of Native peoples from hundreds of nations, intent on asserting their own sovereignties, pushed back against federal policies that brought white Americans into their territories.

The scientific exploration of Yellowstone became part of this larger struggle over the expansion of federal power during Reconstruction. Three men shaped its course. They were all in their forties and fifties and prominent leaders in their communities. They wielded a tremendous amount of power, which they each used to advance their interests and to assert their rights to Yellowstone.

Ambitious and self-absorbed, surveyor and scientist Ferdinand Vandeveer Hayden had already built a fifteen-year career bringing the landscapes of the West into the American consciousness. He had been a member of the military expedition that turned back from the Yellowstone in 1860 and had chafed at that failure ever since. By 1871, he held the position of U.S. geologist with funding from the Department of the Interior to survey the western territories. He was determined to launch his own expedition to Yellowstone, a project of national importance that he felt would secure his status as America's most renowned scientist-explorer.

Hayden's survey would be a boon for Jay Cooke, a fiercely competitive investment banker who saw in Yellowstone a way to build his business in the rocky financial waters of Reconstruction. Cooke specialized in selling government bonds but had grown interested in developing and promoting the West in the years after the war. In 1870, he took responsibility for raising funds to build the Northern Pacific Railroad, which would cross from the Pacific to the Great Lakes. Its tracks would come within fifty miles of Yellowstone. If the railroad could transport tourists as well as prospective white farmers and ranchers to the Great Northwest, the Northern Pacific would be a financial success— and Cooke's greatest accomplishment.

Another powerful man was working against Cooke's and Hayden's visions for the Reconstruction West. Tȟatȟáŋka Íyotake (Sitting Bull) and his band, the Húŋkpapȟa Lakota, had not encountered many Mílahaŋska (Long Knives, or American soldiers) until the early 1860s, when they appeared on the eastern horizon

31

to protect white migrants and gold miners intent on traveling through Lakota territory. In the early 1870s, Cooke's Northern Pacific surveyors also crossed into their homelands, measuring distances, pounding markers into the ground, and attempting to claim Lakota land for themselves. Sitting Bull was determined to expel Cooke's workers, and the U.S. Army soldiers who protected them, from his people's territory.

Hayden, Cooke, and Sitting Bull staked their claims to Yellowstone at a critical moment in Reconstruction, when the Grant administration and the Forty-Second Congress were testing the reach and the purpose of federal power across the nation. These federal government officials— most of them Republicans—were intent on controlling the South *and* the West, bringing both regions into the nation and shoring up their political power in the process. Hayden and Cooke saw their work as part of this larger vision and lobbied Congress to pass legislation beneficial to their projects, while Sitting Bull's actions in defense of Lakota sovereignty undermined these and other congressional aims.

Yellowstone was a site of contention and a perfect symbol of what the United States had become by 1871: a nation whose "best idea" required Indigenous dispossession and whose white politicians embraced but then quickly abandoned the cause of racial justice. In this moment, the fragile crust of American democracy and political reunification barely contained the roiling, violent forces that lay beneath.

1

The Interest of One Is the Interest of All

Washington, D.C. January 1871.

I t was already dark when Ferdinand Hayden hurried out of his office at the Smithsonian Institution and across the lawns of the Mall. The gas lamps placed along Pennsylvania Avenue were tiny pinpricks in the distance. Hayden strode across a wooden footbridge that spanned the Washington Canal, its sludgy depths covered with a skim of ice. He followed the canal toward the Capitol for a few blocks, then turned left onto 9th Street.

Soon Lincoln Hall rose before him, its four stories of arched windows glowing with light. Hayden fell in with the crowd streaming into the main entrance. After presenting his thirty-cent ticket, he made his way to the auditorium and found a seat. The space was impressive, with soaring ceilings, chandeliers, and neoclassical décor. Hayden settled in and waited for the evening's lecture to begin.

Soon a man with small eyes, furrowed brows, and a full, bushy beard stepped out onto the stage. The audience had been promised a speech from this lecturer, "describing a trip during the past season to a hitherto unexplored region at the head-waters of the Yellowstone, including discoveries of CATARACTS MANY HUNDRED FEET HIGH, ACTIVE VOLCANOES, FOUNTAINS OF BOILING WATER TWO HUNDRED FEET HIGH, and many other features of scenery, interesting and striking in the highest degree."

Nathaniel Langford did not disappoint. The Montana Territory booster recalled his expedition's journey in the summer and fall of 1870, describing the party's struggles through "narrow defiles, and up sharp declivities." He held forth on the beautiful sights they beheld, including "the glowing peaks of the Yellowstone, their summits half enveloped in clouds, or glittering with perpetual snow." The audience applauded throughout Langford's graphic portrayals of Yellowstone's massive waterfalls, towering basalt columns, and hot and cold sulfur springs.

Langford's tone became more solemn, however, as he explained that one of the party, Truman Everts, wandered off near the shores of Yellowstone Lake. The team suspended their explorations for a week to search the trails and mountainsides for their lost man but could not find any sign of him. With their rations running low and storms on the horizon, Langford lamented, they gave up the search and headed back to Helena. All turned out well in the end, the speaker assured his audience. Truman Everts was found.

This was extraordinary, as were Langford's subsequent descriptions of Yellowstone's geyser basin, which the expedition members discovered on their return journey. These marvelous geothermal features erupted from the ground "in every direction, projecting water to various heights."

"We were convinced," Langford intoned, "that there was not on the globe another region where . . . nature had crowded so much of grandeur and majesty with so much novelty and strangeness."

Ferdinand Hayden listened to Langford with a mixture of interest and concern. He had already been planning a survey to Yellowstone for the 1871 season. Langford's lecture convinced him that he must move forward, or this land of wonders would be overrun with amateur outfits. It was vital that Hayden claim the area for science—and for himself—before that happened. His mentor at the Smithsonian Institution, Spencer Baird, agreed.

"You will make more capital and accomplish more for science," Baird suggested to him, "by concentrating effort upon one region like the Yellow Stone, than by attempting to traverse an immense section of country."

If Hayden could focus on this single extraordinary area and come to understand its geology, hydrology, and geothermal features, he would establish his scientific reputation in America and Europe and become the nation's most famous explorer. His survey would also allow the federal government to assess, distribute, and sell its lands to white settlers and entrepreneurs, changing the demographics of the region and shaping the future of the West.

A child of divorce who grew up in poverty, Hayden learned early on that he had to hustle to make his way in the world. His intelligence was evident to his family, and they managed to send him to Oberlin College in the late 1840s. There, he captivated some classmates with his intensity, his bright blue eyes flashing when he talked about his projects. Others found his nervous energy and competitiveness off-putting. He became interested in geology, and in the major debates of the day in that field: Was the earth old or young? How did geological change happen, in short bursts or long periods of change? What forces had created North America's mountains and canyons and broad river valleys?

Because medical school was the only path available to men interested in studying natural sciences in the mid-nineteenth century, Hayden enrolled in Albany (New York) Medical College in 1851. His background meant he was an outsider in the elite world of American science, and he worked throughout his career to gain acceptance from his fellow scientists. He soon became interested in animal and botanical fossils, tiny specimens that could be used to establish the age of different landforms and reveal the secrets of the earth's history. Two years into his studies, Hayden set out on his first important fossil-collecting trip to the White River Badlands west of the Missouri River.

The clay and silt hills of that region, eroded into needles of rock, exposed at least ten substrata that were packed with the fossils of ancient animals. Oglála Lakotas were likely the first to excavate these specimens, but once American scientists began to explore the region in the 1840s—without Lakota consent and in violation of several treaties the U.S. government had made with them—they claimed it as their own and called it "The Boneyard." When Hayden arrived there, he was one of a growing group of collectors excavating fossils from these lands. They all hoped to make their reputations in the study of geology by using specimens stolen from Indian country.

In the Boneyard, Hayden discovered that he did not merely enjoy collecting fossils, he excelled at it. He had a talent for spotting important rock shards, and the speed with which he gathered them was impressive. Hayden liked to tell anyone who would listen that during a subsequent trip to the Upper Missouri in 1854–55, the Lakota warriors who tracked him as he collected fossils in their lands gave him a nickname: Man Who Picks Up Stones Running. It was a likely apocryphal but useful story, one that suggested that he secured permission to hunt fossils on Lakota land (he had not), and that he also earned their admiration for his skill (he did not).

At first Hayden believed he could make a living collecting fossils and selling them to other scientists. He had no family money like many of his fellow scientists, so he had to work constantly to support himself. He often dreamed of becoming wealthy from the fossil trade.

"A man without money," he told a friend, "is a bore."

But he also craved recognition in the scientific community and a more expansive, nationwide fame. To achieve these goals, Hayden thought, he would have to attach himself to the geographic surveys that were already underway in the West during the 1850s, funded by the federal government and organized by the U.S. Army.

Territorial surveys were almost as old as the nation itself. Meriwether Lewis and William Clark set out for the West in 1804, sent by President Thomas Jefferson to explore the region's rivers and find a pathway to the Pacific. They were also meant to impress upon the Native peoples of the region, particularly the Lakota who controlled access to the upper Missouri River, that the American federal government had power they could not resist. Their two-year expedition demonstrated that the continent was massive and that it would take many more surveys to map it. Lewis and Clark's reports also suggested that the Lakota were not particularly impressed with their demonstrations of power and would likely act to protect themselves, their river access, and their lands. The military academy at West Point trained a corps of engineers to do this work, and the wars of expansion and empire that the United States fought in the 1830s and '40s provided them with opportunities to examine the western territories won in these conflicts.

When the opportunity arose for Hayden to join an army expedition into the northern reaches of the Rocky Mountains in the summer of 1856, he lobbied hard for a job as the expedition's geologist and naturalist, and got it. Hayden took advantage of the army's supply chain and protection to gather a large new collection of fossils on Lakota lands and to cultivate contacts among the U.S. territorial officials across the West.

It was on this trip that Hayden first heard stories about the Yellowstone Basin. Jim Bridger, a legendary guide who joined the expedition, claimed to have stumbled on the geysers and hot springs there during his travels.

It was a place, he liked to say, "where hell bubbled up."

Hayden came close to seeing those sights for himself in 1856, and then once again in 1860, during a U.S. Army survey into the Rockies north of Colorado. That expedition, under the command of Captain William F. Raynolds, moved through Cheyenne, Arapaho, and Eastern Shoshone territory, but then stalled. They found no cut through the Wind River Range, and no safe passage up and over their ragged peaks. The heavy snows of early fall pushed them back eastward, and the expedition was forced to disband.

These failures nagged at Hayden. He planned to go back and try again, but the outbreak of the Civil War halted all government surveys. He avoided the war at first, living in rooms at the Smithsonian with a group of young scientists and joining their Megatherium Club, a social group named after a giant extinct South American sloth.

"There is no voice for science here now," Hayden complained. "The cry is all war! War!"

Reluctantly joining the U.S. army in 1863, Hayden served as a regimental surgeon until the end of the war in the spring of 1865. After mustering out, he moved to Philadelphia, hoping to join that city's revered scientific community. They did not know what to make of Hayden at first. His talents were obvious, but his origins were distasteful. He could be brash and resentful, and his ambition was uncomfortably obvious. To earn money, Hayden began teaching classes at the University of Pennsylvania. He found the time to head out on short collecting trips only when school was not in session.

Hayden's next big opportunity came in 1867. Nebraska had just entered the Union, the first state to join the postwar nation. Local boosters wanted to establish a survey to map the new state and give a full report of its natural resources. Hayden lobbied state officials, using all the western contacts that he had cultivated during his explorations before the war, and got the job.

What started as the Geological Survey of Nebraska expanded over the next two years to encompass all the U.S. territories west of the 100th meridian. In 1869, it was reorganized into the Geological Survey of the Territories of the United States. The Department of the Interior oversaw Hayden's survey, and in 1870, he secured a large appropriation from Congress to take a team of scientists to Wyoming, another recently created territory. Hayden was the first civilian to lead a federal government survey, a fact that pleased him immensely. He believed that his work producing scientific knowledge of the West was of national importance.

"We have beheld, within the past fifteen years, a rapidity of growth and development in the

Northwest which is without parallel in the history of the globe," he wrote in his survey report that year. "Never has my faith in the grand future that awaits the entire West been so strong as it is at the present time."

As Hayden left Lincoln Hall after Nathaniel Langford's lecture, he made plans to accelerate his organization of the 1871 survey. He had already written letters to several men who had joined him on previous expeditions to gauge their interest. He would write again to secure their services and attain the commitments of his most talented scientific colleagues to analyze and write up descriptions of the specimens the survey collected. And he would convince the members of Congress to give him enough money to make a thorough investigation of Yellowstone Basin.

During the next month, Hayden made several trips to the Capitol, a massive building whose awe-inspiring dome had been completed five years before. There he met with members of the House and Senate appropriations committees, describing to them the importance of funding an expedition to Montana and Wyoming. If the rumors of Yellowstone's wonders were true, it was imperative that the scientific community and the federal government exert control over these public lands, to understand and exploit their riches.

Although he was already well known in

Washington, Hayden had competition for expedition funding. The postwar years had been productive for surveyors, as Americans began to embrace science as a source of knowledge vital to the nation's interests. In 1870–71, Civil War veteran John Wesley Powell was out on the Colorado River, exploring the canyon lands of the West, while an army engineer named George Wheeler mapped the high deserts of the Southwest for the U.S. military. Hayden was particularly irked by the swift progress that fellow explorer Clarence King had made in establishing his survey of the 40th parallel. King was younger than Hayden by ten years and an accomplished mountaineer, fond of having his picture taken hanging from rocks or looking over precipices high in the Sierra Mountains of California. He was also a talented writer, and as adept as Hayden at cultivating patrons in Congress.

The halls of the Capitol were busy in the early months of 1871, teeming with politicians and their staff as well as lobbyists like Hayden hoping for an audience. There were only a few weeks left in the final session of the Forty-First Congress, and everyone was trying to push their pet projects through to the floor. As had been the case since the end of the Civil War, it was hard to find money for these ventures while also paying government officials, funding the army and navy, and improving infrastructure across the nation.

Making matters more complicated was the fact that three of the final four states of the former Confederacy (Virginia, Mississippi, and Texas) had finally met requirements to rejoin the Union: they repealed their secession laws, ensured that their citizens would not be taxed to pay the debts of the former Confederacy, and ratified the Thirteenth, Fourteenth, and Fifteenth Amendments (the latter securing the right of Black men to vote). After rewriting their state constitutions and submitting them for readmission, these states held elections and elected representatives and senators to send to Washington, D.C. In March 1871, when Georgia's senators and congressmen traveled to the nation's capital to be seated for the first session of the Forty-Second Congress, the United States would be politically reunited.

This could be good news for Hayden, or bad. Southern senators and congressmen were mostly moderate Republicans, but some were Democrats. Republicans were likely to back Hayden's survey plans; they usually favored federal projects that they believed would benefit the nation in some way. Democrats were a harder sell. Even in the wake of the Civil War they continued to argue for the supremacy of states' rights over federal power. It was up to Hayden to convince them that the scientific exploration of Yellowstone would benefit their constituencies as well.

While Hayden made his rounds lobbying members of Congress, President Ulysses S. Grant was working in his office at the Executive Mansion. He did not know the particulars of Ferdinand Hayden's Yellowstone Expedition plan, but he had always supported this aspect of the federal government's work. Early in his military career, when he served at forts along the Pacific coast, he outfitted several army surveys for their explorations of the towering stands of redwoods and wide, roiling rivers of California and Oregon Territory. Some were sent out to establish railroad routes through the Cascades, and others were mapping the region's natural resources. Grant had supplied them all, providing pack animals and provisions for their travels through the wilderness.

As the General of the Armies in the years after the Civil War, Grant continued to approve requests for government survey supplies, some of them submitted by Ferdinand Hayden. The military's forts, scattered across the states and territories of the West, were useful depots and base camps for survey teams. Grant had visited some of them on a short trip in the summer of 1868, before his election to the presidency. With his most trusted friends and fellow officers, William Tecumseh Sherman and Phil Sheridan, he took a series of trains and stages from fort to fort in Kansas, Colorado, and Wyoming, inspecting the garrisons and making sure the soldiers there were well trained and equipped for "frontier service": guarding wagon trains and work camps along the roads and trails of the West, and riding out in campaigns against Indigenous enemies.

The 1868 trip "gave me the key to the topography of the country," he told a good friend, "so that now when Indian hostilities are reported, or the establishment of a new post, at a particular place is recommended, I can have more distinct ideas about what should be done than can be got merely from maps."

Grant had taken along his oldest two sons, Fred and Buck, on that summer tour. He wanted them to see the Great Plains before its "frontier" character faded away.

"It will be something," he wrote to his wife, Julia, "for [the boys] to know that [they] had traveled on the plains whilst still occupied by the Buffalo and the Indian, both rapidly disappearing now."

Grant himself did not see the contradiction between his belief that Indians were vanishing and the regular reports about Indian hostilities in the West. He continued to staff an Office of Indian Affairs, whose employees had a range of relationships with Indigenous communities across the nation. The many forts that Grant visited that summer had been built so that the army could monitor the activities of Native peoples in the region, negotiate treaties with them, and initiate military campaigns against them if the federal government deemed them necessary.

Despite the obvious evidence of Indigenous resistance to the encroachments of white miners and farmers in their homelands, Grant did not believe that war should be the federal government's first response. His 1868 presidential campaign slogan, "Let Us Have Peace," applied both to the reconciliation of northerners and southerners after the Civil War and the federal government's relationship with Native peoples across the country.

"I will favor any course toward [Indians]," he stated in his inaugural address in 1869, "which tends to their civilization and ultimate citizenship."

That spring, Grant kept an eye on the West. He was also deeply concerned about the progress of Reconstruction in the South. The 1867 Reconstruction Act enfranchised Black men to vote in statewide elections in 1868, and the passage of the Fifteenth Amendment in 1870 gave them the right of franchise in national contests. After these new voters attended Republican political rallies and appeared at polling places to vote, the Ku Klux Klan donned their disguises and rode out to whip, beat, rape, and kill them in retaliation. Radicalized by reports of this racial violence even before he was elected to the presidency, Grant helped frame congressional legislation to protect Black southerners and their white allies in his first term as president.

In May 1870, the Forty-First Congress had passed the first Enforcement Act, to prevent the Ku Klux Klan from gathering in the streets at night to intimidate Black voters. In February 1871, Grant had signed the Second Enforcement Act, which outlined a specific procedure for oversight of federal elections in southern states, and the protection of all voters who came to cast their ballots at polling places.

By this time, Grant had fully embraced the power of the legislative and the executive branches to fight for and protect civil rights. The Republican majority in Congress did as well. But Grant was doubtful that these measures would stop the Ku Klux Klan from attacking people in their homes, in towns, or on the roads across the South. His wartime experience showed him that white southerners would defend their own power, no matter the cost. The violence that was occurring almost daily in the states of the former Confederacy would turn into another full-fledged rebellion, Grant believed, if his administration, Congress, and the U.S. military did not work to check it. There were too few days left in this final session to push another piece of major legislation on this matter. It would be up to the Forty-Second Congress, which would convene the day after the Forty-First disbanded, to pass another measure to protect Black rights across the South.

Up the hill at the Capitol, lawmakers continued their work. They turned to the annual Indian Appropriations Act and to the proposal to fund Ferdinand Hayden's survey of Yellowstone. The House Appropriations Committee, chaired by Henry L. Dawes, an influential Republican from Massachusetts, recommended financing the expedition. On March 3, the last day of the Forty-First's final session, Congress included a line item in a bill appropriating funds for civil purposes.

"For continuing the geological survey of the Territories of the United States, by Professor Hayden," it read, "forty thousand dollars."

It was an immense sum, the most ever dedicated to the production of scientific knowledge on behalf of the nation. Within two weeks, Hayden had put together his plan.

"I expect to start from Salt Lake City and go northward to Helena, Montana," Hayden wrote to his former Oberlin geology professor, George Allen, "[and] explore the Missouri and Yellow Stone [Rivers] from their sources down." He would outfit the survey in Salt Lake City and explore as much of Yellowstone as practicable in five months, from May to October.

As news of the appropriation spread, letters and telegrams began to arrive at Hayden's Smithsonian office, from established and aspiring scientists. He had to turn away more than fifty qualified applicants, but he kept a space open for Allen, who had been his mentor. Hayden believed in returning favors, and he knew Allen had always wanted to go to the West. Perhaps the geologist could help him with the mineralogical and metallurgical specimens, "testing ores, minerals, rocks, also saline waters, and as much geology as possible." Or perhaps he could work with a young botanist Hayden was hoping to bring in. The boy was talented but inexperienced, and Allen's wide-ranging knowledge could help him with his collecting.

Hayden was worried, however, that the older man was not up to it. Survey expeditions could be tough going, and members of the party had to be willing to "rough it" in the wilderness for months at a time. He was not sure if Allen had even the most basic of skills—like riding a horse—for long-term work in the field. If Allen slowed down the expedition, Hayden would not hesitate to send him home.

The same policy would apply to several other men he was taking along, like an untested ornithologist from Chicago, whom Smithsonian

Assistant Secretary Spencer Baird had championed. And the sons and nephews of congressmen who had helped secure his appropriation, for whom he had reserved several survey spots. Only one of these political appointees, the brother-in-law of Illinois congressman John Logan, had any scientific experience. Cyrus Thomas had worked on Hayden's 1870 survey of Wyoming, and he would be collecting agricultural data and insects in Yellowstone. The other "political boys" would work as general assistants and, Hayden hoped, behave themselves—as much as could be expected.

In any case, their presence would make Hayden's political patrons feel like they had a stake in the expedition and would help him retain their support. Congressional policy was to fund each survey for one year only. Within weeks of his return from the West in the fall of 1871, he would be back in the halls of Congress once again, lobbying for the 1872 expedition's appropriation. The eyewitness accounts of Yellowstone that the political boys would contribute would help him make his case.

By mid-April 1871, Hayden was in Philadelphia. He wrapped up his teaching responsibilities at the University of Pennsylvania and spent some time with his fiancée, Emma Woodruff, before leaving for the West. He and Emma met in the winter of 1867, when he had come back to the eastern seaboard after his first year as the leader of the Nebraska Survey. She was the daughter of a Philadelphia merchant and at twenty-four years old, eighteen years younger than Hayden. Their engagement a year after meeting surprised many of Hayden's friends, who knew him as a man prone to rampant flirtation and whirlwind romances—and a confirmed bachelor. Most women Hayden had romanced ultimately demanded too much of him. But Emma seemed to understand Hayden's ambition and accepted that his work required that they would often be parted. They were a good match.

Emma and Hayden agreed from the start that they would marry once Hayden had established a national reputation. That he had secured the largest appropriation ever made for a government survey, which included a salary of $4,000 for the coming year, meant that they could finally start their lives together. They set the wedding date for November, after he returned from Yellowstone.

From Philadelphia, Hayden completed his work organizing the survey. Eighteen scientists had signed on already, and he anticipated recruiting ten more. Added to that number would be the packers, hunters, and guides whom Hayden would hire once they reached Utah and Idaho. Then there was the military escort he hoped to secure, to give them some protection against Crow, Shoshone, Bannock—and possibly even

Lakota, Blackfoot, or Nez Perce—bands, who might object to their presence in the Yellowstone.

This would be the largest survey, by far, that Hayden had ever led. His previous expedition consisted of only three fellow scientists and three artists. There would be a lot of men to keep track of, and egos and ambitions to wrangle on this expedition to Yellowstone. As he saw to the final details, Hayden felt a bit overwhelmed. Had he made the right choices? Could his fellow scientists do good work in the rugged mountains of the West, where, as he warned Allen, "all field work must necessarily be of the crudest kind"?

On May 1, Hayden received his official appointment as U.S. Geologist and instructions for the expedition from Secretary of the Interior Columbus Delano. Hayden would be trusted to choose his own team and his own course of exploration, but Congress expected him to produce an accurate geographical map of Yellowstone and to collect as much information as possible about the country.

"You will give your attention to the geological, mineralogical, zoological, botanical, and agricultural resources," Delano instructed him.

These details would help Congress decide how to promote and develop the region. Hayden was required to forward all specimens his team collected to the Smithsonian Institution and submit a report of the expedition with all his findings and illustrations of them with "sketches, sections, photographs, etc." no later than January 1, 1872.

As always, Delano advised, "all your expenditures of the public funds are expected to be made with judicious economy and care."

Those funds, Hayden knew, would not be available until July. Until then, he would pay his scientists their wages and other survey expenses with his own money, loans from Spencer Baird, or lines of credit. Hayden had already sent his friend and survey manager, Jim Stevenson, out to Omaha to establish the first of the survey's rendezvous. He sent off letters to his survey team members, informing them where they could meet Stevenson and gather their supplies.

Hayden himself needed to be in Omaha within two weeks so that the entire expedition could set off toward Salt Lake City. It was imperative that they arrive in the northern Rockies just as spring turned to summer. They needed at least four months to fully explore Yellowstone Basin before the snowstorms came rolling across the mountains in early October. Hayden said goodbye to Emma and loaded his bags onto the train. The 1871 scientific survey of Yellowstone, a project that would expand the federal government's reach into one of the nation's little-known landscapes, had begun.

2

Pulse of the Continent

Omaha, Nebraska. May 1871.

O ne week after leaving Philadelphia, Ferdinand Hayden walked down the plank from
the steam ferry and stepped onto a wide, muddy
street that led to Omaha's busy business district.
The town was little more than fifteen years
old, laid out in a grid system of right-angled
streets on the western bank of the Missouri
River in 1854. In the congressional fight over
transcontinental railroad routes that began that
year, Omaha's founders had lobbied to become
the eastern terminus, arguing that the Platte
River route was the cheapest and most feasible
path westward. Their dreams were realized in
1862, when Congress passed the Pacific Railway
Act, and President Abraham Lincoln, who had
landholdings across the river in Council Bluffs,
Iowa, deemed Omaha the starting point for that
massive technological effort.

Although it had taken the Union Pacific several
years to begin laying track west of Omaha, the
town had benefited immediately. Hayden passed

a large complex of multistory brick buildings, machine shops, and roundhouses belonging to the railroad company. He was making his way to the firm of Wilcox & Stevens, where the members of the 1871 Yellowstone Expedition were expected to check in when they arrived.

Hayden walked into the dry-goods store and found Jim Stevenson waiting for him. The two men had met fifteen years before, as fellow members of an Upper Missouri River survey in 1856, and had hit it off. Hayden appreciated Stevenson's competent, steady, and relaxed demeanor; these characteristics balanced out his own frenetic energy. They had collaborated on three subsequent surveys, including the expedition to Wyoming in 1870. Stevenson had been in Omaha for a month, gathering the scientific and other supplies that Hayden had sent ahead by train and by steamboat (including ammunition cartridges and gun parts), and purchasing provisions that they might not be able to procure farther west.

Several of the other survey veterans, men who had been out west with Hayden and Stevenson on one or more expeditions, were in Omaha already: Cyrus Thomas, in charge of agricultural statistics and catching and classifying insects; the experienced zoologist E. Campbell Carrington; and meteorologist John Beaman. They joined Henry Elliott, an artist whose beautiful landscape profiles and sections Hayden would use to illustrate his survey reports. Hayden was relieved to learn that German-born topographer Anton Schönborn would be joining them. Schönborn lived in Omaha and worked for the U.S. Army, surveying and sketching their garrisons in the Midwest. He was moody and unpredictable, but his expertise in mapmaking was unparalleled in America.

Hayden's students from the University of Pennsylvania had also arrived. George Dixon, Charlie Turnbull, and Albert Peale had all received medical degrees that spring and were eager to begin their careers as naturalists. Robert Adams, Jr., was also in town. A student of classics and law at Penn, Adams was a keen outdoorsman and a hard worker with an interest in botany, so Hayden had agreed to take him on. They were a merry bunch of boys. Some might find them wild and profane at times, but Hayden enjoyed their company. The Penn boys found much to like in the other young men on the survey, particularly Chester Dawes and William Logan, scions of important Republican families.

Stevenson had already made it clear to the political boys that this was no mere adventure in the wilderness. Hayden would demand an immense amount of focused, steady work from them over the coming months. If they proved unwilling or unable to pull their own weight,

Stevenson would send them home on the next train.

George Allen had arrived from Oberlin, Stevenson informed Hayden, along with Frederick Huse, the ornithologist whom Spencer Baird had recommended. Hayden was skeptical about both men. He respected his former professor and was happy to be able to offer him this experience, but it was clear that Allen was physically fragile and might end up being a liability. Hayden assigned Robert Adams to him as an assistant and was hopeful that the younger man would be able to do most of the botanical specimen collecting, preservation, and packing. Hayden did not know Huse at all and was unsure of his abilities, despite Baird's endorsement.

John Raymond, a survey veteran whom the team members called "Potato John," was gathering cooking utensils and sacks of provisions that would keep well on the train to Utah. Hayden was thrilled that Raymond was available to join the expedition. As valuable as his fellow scientists were, a good cook was indispensable for a successful exploration. Stevenson hired teamsters and other workmen in Omaha and would secure hunters and guides in Utah.

After finalizing plans with Stevenson, Hayden left Wilcox & Stevens to check in with another of his survey veterans. He walked down the street to a storefront with a vividly painted sign hanging over the door: two Plains Indian warriors, one riding a black horse and the other white, battling each other with lances on a windswept riverbank.

JACKSON BROTHERS, the sign read, PHOTOGRAPHERS.

In Hayden's estimation, if there was one person who rivaled either him or Potato John in importance to the 1871 Yellowstone Expedition, it was William Henry Jackson.

Jackson began working in a New York photography studio when he was just fifteen years old. Like Hayden and his fossils, Jackson discovered he had a way with the glass plates and chemicals, producing clear, vivid portraits and outdoor landscape scenes. He, too, had been distracted from his work by the Civil War, serving with a Vermont company on the fringes of eastern theater battles in the early 1860s.

After mustering out, Jackson had a turbulent few years, fleeing a disappointing love affair in Vermont and then lighting out for the West with a few friends from his regiment. By the summer of 1867 he worked his way to California as a teamster, and, on his return, found his way to a photography studio in Omaha. Within the year he had bought out the owner, absorbed another studio, and recruited his brothers Ed and Fred to come work with him as clerks and managers. The Jackson Brothers firm was "in full swing" as the town filled with railroad workers and western emigrants, and businessmen eager to sell items to all these new arrivals.

In 1869, Jackson made his name photographing views of the Union Pacific Railroad line and the spectacular landscapes along it. He also made money taking photographs of business owners in towns along the route, posing in front of their establishments. Such images were permanent records of their achievements, Jackson told them, a sign of respectability. While he was in Cheyenne that year, Jackson met Ferdinand Hayden for the first time, in the foyer of Madame Cleveland's. Jackson was delivering a framed photograph he had taken of the women who worked at the brothel. They posed in their finest dresses, facing the camera with hard eyes and grim smiles.

Hayden had been surveying through the Rocky Mountains of Colorado and southern Wyoming that summer, funded by the Department of the Interior. He was at Madame Cleveland's that day with a group of soldiers from nearby Fort D. A. Russell, who were likely there in defiance of orders. Military commanders tried to keep their soldiers away from Cheyenne's brothels and saloons, where the men would spend their meager salaries on sex and alcohol and were often unfit for duty as a result.

Whenever Jackson told this story of his first meeting with Hayden, he noted how surprised he was to see the surveyor at the brothel and how uneasy he appeared. Perhaps it was because Hayden had so recently been engaged to Emma that he seemed to Jackson "like a cat in a strange garret" at Madame Cleveland's. It is possible that Hayden was just nervous to be meeting Jackson, a photographer he admired, while in compromising circumstances.

The next year, Hayden had walked into Jackson Brothers while he and Jim Stevenson were gathering supplies and men for their 1870 expedition to Wyoming. Hayden wandered through the gallery, studying Jackson's Union Pacific prints, and his portraits of Osage, Lakota, Pawnee, and Winnebago men and women. Hayden sighed and turned to the photographer.

"This is what I need," he said, "I wish I could offer you enough to make it worth your while to spend the summer with me."

Jackson was intrigued. He was getting itchy to travel after a year at home in Omaha since his Union Pacific trip.

"What could you offer?" he asked.

Hayden smiled.

Only a meager salary and "a summer of hard work," he said, shaking his head, "and the satisfaction I think you would find in contributing your art to science."

Jackson's wife, Mollie, had walked into the room at that moment, interrupting their conversation. The couple, who had been married for only a year, lived above the gallery. She often worked there as a clerk and assistant.

Jackson introduced Hayden to Mollie and explained that the geologist was off to Wyoming that week, to explore and prepare a series of maps of that territory.

"[I've] been telling your husband," Hayden said, "how much I would like to take him with me, Mrs. Jackson."

Mollie looked at Hayden and her husband and laughed. She knew Jackson could not resist such an opportunity. And he knew that "everything, so far as she was concerned, was arranged."

The expedition of 1870 was out for two months, and for Jackson, the experience was a turning point in his life.

"For me the expedition was priceless," he said, "it gave me a career."

When Hayden invited him to join the 1871 Yellowstone Expedition, of course Jackson agreed. Mollie was coming with him this time for the first stage of the survey. They would travel separately from the rest of the team, booking a sleeper car and traveling straight through to Ogden, Utah. When Hayden, Jackson, and the rest of the team left for Idaho, Montana, and the Yellowstone, Mollie would return to Omaha and manage the studio in his absence. She had done so during her husband's first trip to Wyoming with Hayden in 1870, and had proven herself an able operator.

"I doubt whether Susan B. Anthony herself was ever feminist enough," he declared, "to be willing to take over the management of a Nebraska photographic gallery."

On May 25, 1871, Hayden, Stevenson, and the other members of the 1871 Yellowstone Expedition boarded a Union Pacific train bound for Utah. Stevenson had supervised the loading of train cars with the company's luggage, equipment, and provisions, and several of the men were riding along with the freight, to ensure its safety. The others showed their passes to the conductor and stepped up into a passenger car.

Hayden walked down the center aisle, looking for a good place on either side where he could sit with his notebook and look out a window. The car had a stove at one end and a toilet at the other, carpets, plush seats, and curtains. It was more luxurious than the "emigrant cars" at the rear of the train, with their board seats and plank floors. There was a smoking car ahead for the gentlemen, but no coaches reserved for dining. The trains would stop at hotels along the way, and the team members would disembark for their meals.

The members of the Yellowstone Expedition were riding for free, courtesy of the Union

Pacific, and their freight was carried at reduced rates. The transcontinental, itself a federal project meant to unite the nation by "binding in its iron clasp" the East and the West, was vital to Hayden's expedition. Before the completion of the transcontinental, the long journey from the Missouri River meant that eastern explorers had only a few weeks to try to enter the Basin before the snows came. The Union Pacific also saved Hayden money that he would have spent on provisions and labor. Throughout the expedition, the train cars would transport specimens and survey correspondence from the Rocky Mountains back to Washington, D.C., and Philadelphia, helping Hayden to convert nature into knowledge.

Only two years old, the transcontinental was already changing the demographics of the West, bringing migrants from the East and the West: white veterans of the Civil War, Chinese miners leaving the California diggings for the promise of the Rockies, Black soldiers heading to frontier posts across the region. The trains speeding through the vast prairies and up over high mountain passes were also emblems of motion and power, as the poet Walt Whitman put it. They were the "pulse of the continent."

The train pulled out of the station, moving more quickly as it passed through Omaha's outskirts and then onto the plains west of the city.

The track cut a mostly straight line through the gently rolling prairie, following the Platte River and passing farms and small towns that had sprung up along the route in the past two years, like scrubby weeds in a vast, verdant field.

Interspersed among them were the lodges of Omaha, Pawnee, Lakota, and Cheyenne peoples, whose homelands the transcontinental crossed on its way to Cheyenne. The 1862 legislation that aided its construction had made it possible to "extinguish as rapidly as may be the Indian titles to all lands" along the railroad's route. By doing so, the federal government could claim these millions of acres as public lands. Once they laid forty miles of track, the Union Pacific received alternating sections of that land to sell to white settlers, to fund further construction of the road. Although most white Americans, like President Grant, believed that the Indians were fast disappearing from the West, Native peoples still claimed their homelands along the railroad route, and their hunting rights there had been confirmed by the Treaty of Fort Laramie in 1868.

It took the survey a little more than a day to reach Cheyenne, which had almost doubled in population during the previous year. Hayden gathered his things and disembarked, making his way past the hotels, museums, and theaters of the business district, and three miles beyond, to Fort D. A. Russell, where the survey members began to set up their camp. From there, the men could see the Rocky Mountains to the west. For many of them, this was their first glimpse of that storied mountain range, its snow-covered summits reaching skyward.

"It was a magnificent sight," George Allen sighed, "and I felt fully repaid for coming so far."

Soon a grove of white tents sprang up on the plain, canvas shelters that could sleep anywhere from two to six men in a "mess." As the men milled around, gathering their belongings and choosing their messmates, Hayden had the opportunity to observe them for the first time, together as a team. The veterans knew what to do, stowing their belongings in the tent corners and making up beds of hay stuffed between two scratchy wool blankets. The others milled about, excited about their first experience "sleeping rough." Robert Adams, the botanist who was to act as Allen's assistant, was more circumspect.

In Cheyenne, "our hardships began in a mild form, at least to those of us unused to camp life," he wrote to a newspaper in Philadelphia. "A pair of blankets, with your clothes for a pillow, is a hard substitute for a spring mattress; and our rations differ somewhat from city cuisine."

For George Allen, it was not the rustic accommodations that rankled as much as the total lack of privacy. The very evident difference in age and habits between him and the rest of the company also bothered him. The young men treated him with respect, but they were a rowdy bunch already prone to late-night carousing. Allen hoped that once the tent assignments were sorted out, he would be able to get along. Over the next few days, he explored around the camp, collecting samples of bright yellow evening primrose and vivid purple blooms of tufted phlox, to press between clean sheets of paper. Allen was not a botanist by training, but Hayden assigned this task to him after evaluating the strength of his survey team. At least Allen would learn a fair bit about flowers while being compelled to attend to them.

While the scientists collected specimens, Hayden and Stevenson walked over to Fort D. A. Russell to consult with the fort's commander. The fort had twelve storehouses that contained several million pounds of supplies: food, fodder, weapons, blankets, saddles. Hayden presented his paperwork, signed by President Grant, which allowed the expedition to purchase food and other supplies at cost and to procure horses. This arrangement, like the transcontinental, was essential "to the complete success of a party exploring the remote sections of the interior of our continent," Hayden knew. It allowed him to avoid dealing with frontier merchants, who would have driven up the prices.

A short time later, Hayden and Stevenson left

the general's headquarters with orders for the quartermaster to supply them with whatever they needed—and with the general's son, who would be joining the survey as a "general assistant." As they walked toward their expedition camp, Hayden was annoyed to find another group of surveyors in the area. It was the 40th parallel team, led by his most hated rival, Clarence King. Thankfully, Hayden did not have to endure a falsely polite meeting with King, for he was not there. King sent his men to finish up the season's fieldwork while he went to California to climb the volcanic peaks of the Sierras. Hayden was relieved to know that the two surveys would not be crossing paths again or duplicating each other's work. And it was imperative that King did not get any ideas about joining Hayden's expedition or dropping by the Yellowstone on his way back from California. Hayden wanted the Basin to himself.

The team was ready, Hayden thought. And they had everything they needed.

"We have a splendid outfit," he bragged to Spencer Baird from Cheyenne, "better than ever if anything."

On May 30, in a driving rain, the survey's wagon masters, ambulance and mule drivers, and general assistants loaded the last of the company's freight onto five train cars waiting at the Cheyenne depot. More than thirty horses went in last, the men pushing on their rumps to get them up the plank and into the cars. The horses, hardy ponies Hayden had procured at Fort D. A. Russell, would carry the survey team members. Hayden and Stevenson would purchase mules in Utah to carry their supplies.

Their cargo loaded, the expedition members split up again. The teamsters settled into the freight cars and the scientists in the passenger coaches. As the train left Cheyenne, Hayden looked around for Jim Stevenson and did not see him. When they pulled into the next station, a single engine followed and slowed to a stop behind them. Stevenson jumped down from the engine and made his way over to the transcontinental. Sheepish, he explained to Hayden that he had misunderstood the departure time.

"The boys turned his coming into an ovation," Adams reported, "and, lifting the new arrival upon their shoulders, deposited him upon the train."

The whistle sounded and the train moved on, now with the entire Yellowstone survey team aboard. Hayden gazed out the windows at the landscape moving by. Red rocks (syenite, most likely) towered over the earth, their surface dotted with gray-green lichen. Bright white patches of snow melted into rivulets that fed the wildflowers already blooming. Rich grasslands whipped by, covering rolling prairies.

Towering bluffs appeared along the Green River in southwestern Wyoming, suggestive of the geological changes that had shaped the land over thousands of years. This landscape was of great interest to Hayden because of his work on the processes of geological transformation and the nature of time. Geologists had determined that when the ocean covered this valley it had laid a band of clay. As the saline waters withdrew, some lakes were left behind, surrounded by green forests of lodgepole pines and firs. Ribbons of rock and soil were deposited on top, bearing within them evidence of volcanic eruptions, uplifts and foldings, and changes in climate. All of it was topped by red sandstone, which had been sculpted by wind and water into fantastical forms: castles, ruined cities, narrow minarets. It was America's ancient history, written upon the rocks.

Once the train began to wind its way along the steep mountainsides and across the deep canyons of the Wasatch Range, there were man's works to marvel at as well. Trestlework bridges, impossibly long and looking like precarious heaps of matchsticks. Dark tunnels bored through the granite and limestone peaks. Curves along high embankments that made the survey team members clutch at the back of their seats, hearts in their throats.

The track dropped them down into a valley

and began to move north between the Wasatch foothills on the right and the Weber River on the left. Soon the brakemen jumped up from their roosts on the top of the cars. Each of them took hold of a wheel at each end of a car and began cranking them clockwise to apply the brakes. Metal screeching on metal, the train pulled into the station at Ogden.

It was a brief stop. The survey members climbed down from the Union Pacific cars and stretched their legs in the short walk to the Utah Central Railroad platform. Although the survey's base camp for the next week would be established at Ogden, the team members were intent on seeing the most famous curiosity in the West: Salt Lake City.

The train moved south on an easy grade, skirting the Great Salt Lake and passing through several small towns before arriving at the city depot. Hayden and most of the others stayed the night in the Townsend House Hotel, a Mormon-owned establishment on Main Street.

Salt Lake City had been founded in 1847 by members of the Church of Jesus Christ of Latter-day Saints fleeing religious repression and attacks on their community in the Midwest. The town teetered on the edge of failure for two years before the California Gold Rush saved it. Salt Lake City became a way station for argonauts, a place for them to rest and restock on the way out to the goldfields or on the return. For merchants, blacksmiths, wagonwrights, and hoteliers, business boomed and the city grew.

Mormon resistance to U.S. federal oversight, both political and military, ultimately put them in direct conflict with the government. In 1857, President James Buchanan sent more than 2,000 troops to Utah to quell the Mormon uprising. There were no major battles; Brigham Young negotiated a peace deal with Buchanan and spent the next decade building his economic power in the region, centered on the western emigrant trade.

The construction of the transcontinental had been a marvelous opportunity. Young lobbied for the placement of a depot at Ogden, negotiated contracts with the Union Pacific for Mormon workers to grade elevations through the Wasatch Range, and invested $5,000 in company stock. With the money he made, Young financed the construction of the Utah Central Railroad, which brought goods and tourists down to Salt Lake from the depot at Ogden.

After a refreshing night's sleep in the Townsend, the Yellowstone survey team members went for a walk around town. The wide streets were graded and graveled and planted with cottonwoods and poplars. On every block, cobblestone-lined irrigation ditches delivered clear and sparkling water to houses and businesses.

They visited the Tabernacle, probably the most famous building in the West, a massive ellipse with a shingled dome soaring 250 feet above the street. They were allowed into the sanctuary and gawked at the immense pipe organ under construction at one end, encased in elaborately carved wood. The Great Temple next door was also only half built, the large granite blocks that would form its walls sitting in heaps on the ground. They peered through the main entrance gates at Brigham Young's house, called "The Beehive," a reference to a common symbol in the city and in the Mormon faith, referencing the hard work and unity required to build the Kingdom of God. The building next door housed Young's many wives. The extensive complex was surrounded by a high cobblestone wall, signifying the president's powerful position in Mormon society.

George Allen and Robert Adams entered a small reception room near the gates, where they waited to see if Brigham Young himself would appear. They left disappointed, informed that the president was not taking visitors until the next day. On their ramble through Salt Lake City's central business district, however, they had a bit of luck. Young had gone into a photographic studio and was talking to the proprietor. Allen and Adams lurked outside, pretending to examine the works exhibited in the windows but really sneaking looks at the president and assessing his physiognomy.

"We were entirely satisfied with the opportunity," Allen decided, "and felt that we had seen the great lion of the city."

From there the two scientists went to the city's natural history museum to see, as Allen joked, "the smaller lions." In 1867, Brigham Young's son John had first proposed the idea of a gallery to showcase Utah's natural resources and its Mormon history, and the Deseret Museum opened two years later. Allen and Adams walked up the creaking wood steps of the adobe building across from the Tabernacle, paid their fifty-cent admission fee, and wandered through the collections for most of the afternoon.

Specimens of silver and other minerals, collected by miners in the region, were displayed in handsome cases, along with artifacts from the community's early history, including cloth and paper currency produced in the 1840s. But the real showcase was the museum's menagerie, a collection of live animals gathered in cages in an open area.

Here there were bears, pumas, lynxes, foxes, porcupines, and golden eagles. Allen was particularly entranced by an old camel, a veteran of Secretary of War Jefferson Davis's dromedary importation scheme in the mid-1850s. With Davis's urging, Congress had appropriated

$35,000 to bring nearly one hundred camels from the Middle East to Texas, to be used in cavalry battles with Apaches and Comanches. The experiment failed, and in 1861, when federal troops abandoned the Texas posts at which the camels had been corralled, the animals were dispersed throughout the Southwest. How this one had ultimately made his way to Salt Lake City was unclear.

The next morning, Allen went out with Adams to collect flowers in the hills outside of town. On their way back to the Townsend Hotel they stopped to stare at a procession making its way up Main Street.

"A mounted band of Indians," Allen remarked with awe, "in all their native paint and glory."

They had come to town with animal skins to trade. After twenty years of fighting with Mormons for control of their homelands and fending off efforts to convert them to the Mormon faith, Northern Utes had signed a treaty with the federal government in 1868. Giving up most of their lands in exchange for annuities and rations, they lived on a large reservation in the Wasatch Mountains southeast of Salt Lake City. The men dismounted and tied up their horses along the street and went into stores, browsing among the items and buying some, negotiating with the clerks in English. They carried the packages back out to the horses, where two women waited on ponies with travois attached to their saddles. Allen was fascinated by the paint on their faces—some wore vermilion and others yellow and green—and their clothes, a mixture of red flannel and buckskin.

Allen and Adams watched the Ute men and women remount their horses and ride out of town, then turned back to the hotel and gathered their belongings. In the afternoon they took the Utah Central back to Ogden. The survey had set up camp near the depot, and Hayden and Stevenson were already there, making final preparations for the journey northward.

That day, a journalist from the *Ogden Junction* came to see Hayden, inquiring about the business they had in Utah, how long they were staying, and what route they would take to the Yellowstone. Utah's Mormons had spent much of the past twenty-four years resisting federal oversight of their territorial government, church leadership, and religious practices. They were suspicious of Hayden's men, who were federal officials on a government-sanctioned expedition. Hayden reassured the journalist that the survey was merely "taking observations, making sketches, taking photographs, &c." around Ogden, and that they would leave soon for the Yellowstone. He was only waiting for a few more scientific supplies to come in on the train from Washington, D.C., and then the expedition would be on its way. In the meantime, the merchants of Salt Lake City and Ogden were proving very helpful to their work; like the U.S. Army and the Union Pacific, the Mormons of Utah were vital to launching this expedition into the wilderness.

In early June, the team members explored the hills and canyons near Ogden, collecting samples of plants, rocks, birds' eggs and nests, and fossils. William and Mollie Jackson arrived, and the couple and a few other survey members took a trip up into Ogden Canyon. The geologists inspected the walls of the ravine, their stratifications exposed by a combination of both the upheaval that created the Wasatch Range and the erosion produced by Ogden Creek, which rushed by in a frothy blur. The layers in the uplifted rock were like tree rings, tracing the change over time. Newer strata of rocks were laid down over the older, and the fossils that explorers dug out of these landforms could be compared and used to develop a timeline of the earth's history.

Jackson took photographs of the creek as the party gathered at the base of a precipitous canyon wall, picnicking among the rocks tumbled down from the heights. Mollie left Ogden the next day, boarding the eastbound train for Omaha. Neither she nor Jackson knew it yet, but Mollie was pregnant with their first child.

For more than two days, Hayden oversaw the packing of all their specimens, instructing his scientists how to write the name of the item, the size, color, date and location of collection, and the name of the collector on a tag they affixed to each specimen. Spencer Baird was very particular about this labeling process, so the men needed to identify everything correctly. Hayden was relieved to receive a box of barometers from the Smithsonian, courtesy of Baird, just in time for their departure. The devices would help them measure atmospheric pressure and determine elevations along their route.

On June 10, the survey team—referred to alternatively as the Hayden Expedition or the Yellowstone Expedition in the papers—left Ogden, following a northbound road that had been improved and graded by the Wells Fargo stage company a few years before. From this point on, the real work of the expedition would begin. Hayden and his fellow scientists would decipher the records of the past, long buried in the rocks and rivers and boiling springs of Yellowstone. They would analyze and measure and record its features. This process, Hayden assured Baird, would produce a tremendous amount of knowledge of these regions so little understood by white Americans. It would "strip the region of all romance."

They were a large party: thirty-two men on horseback, with more than ten mules in tow carrying a variety of supplies. Five wagons and two ambulances followed, transporting the more fragile pieces of scientific equipment and William Henry Jackson's mobile photographic "studio," along with many wall tents, trunks, and boxes for packing specimens.

"We make a formidable camp," Hayden thought proudly, "almost an army on the march."

3

The Grandest Achievement of Our Lives

Gibraltar Island, Lake Erie. June 1871.

As Hayden and his survey team made their way into northern Utah, Jay Cooke hauled several baskets of fish out of the hull of his boat. The June afternoon on Lake Erie had been blustery, but the catch was impressive: a mess of black bass, along with whitefish, rock bass, pike, and pickerel. Lesser fishermen would have seen the weather and stayed inside to nap or read. But Cooke knew that when the winds blew strong from the northwest, the bass would be running fast and in large numbers. When that happened, the east side of Gibraltar Island was the best place to fish on Lake Erie.

Cooke took the catch up to the house, the final step in his fishing ritual at Gibraltar. Reading the signs in the sky and the waves. Jumping into the boat. Navigating the chop. Taking a hook from the crown of his broad-brimmed hat. Pulling the fish from the lake. And then, finally, presenting the catch to Mrs. McMeens, the household manager who kept Gibraltar running while the Cookes were there and while they weren't. The fish were his daily offering to his family and to God. A way to make good on the many blessings in his life.

Cooke relished his hours out on the open water, time that he spent meditating upon his life and his business. There was much to occupy his mind these days. His work recruiting investors for the Northern Pacific Railroad, whose track would come within fifty miles of Yellowstone Basin, was proving much trickier than he had imagined. But he had always found that fishing helped him to think and to pick his way through thorny financial problems.

Cooke had been an outdoorsman from his youth, roaming through the countryside outside Sandusky, Ohio, with a gun on his shoulder, in the company of his brothers, Pitt and Henry. He had grown up in a household of means, with parents who were supportive of his ambition. He was not a large boy—he would ultimately grow to five-foot-eleven and was always slight—but he was dogged and focused on the hunt.

Eager to quit school and start working, Cooke left Sandusky when he was just fourteen years old, taking jobs in merchant stores and transportation companies. He went to St. Louis, then to Philadelphia. With a talent for accounting and a prodigious memory, Cooke worked his way up from general assistant to clerk in a brokerage house. By the time he was twenty-one, he was a partner in one of Philadelphia's first investment banks, working from eight in the morning until eight at night, Monday through Saturday. He always observed Sunday as a day of rest, going to church and then out for long walks through the city streets, or along the Schuylkill River.

Although he loved his life in Philadelphia, Cooke always felt an attachment to northern Ohio and its rocky lakeshore. He made as many trips home as his work schedule allowed. In 1843, right after he made partner at his firm, he decided to stop on the way to Sandusky and see his brother Henry, who was a student at Allegheny College in northwestern Pennsylvania. There he met the brown-haired, vivacious Dorothea Elizabeth Allen. Libby, as Cooke came to call her, was the sister of one of Henry's professors.

"I lost my head that first day," Cooke said, "and the second day we were sworn friends and lifelong lovers."

Cooke and Libby were married in August 1844 and moved into an apartment above his firm in the financial district of Philadelphia. Their first son, Jay Jr., was born the next year. Seven more children arrived by the late 1850s, and four of them survived to adulthood.

The family did not make as many trips to Ohio after the Civil War broke out in the spring of 1861. Cooke had just started a new investment bank of his own, Jay Cooke & Co., and was looking for ways to serve his country. When it became clear that the war was not going to end during the first summer, and that the federal government desperately needed money to recruit soldiers and keep them on the field of battle, Cooke saw his chance.

With the help of his younger brother Henry, who was skilled at hobnobbing with politicians, Jay lobbied for the chance to sell U.S. government bonds to fund the war effort. In 1862, the government decided to issue $500 million in bonds, which Jay Cooke & Co. would advertise, sell, and distribute to investors loyal to the Union. For $50, individuals or institutions could purchase a bond and cash it in after five years for their original investment plus 6 percent, payable in gold. Americans could demonstrate their financial patriotism by investing in the federal government, and the government's fully funded effort would sustain the Union.

Cooke sent out hundreds of agents to sell the bonds to regular people: farmers, war widows, businessmen. Over the course of the war, he helped to sell more than $1 billion in war bonds, taking a commission on all the transactions. His fellow businessmen began to call him "The Tycoon." Cooke relished the attention and the new national prominence that his sale of Union war bonds had given him.

"Like Moses and Washington and Lincoln and Grant," he boasted, "I have been—I firmly believe—God's chosen instrument, especially in the financial work of saving the Union."

By 1864, Jay Cooke had made enough money to establish a permanent foothold in the Lake Erie islands, buying Gibraltar and sending his older brother Pitt there to supervise the construction of a house.

Mrs. McMeens took the fish away to the kitchen, and Cooke walked up the steps to one of the mansion's two porches, its pillars painted a creamy yellow. The main house (the family called it "Gibraltar," but everyone else called it "Cooke's Castle") was pleasingly symmetrical. Its porches flanked a massive two-story square block of stacked gray limestone bricks, each face boasting ceiling-high rectangular windows. On one side of the house, jutting out into the island's promontory, was a four-story, seven-sided turret with an observation deck on the roof. From its heights, the Cookes could see the ships coming and going from Put-in Bay, the small town on a larger island to the south, and listen to the American flag atop the turret whipping in the wind.

The house had fifteen rooms, but the turret was Cooke's favorite place in Gibraltar. It housed his library, the books stowed away in glass-fronted, gleaming dark wood cabinets. Cooke was not an intellectual, nor a great reader. But he liked to have books around him and a quiet place to conduct business during his twice-yearly visits to Gibraltar. The architect had built gently curving stairways in the tower without impeding the windows, so the light poured into each floor on three sides.

Cooke settled into a chair at a desk built into one of the cabinets. Then he took up his pen and began writing letters to a host of correspondents, including his brothers and the other partners in Jay Cooke & Co. At the end of the war, Cooke had remained focused on government finance, opening a branch of the investment bank in New York City to handle that business. After the excitement and pressure of the Civil War years, however, his work during peacetime seemed like less of a challenge and sometimes even a bore. Entrepreneurs brought him all kinds of proposals these days: inventions destined to revolutionize daily life; steamship lines that would exploit the lucrative China trade; and iron, coal, and silver mines sure to provide him with riches beyond imagination. He had opportunities to make investments in the South—and believed that former Confederates and freed people deserved a chance to better their lives—but he turned instead to the West, that region of seemingly inexhaustible natural resources. Here, Cooke believed, he could really make his mark and regain some of the national prestige he had attained during the Civil War.

As the sun began to dip below the horizon, a boat arrived at the dock, bearing the evening mail. Cooke sifted through the letters and papers until he found the *Philadelphia Inquirer*, dated June 13.

There it was, on the front page.

THE GREAT NORTHWEST, the headline read, A MASTERLY EXPOSITION. THE AUDIENCE GROWS ENTHUSIASTIC. A GREAT FURORE CREATED.

The night before, at the Academy of Music in Philadelphia, Republican Congressman William D. Kelley had talked for two hours about the lands extending from the Great Lakes to the Pacific, along the northern border of the United States. There had been "strange whisperings of wonderful resources . . . coming to the ears of the people in the East" about this region for years, the editor noted, and Kelley was there to confirm whether the rumors about the Great Northwest's marvels were true.

Kelley, who had served in Congress representing Pennsylvania since the start of the Civil War, was an "eloquent champion of Philadelphia's interests" who earned the nickname "Pig Iron" Kelley for his vociferous advocacy of iron and steel legislation. The businessmen and investment bankers in Philadelphia trusted him to tell the truth about the prospects of the Great Northwest.

Kelley was also a frequent visitor at Ogontz, Cooke's sprawling fifty-three-room estate outside of Philadelphia, which the banker had built two years after Gibraltar. Cooke had named the estate after an Ottawa chief who, family legend had it, had welcomed the Cooke family to the Sandusky area with open arms. Ensconced in comfortable leather chairs in one of the mansion's many parlors, Cooke and Kelley had long and productive conversations about America's economic prospects, discussing how to promote new businesses in the aftermath of the Civil War. To build these businesses, they would take lands from Native peoples and sell them to white Americans. Kelley had grown interested in the territories of the Great Northwest in recent years, seeing them as an ideal place from which to launch a prosperous trade with China.

It was for all these reasons that Jay Cooke had picked Kelley, and paid him handsomely, to make the "Great Northwest" speech. He needed to create some buzz around the region to promote the Northern Pacific Railroad.

In January 1870, Cooke had officially signed on to direct the financing of the railroad, whose route would connect Minnesota to the Pacific coast along the 46th parallel. He agreed to market and sell bonds to fund construction, taking a percentage of the sales for Jay Cooke & Co. It was a move that befuddled many of his friends and investment banking competitors. The transcontinental railroad business was a risky one. It depended on the goodwill and largess of Congress for company charters, public land grants, and financial backing. Almost always, transcontinentals were built in anticipation of demand, which meant that Cooke would have to advance the Northern Pacific money from Jay Cooke & Co.'s reserves to keep the railroad going as the workers laid the tracks. Jay Cooke had become the most successful banker in America by avoiding such schemes in the past.

By 1870, however, Cooke had been casting about for a new undertaking. He was in his late forties, and most of his children were grown, but he was not yet ready to stop working. The Northern Pacific appealed to his patriotism and his conviction that he still had a role to play in the development of the nation. The railroad had been chartered in 1864 as the second transcontinental, a "Centennial Line" that Congress expected would be completed by the nation's 100th birthday in 1876. But the project had stalled, mired in the sluggish postwar economy and fights over Reconstruction politics in Washington, D.C.

A great national project, Cooke believed, would bring northerners and southerners back together again in a joint effort. Farmers and ranchers had already laid claim to much of the lands along the first transcontinental, from Omaha to San Francisco. If Americans would invest in the Northern Pacific, migrants from the North and the South would flood into the Northwest, taking lands from the Lakota, Cheyenne, Arapaho, Crow, Nez Perce, Shoshone, Yakima, and Chinook peoples. Under the Homestead Act of 1862, these white settlers would convert Native lands into verdant farms of golden wheat and produce wealth for the entire nation. Cooke had always believed that the country's strength was measured in its natural resources, and they were abundant in the rolling prairies and hills of the Great Northwest.

Like President Grant, Cooke felt that the sacrifices of the Civil War must not be lost during Reconstruction, and that people must come together to defend the values that so many northern soldiers had fought for: the ability to labor freely, wherever they chose. Cooke was also convinced that building the Northern Pacific would be a feat unsurpassed in American history.

If they could pull it off, his brother Henry wrote to him in 1869, "it would be the grandest achievement of our lives."

Conquest, Cooke knew, required capital. Laying down two thousand miles of track through the Northwest would cost almost $100 million. The Northern Pacific's 1864 charter did not provide government funding, nor did Congress promise to secure any bond offerings. The government did, however, grant the company alternate sections of land along the route: ten sections to the mile in the state of Minnesota and twenty sections per mile in the territories of Dakota, Montana, Idaho, and Washington. This land, Cooke was sure, would be the draw for investors.

The Northern Pacific had to build twenty-five miles of track, however, before any of the adjacent land would be granted. Without ready land to dangle in front of businessmen and investment banks, Cooke had problems raising money. He and Henry successfully lobbied Congress to pass amendments to the railroad's charter to allow bond sales, but the response had been tepid. Then he had tried to sell the bonds at a discount, taking $88 for a $100 bond, and promising a high interest rate of 7.3 percent. Even then, Cooke had managed to raise only $30 million by the time he left for his summer trip to Gibraltar in 1871.

These funds were disappearing quickly. Although the route through Minnesota was relatively flat, the engineers and construction crews had been forced to start building track in the freezing winter months. When the snow melted away in the spring of 1870, it revealed a vast expanse of black mud. The rails already laid began to buckle, sinking into the muck. In some areas that had appeared to be firm prairie land, water was discovered just under the surface, creating more engineering problems. Despite these issues, workers had managed to build a few hundred miles of track by the summer of 1871. This was too slow for Cooke's liking. To compound his problems, some of the money that Cooke sent to his managers had vanished, with no explanation from the railroad's president or board of directors. Cooke needed to raise more funds as soon as possible.

And so Cooke had hired Pig Iron Kelley to give a speech in Philadelphia to an audience of wealthy manufacturers, bankers, and other men of influence, all of them potential buyers of railroad bonds.

"Every doorway was filled," the *Inquirer* noted, "and the aisles were occupied by those who preferred to stand rather than lose the intellectual treat spread before them for their enjoyment." It was rumored that more than two thousand hopeful attendees had been turned away.

Cooke turned to page 2 of the paper, where the story continued, filling all six columns. Kelley had touched on all the topics that he and Cooke had discussed.

Some naysayers, Kelley noted, argue that the Northwest "is unfit for the occupation of communities by reason alike of its latitude, its topography, and the character of its soil and mountains." He paused. "These objections are without foundation."

Future immigrants would enjoy the Northwest's vast resources, including gold, silver, coal, iron, copper, and other minerals. They would have plenty of timber to build their houses, and water and grass to nourish their cattle and sheep. The winters were no harsher than those in Boston or Philadelphia, Kelley argued. While the mountains might be rugged and snowcapped most of the year, the valleys abounded with buffalo, elk, and antelope, fattening themselves on grasslands that were rich and green even as the temperatures fell.

One had only to look at the shining example of Brigham Young's flourishing town at the base of the Wasatch Mountains in Utah, Kelley noted, to see what could be done in a place previously thought to be a "Great American Desert."

"The Mormons have demonstrated that by conducting the melting snow of the mountains to the foothills and valleys," he explained, "they can be made to bloom as the rose."

American migrants to the Northwest would have no need of irrigation canals, however. The Northern Pacific line would cross multiple major waterways on its route from Lake Superior to the Pacific, including the mighty Missouri and the Yellowstone. Even with these crossings, the railroad's grades were easy, with low profiles across extensive prairie lands and a peak elevation of little more than four thousand feet. It was a region of unsurpassed fecundity and unlimited promise.

"This is nature's own route," Kelley declared, "for a Pacific Railroad."

Kelley made no mention of the fact that this route crossed numerous lands currently claimed and inhabited by Native peoples, who were persistent in their assertions of sovereignty in the region. The Lakota had been defending their dominion against Indigenous enemies for thousands of years and against Americans since the early 1860s, attacking wagon trains moving through their lands and U.S. forts built west of the Missouri River, warning future migrants to stay away. Kelley never acknowledged this. Both he and Cooke felt that it was only a matter of time before the government forced these tribes, particularly the Lakota, into submission and onto reservations.

At the end of his remarks, according to the *Inquirer*, Kelley was greeted "with a perfect storm of applause."

This signaled the end of the event itself, as the second speaker of the evening, Selucius Garfielde, had been taken ill and withdrawn from the program at the last minute. Cooke was disappointed. Garfielde was a delegate to Congress from Washington Territory and a seasoned speaker on the climate of the Northwest. His remarks would have bolstered Kelley's claims about the richness of the prairie soil and the salubrious effects of the brisk climate for people and their animals.

Cooke folded up the paper. Hopefully Kelley's talk had had its intended effect. The governor of Pennsylvania, it appeared, was convinced.

"I am overjoyed," the governor said at the banquet following the lecture, "that sectional differences [between the North and South] could be forgotten in the consummation of a great enterprise like . . . this great railroad."

Perhaps Kelley had managed to sway others, particularly the bankers and industrialists with money to invest. The coverage in the *Inquirer* had been extensive and detailed. Cooke expected nothing less, given how much he had paid for it.

Cooke understood, better than most other Americans, that conquest also required advertising. He had written ad copy for businesses as a teenager and had been convinced ever since that publicity was a vital and underutilized strategy for bankers. When he founded Jay Cooke & Co., he placed regular ads for the bank in local and national newspapers, and published pamphlets and posters promoting the government bonds he sold during the Civil War.

To promote the Northern Pacific, he had also hired an old friend and newspaper editor from Sandusky, Colonel A. B. Nettleton, to run the publicity campaign. News coverage, Cooke knew, could be purchased. Nettleton was a U.S. Army veteran who fought under George Armstrong Custer, and the part owner of the *Sandusky Register*. From his office on the second floor of Jay Cooke & Co.'s Philadelphia headquarters, Nettleton launched a variety of promotional schemes to spread the word about the Great Northwest and the riches an investment in the Northern Pacific would bring. Cooke had already spent $140,000 on these publicity efforts. It was not yet clear if any of them would pay.

Mrs. McMeens came to fetch him for supper. They would eat some of the bass he had caught and then have ice cream, churned on the premises, for dessert. Devotions would follow, and then to bed. It was a small group this evening, just Cooke and his youngest son, Harry. His other son and daughter had chosen to remain in Philadelphia for this summer's trip, as each of them had young babies.

Dear, sweet Libby was not there either. She had been too ill to make the boat trip to Gibraltar in the turbulent weather of the past two weeks. Cooke had visited her a few days before in Sandusky, and she seemed better. He would go the next day and try to bring her over. He firmly believed that a few days of lake air, and suppers of lake bass, their flesh "hard & firm & sweet as honey," would do Libby a world of good.

When Libby arrived a few days later, the seas were rough. Several of their friends who made the trip with her became seasick.

"Wifie bore the sail splendidly," Cooke reported proudly, "& improved every moment." The doctors in Philadelphia had not been able to decide what was ailing her. Something to do with her heart, perhaps. Or just a general malaise. The fresh air of Gibraltar seemed to benefit her health and spirits, Cooke observed. She was still weak, but able to sit on the porch and in the hall during the day.

"This sweet Island home is indeed blessed to us all," Cooke wrote in Gibraltar's house journal. "The prayers, that a prayer hearing God listens to from this place . . . are *not unanswered*."

The next week proceeded as vacations at Gibraltar always did, with excursions and reading and laughter in the evening light.

Cooke attended to Northern Pacific business, sending orders for equipment and transferring funds to the railroad from Jay Cooke & Co.'s coffers. Nettleton had written to him about a new idea he had to fund an expedition of newspaper editors to Minnesota and Dakota. Nettleton would wine and dine them and show them the full bloom of the country in midsummer. Then the editors would write glowing reports about their experiences for their respective papers. The group would include Bayard Taylor, the Pennsylvania-born travel writer who penned vivid pieces for the *New York Tribune*, and Charles Carleton Coffin, a former Civil War correspondent whose 1870 book about the "glory and grandeur" of the Northwest, *The Seat of Empire*, included a final chapter lauding the Northern Pacific.

"Go ahead!" Cooke wrote to Nettleton. "I have great faith in being kind to editors."

Nettleton also let him know that the Phila-delphia painter Thomas Moran was on his way west to join Ferdinand Hayden's Yellowstone Expedition, with a letter of introduction from Nettleton tucked into his carpetbag.

The previous summer, Yellowstone had become a part of Cooke's promotional plans for the Northern Pacific when Nathaniel Langford con-tacted him about planning an expedition to that storied wilderness. Cooke had encouraged him and then paid for his lecture tour to Lincoln Hall in Washington, D.C., and other locations in the East after his return. Langford's article about the journey had just been published in the May 1871 issue of *Scribner's Monthly*, a new magazine marketed to middle-class Americans who wanted to read stories that amplified America's greatness.

Just fifty miles south of the planned route of the railroad, Yellowstone might attract tourists who would pay full price for passenger-car tickets on the Northern Pacific. A trip to Yellowstone would serve as an introduction to that region for many curious Americans and could convince thousands of them to buy lands along the tracks.

For weeks, the newspapers had been publishing reports on the progress of Hayden's expedition. Cooke knew Hayden had taken the artist Henry Elliott and the photographer William Henry Jackson with him. The financier approved. Like Hayden, he knew the value of images in communicating the potential of unfamiliar landscapes. He often used illustrations and maps in his posters and circulars to promote investment in his projects. They helped people visualize their future.

Earlier that spring, Cooke and Nettleton had discussed sending Albert Bierstadt to Yellowstone with Hayden. Since the early 1860s, Bierstadt, the most famous landscape painter in America, had been producing huge, sublime pictures of the American West that erased Native presence and promoted dreams of white Manifest Destiny. But Bierstadt was unable to go; he had already committed to join Clarence King's 40th parallel survey. Cooke turned to his second choice, Sanford Gifford. A painter of scenic landscapes suffused with warm light, Gifford had accompanied Hayden on his 1870 expedition and was familiar with the survey team. But Gifford was not able to join the expedition either.

Thomas Moran, however, had been available. And eager. The painter had come to Philadelphia from England as a child in 1845, at around the time Cooke was beginning his banking career. He was the fifth of seven children, almost all of them demonstrating talent in painting and photography. Like Cooke, Moran had launched himself into the working world as a teenager, learning the craft of engraving and then lithography, as part of Philadelphia's burgeoning book and magazine industry. He developed his skills as a painter as well, selling watercolors for $10 to $15 apiece or trading them for books.

Instead of volunteering for the U.S. Army, Moran went to Europe to study the great French and English landscape painters and returned to begin building a reputation for himself as an American artist to be reckoned with. One of his boyhood friends, Richard Watson Gilder, was an editor at *Scribner's Monthly* and had secured work for Moran there. It was Moran who had illustrated Nathaniel Langford's "Wonders of the Yellowstone" article that was published in the May issue.

In late May 1871, when Nettleton suggested to Moran that he join the Hayden Expedition, the artist jumped at the chance. The scientists were in Ogden when the decision was made, so Nettleton sent a letter to Hayden there. Hayden would not be expecting Moran, but Nettleton had no doubt that the scientist would see the utility of having a landscape painter along—and of making Jay Cooke happy.

"My friend, Thos. Moran, an artist of Philadelphia of rare genius," the PR man wrote, "has completed arrangements for spending a month or two in the Yellowstone country taking sketches for painting." Nettleton assured Hayden that he did not want to burden him with "more people than you can attend to." Moran was prepared to pay his own way (he borrowed funds from *Scribner's* and from Jay Cooke) and would be "no trouble at all." And, of course, Nettleton and Cooke would appreciate any details about Yellowstone that Hayden cared to share as the survey team moved through the region.

"We shall be pleased to receive occasional letters from you," Nettleton wrote, "telling of your expedition, your discoveries, your opinion of things, etc. and if there is any way in which we can serve you, be sure to let us know."

And so Moran left his wife and three children at home in Philadelphia and set out for Omaha, to catch the transcontinental line to Ogden. Cooke was pleased that he was on his way. The painter had promised him sixteen watercolor paintings of Yellowstone, some of which he would hang in the halls of Ogontz and all of which he would use in promotional materials for the Northern Pacific.

• • •

In late June, the Cookes set out from Gibraltar for a sail back to Sandusky, to attend a family wedding. When they returned, they brought Milnor Roberts, the chief engineer of the Northern Pacific Railroad, with them. Cooke had met Roberts in the 1850s and first hired him as an engineer when he started investigating the railroad business during the Civil War. By 1871, Roberts was one of America's leading civil engineers, and Cooke hired him to survey the region that would be the most challenging for the Northern Pacific's workers: the mountains and valleys of the huge territories of Dakota and Montana.

Cooke and Roberts knew almost nothing about this region, as they had not yet been able to secure a military escort for Roberts's surveying team. This area was Lakota and Crow territory, and Cooke assumed that neither of these Indigenous peoples would welcome his surveyors. The U.S. Army had finally agreed to assign a few soldiers to Roberts's crew, and he was leaving the next day for Montana. His surveying route would take him just north of Yellowstone, within shouting distance of Hayden's expedition. Before that, however, Cooke wanted Roberts to take several European investors on a tour of the Great Northwest.

Roberts left the next morning, and after bidding

him goodbye Cooke returned to the house. There he found Libby, looking worse than she had during her entire stay at Gibraltar. They decided that they must return to Philadelphia so she could consult the doctors there and enjoy the comfort of her rooms at Ogontz. Cooke arranged transportation and had their luggage taken to the dock. Before leaving, Cooke sat down before the house diary and scratched a few sentences.

"Our visit is ended," he wrote. "It has been saddened by the dear Wife's sickness. . . . May God protect and keep us & bring our dear one safely to Ogontz—Goodbye dear Gibraltar."

After saying goodbye to Mrs. McMeens, the couple left on a steamer for Erie and then caught a special train car to Philadelphia, which had been held for them. Cooke stayed close to Libby, tucking in her blankets and praying over her. He would not leave her side until her health improved. If she continued to decline, Cooke did not know what he would do. He was not sure that he could live his life without her.

4

A Wilderness of People

The Junction, Montana Territory. Late June 1871.

Ferdinand Hayden was in his tent, balancing a small box on his knees as a writing desk, when his survey manager, Jim Stevenson, hallooed at him.

"Thomas Moran has just arrived," Stevenson told him, "on the stage from Utah."

Hayden nodded. He had received the letter from Jay Cooke's man Nettleton about Moran's intent to join the expedition. He did not know Moran, but if Cooke wanted him to join the survey and he would not cost much in terms of salary or provisions, Hayden was prepared to welcome the painter. Cooke, who had abundant connections in Philadelphia and in Washington, D.C., would be a good friend to have, especially when it came time to lobby Congress again for his annual funding.

"The thing is," Stevenson added, "he's got two Saratoga trunks with him."

"What!" Hayden exclaimed, leaping up. The expedition's wagons had very little room for extra luggage. Hayden had been clear about his expectations that the men bring only their essentials.

"Send him to me! I'll fix him."

Stevenson beckoned to Moran, who was standing nearby. A frail man wearing a red flannel shirt, trousers, heavy boots, and a wide-brimmed hat, Moran carried a single carpetbag in his hand. Stevenson's eyes began to twinkle. Hayden grimaced and then laughed. His old friend knew that Hayden, who was always a little keyed up during expeditions, needed something to lighten his mood every now and again.

Everyone thought that geological surveys were the height of romance: a group of men, headed off into the unknown, in search of truth and self-knowledge. The truth was, exploring was hard work.

"Sharp and rugged ridges are to be ascended," the mineralogist Albert Peale reported, "treacherous rock-slides, that give way beneath your feet, to be crossed; bluffs to be scaled, and dangerous precipices surmounted, involving toil and fatigue." When the weather did not cooperate, the men spent dreary days in their tents. Then there were "nights when, after a hard day's work, camp is not reached, and supperless and blanketless, you lie with your feet to the fire with no covering save the cold and comfortless vault of heaven."

As the leader of the survey, Hayden was busy

from dawn to late at night every day, collecting fossils, managing the men, and keeping tabs on supplies. It had been a long slog on the road from Ogden. The summer heat had reached ninety-five degrees for several days in a row. Strong winds whipped up dust storms that drove grit into their eyes and uprooted their tent stakes, sending the men chasing after them half-blind. On one stretch, the road wound through a low, marshy plain, bringing swarms of mosquitoes into camp.

"Every man was obliged to give himself up to self-defense," George Allen noted in his diary. "Some had their mosquito netting around their heads—others their blankets or overcoats. All were in Motion, raving about the camp like so many madmen. . . . Everybody laughed, but everybody was tormented beyond endurance."

Despite these trials, Hayden was happy to report in a letter to the Smithsonian's Spencer Baird, the Yellowstone Expedition had already been productive. Each morning at around 4:30 a.m., the scientific team met around the campfire while the laborers packed up the camp into the wagons. Over pan coffee and Potato John's cooking, they peered at maps in the firelight, discussing the route for the day and what might lie along it. Once the dawn sky lightened, the men started off down the road and set to work.

Hayden had not assigned collecting groups. In his experience, men who chose their own workmates felt a sense of independence during their excursions, and this made them more effective collectors. Hayden did insist, however, that no man wander off by himself. He did not want to lose anyone like Nathaniel Langford had lost Truman Everts the year before. The political boys went off with the zoologist Campbell Carrington. They dashed about the hillsides, catching tiny prairie lizards with black and tan scales and teal bellies, and delicate butterflies with white bodies, orange spots, and gray-tipped wings.

Hayden himself found many fine fossils in the limestone and quartzite outcroppings along the route: the thin leaves of ancient ferns; round skeletons of coral, clustered together; the arcing fans that had been the outer shells of marine animals called brachiopods. They were evidence of life that bloomed and died here two hundred million years before. He chipped them carefully out of the rock and stored them in his bag.

"Nothing escapes our party," the botanist Robert Adams wrote to the *Philadelphia Inquirer*. "Birds' nest, fishes, plants, butterflies, bugs, and insects fall prey to our eager collectors."

The expedition members reconvened at a campsite each afternoon, unloading specimens from their bags and buckets, preparing labels, and packing items carefully in envelopes, boxes, or barrels. This laborious work required much patience after a day of tramping at high elevation, but the men did not seem to mind. In fact, Hayden believed that most of them were thriving.

The exception was George Allen, Hayden's friend and former professor. He could sit in the saddle for only a few hours every morning, and even during that short time, his hands became badly chapped and sore from holding the reins. By noon every day, he gave up and rode in one of the wagons. The elevation and heat brought on a series of sick headaches. Allen was also grumpy about the expedition schedule. A devoutly religious man, he disapproved of the fact that Hayden allowed the survey to continue on Sundays rather than observe the Sabbath. Allen had been able to collect some fine botanical specimens with the help of Robert Adams, but lately Hayden could tell that he was distracted, his thoughts turning homeward.

The expedition was moving slowly—fifteen miles per day—but steadily. As they progressed from the mountains of Utah into Idaho, Anton Schönborn prepared notes and sketches for the most detailed map of the region ever produced. William Henry Jackson found much to captivate him, taking more than fifty negatives from the steep hillsides.

Hayden need not have worried about his men getting lost in this first part of the journey. The road had been pulverized into ruts by Wells

Fargo stages, wagon trains, and cattle herds. All along it were ranches and farms, flanked by wheat fields, as well as an abundance of fruit and root vegetables, cultivated by Mormon families. Brigham Young had sent them north from Salt Lake City, seeking to expand his own empire in the West and to secure more food supplies for residents in the city. Their fields were lush, fed by irrigation ditches planted in a series of broad terraces. The survey members stopped frequently to buy milk and food from these farmers. There they heard stories about these migrants' journeys, and their belief that Mormons were at the center of the nation's narrative of Manifest Destiny. It was God's will, they believed, that they settled here.

These Mormon farmers had displaced Shoshone and Bannock peoples, who had emerged into these homelands thousands of years before. They established communities, hunted animals and harvested vegetables, gathered plants for medicines and weaving into baskets. Their histories and identities were rooted in these lands, where their creators had brought them out of the earth. When Mormons appeared in their homelands in the 1850s, Shoshones and Bannocks monitored the trespassers and then coordinated successful attacks on white settlements and wagon trains. The U.S. Army struck back in January 1863, massacring a camp of northwestern Shoshones at Bear River, almost wiping out an entire band. After this devastation of their community, Shoshone survivors negotiated with the federal government, and the army created a reservation for them near their garrison at Fort Hall.

The reservation was established as part of the 1867–68 Indian Peace Commission, a congressional effort to negotiate with Indigenous nations across the Northwest and the Great Plains. The commission was only the most recent effort to establish a U.S. Indian policy focused on the removal of Native peoples from their homelands and their subsequent "civilization" through conversion to white language, land ownership, politics, and culture. This policy had taken hold in the 1830s, after the passage of the infamous Indian Removal Act, but it was based on much older approaches to "Indian relations" in America. Since the seventeenth century, Euro-Americans had been trying to corral and contain the Native peoples in their midst and destroy their cultures.

The Peace Commission was one of the few Johnson administration projects that Ulysses S. Grant embraced. Grant and Ely Parker hoped that reservations like Fort Hall would establish a long-lasting peace between Native peoples and white migrants across the West. They also hoped that the 1868 treaties would reduce the costs of frontier warfare and secure the safety of white migrants and settlers.

In mid-June, Hayden and the others had stopped at Fort Hall for several days, enjoying a much-needed rest and camping among the many irrigation ditches through and around the grounds. The Shoshone were farther north just then, hunting for deer and antelope and digging camas roots out of the ground. The roots were a nutritious staple, a type of lily they would mash or boil and eat with dried meat or in a stew. As the survey moved northward, they sometimes saw families returning from these summer harvests. Leading ponies packed with their haul, Shoshone women and men stopped in the expedition's camps to talk to the guides and barter or ask for additional provisions.

Hayden counted himself lucky that the expedition did not encounter any highwaymen, gangs of white men who had been attacking and robbing stages between the gold mines of Idaho and Montana and Salt Lake City. He was wary, though, and instructed Stevenson to ride ahead of the wagon train and keep a sharp eye out. The closer they came to the mining region, a cluster of ravines on the eastern slope of the northern Rocky Mountains, the more likely it was that highwaymen would launch a surprise attack. Virginia City, the epicenter of the Montana gold rush in the early 1860s, was just a few days away.

In camp at the Junction, Hayden sent Moran to William Henry Jackson's tent to get settled and turned back to the letters he was writing. Some he would send back to Ogden, to be packed on railcars and delivered to correspondents in the East. Others were going with Jim Stevenson and the political boy, Chester Dawes, who had taken a shortcut through the mountains to Virginia City. They would notify the town's officials that the expedition was on its way and would send back word to Hayden if there was any trouble on the road ahead.

As the men guided their horses along Alder Creek into Virginia City, they gazed with astonishment at the landscape. It looked like a severe flood had ravaged the slope, carving deep cuts into the soil from the mountainsides. But these were marks that the miners had made.

The bedrock in the area was buried deep beneath the surface and getting to it required digging shafts more than twenty feet deep. To wash the dirt out of these holes in the ground and into their rockers (which would sift the gold dust and nuggets from the dirt), they carved out long irrigation ditches from Alder Creek to their shafts. These had the same effect on the landscape as a sudden flood would, wiping the ground clean of topsoil and exacerbating erosion. Piles of pebbles, driven out of the ground by the water, were scattered across the rolling hills. There were only a few men at work in the diggings, most of them Chinese miners, who immigrated to California in 1849 and moved east to the Rockies in the 1860s.

William Henry Jackson stopped and unloaded his camera, determined to capture the scene. Although several of his fellow explorers did not understand why he would want to take photographs of the mining town, Jackson was attracted to any landscape that presented contrasts in texture and shape. These were pleasing to the eye and made a landscape picturesque. Also, part of his job was to document places along the expedition's route that would appear on Schönborn's maps and in Hayden's reports. These would give politicians, scientists, and other interested readers a three-dimensional sense of the landscape of the northern Rockies and provide proof that the surveyors had really been there. He was taking negatives of all the scenes that they passed through on their way to Yellowstone, both natural and seemingly unnatural.

Jackson set up his camera on the hillside and adjusted it to capture the mounds of rubble in the foreground, the jagged creek bank cutting through the valley, and the town's cluster of low-slung wooden buildings on the rising land beyond. He waited to let the plates expose and adjusted the aperture of the lens to achieve maximum depth and definition. After five or ten minutes, Jackson removed the plate and developed it in his mobile darkroom. After he packed the negative away, the photographer gathered up his materials and mounted his horse.

He caught up with the expedition as it entered Virginia City, arriving at an auspicious moment. There was a parade forming at the foot of the main street that straggled through the center of town. It was July Fourth,' and everyone had turned out for the festivities.

"The American Flag was flying," the mineralogist Albert Peale noted. "A brass band headed the procession consist[ing] of three or four lodges of Good Templars, and a wagon containing a number of young ladies representing the different States and Territories."

Peale, Hayden, and the others urged their horses into a more formal line so they could join the parade properly as a cavalcade. When the other revelers moved off onto side streets, the expedition members and their wagon train kept moving up a hill about a mile above the town, where they established their camp. That night, several of the boys attended a ball to celebrate the nation's founding—and the ability of white adventurers like themselves to pursue life, liberty, and happiness in the gulches of the Rocky Mountains.

American miners came to the northern Rockies almost ten years after the first strikes in California taught Americans to dream of wealth built on a mountain of gold. In 1858, a pair of brothers from Iowa named James and Granville Stuart prospected the creeks of the northern Rockies and founded the mining town of American Fork. By the summer of 1862, thousands of miners—most of them white Americans but some Chinese and Mexican prospectors, and a smattering of Europeans—made their way across rugged mountain passes and through Nez Perce and Flathead territories to stake their claims in the diggings around American Fork.

In 1863, just as U.S. and Confederate armies were facing each other across the rolling green fields and sharp hills of Gettysburg, James Stuart and a group of miners set out through Crow homelands to the east. They were headed for the Bighorn River, where trappers had reported signs of gold buried in the riverbanks. Crow warriors tracked their movements and then attacked the party, forcing the miners back where they came from. They hunkered down along Alder Creek, named for the green, leafy trees that clustered along its banks. While dodging gunfire, they panned its waters, and a significant amount of gold dust settled in the bottom of their pans. The miners sent word back to American Fork. Within months, ten thousand men and a handful of women arrived in Alder Gulch and founded the town of Virginia City along the creek.

For the miners who came to Virginia City in those first couple of years, the work was hard and the outcome uncertain. This was the nature of gold mining and the root of its allure. It was the sense of possibility—the not knowing—that drove gold seekers into frenzies and stampedes. This desire was also rooted in a sense of entitlement, a belief that these lands and all the mineral wealth that lay beneath them were theirs for the taking.

Alder Gulch, it turned out, repaid many of the miners for their labor. These diggings and others across Montana, which had been founded as a territory during its gold rush in 1864, produced more than $100 million in gold between 1863 and 1870. By July 4, 1871, when Hayden and his Yellowstone Expedition arrived in Virginia City, however, most of the miners had gone, and the diggings were mostly played out. Some workers did remain, like the Chinese miners Hayden and the others saw on their way into town, staking claims until all hope was lost. A few hundred white residents also stayed on in Virginia City, their labor and services supporting the increasing numbers of people and goods moving through the Great Northwest.

The day after the expedition's arrival, the men explored Virginia City and several of the surrounding mines. George Allen wandered through the diggings and visited William Marshall, a businessman from Massachusetts, and his wife and five-year-old daughter, Nellie. After showing Allen the entire process of placer mining—the washing of the dirt out of the shaft, its transportation to the rocker, the sifting of the gold from the dirt—Marshall cooked them all lunch. Allen was delighted with his visit, especially his conversations with Nellie.

"It really does seem so good to see and hear a little child again!" he wrote wistfully in his diary.

Before Allen left to go back to the expedition camp, the Marshalls gave him a handful of tiny gold nuggets to take with him. He could keep them as souvenirs or send them back to the Smithsonian as proof of the region's prospects.

"The kindness of these Western friends I cannot soon forget," Allen wrote.

Hayden and Peale also went visiting. Judge William Lovell, one of the first residents of Virginia City, invited them to his house to meet his teenage daughter, Fanny, and to look over his prodigious collection of silver and gold ore. The scientists were particularly interested in the specimens reportedly retrieved from the banks of the Yellowstone River. Interior Secretary Delano had ordered Hayden to determine the extent of the mineralogical resources in the region. If it was rich in quartz that promised gold, this would be a significant discovery for the Yellowstone Expedition and the federal government. Although Americans had been using paper money as the currency of exchange since the Civil War, gold backed its value, and the value of government bonds. A steady supply of gold from the western mines meant a more stable national economy.

Judge Lovell did not give Hayden any of his gold, but he did present him with a giant mastodon tusk, which miners unearthed in a gulch near the city. It was a marvelous specimen, one that the Smithsonian would welcome into their collections as a record of the nation's long geological history. Mastodon fossils had enraptured American scientists since the early eighteenth century, when they were first discovered in the Hudson River Valley. Their size was astonishing, as was the fact that they were not related to any other ancient pachyderms that geologists had found. The giant animals had clearly gone extinct, a fact that flew in the face of biblical teaching about the orderly emergence of animals out of the Garden of Eden. This was an important discovery. The mastodon suggested that North America's past was one of chaos and rupture. This was a violent vision of geological change and its effects on the earth's animal life.

Albert Peale had another reason to be interested in the tusk. His great-grandfather Charles Willson Peale had first examined mastodon bones in the late eighteenth century, and credited the experience with provoking his interest in natural history. He went on to open the Peale Museum in Philadelphia, the first institution of its kind in America, which displayed both artistic works and natural-history specimens. Several years later C. W. Peale funded the excavation of mastodon bones on a farm in upstate New York; he commemorated the event in one of his most famous paintings, *Exhumation of the Mastodon* (1806–08).

Hayden and Peale carried the seven-foot-long tusk back to camp, where Peale and Jim Stevenson packed it carefully in sawdust and then wrapped it in old saddle blankets and gunnysacks. They placed it in the pile of specimens to be sent by stage back to the Union Pacific rail line and then forwarded to Washington, D.C.

Expedition members spent the next morning finishing letters and packing up their belongings. After lunch, they set out on a road winding up into the mountains northeast of Virginia City. The next day they descended into the Madison River Valley.

"A more beautiful stream we have not yet encountered," Robert Adams observed, "flowing placidly between its grassy banks, and sometimes has cut its course between the hills, forming lovely canyons rich in floral growth, a perfect harvest for a botanist."

Adams walked behind the wagon train, leaning down to pull out flowers by the roots and place them in his collecting can. He filled two cans with clusters of blue low larkspur, the sky pilot's small bunches of purple petals, and shooting stars, their green stems drooping and their white petals opening skyward.

"The very air was perfumed with their fragrance," he reported to the readers of the *Philadelphia Inquirer*, "and with the surrounding scenery, one's esthetics had full chance for indulgence."

George Allen was no help to Adams in this latest effort at collection. He had fallen ill again and had to stay in the wagon. He and Hayden decided that once the team reached Fort Ellis in a few days, Allen would leave the survey. The entomologist Cyrus Thomas would go with him. Hayden was disappointed to lose both men, but also relieved that he would not have to worry about Allen's comfort any longer. Robert Adams had proven himself an able botanist and could easily take over Allen's role in the expedition. And Carrington and the political boys could gather insects to add to Thomas's collections. They were about to reach the most difficult part of the journey, and Hayden could not afford to have any weak links in his party.

The road to Fort Ellis wound through the mountains until it pitched up to a divide that separated the Madison and the Gallatin river valleys. The men paused at the top of the pass, reveling in the view: extending fifty or sixty miles across a grand amphitheater, the valley was surrounded by jagged mountain ranges. The mining town of Bozeman, founded a year after Virginia City and currently boasting five hundred permanent residents, lay below them. Beyond it a thin ribbon of road moved eastward, a trail blazed by John Bozeman in 1864 as a shortcut to the mining district of Montana from the Oregon Trail. Bozeman carved it through the heart of Lakota and Crow territories and brought the first large groups of white migrants into their homelands. Soon the U.S. military began to build forts along the route to protect these migrants, material markers of the federal government's desire to colonize the Northwest. Crow and Lakota leaders refused to make way for the new arrivals.

"The Crow country is in exactly the right place," the chief Rotten Belly told a white trader who suggested that his people move westward to allow for white settlement. They would not leave it.

In defense of their homelands and their way of life, Crow and Lakota warriors fought U.S. Army soldiers in a series of battles. In 1866, these clashes culminated in the Hundred Men Killed Fight (remembered by whites as the Fetterman

Massacre), a Lakota ambush of soldiers who had been sent to rescue woodcutters besieged by Lakota warriors along the Bozeman Trail. Soon the U.S. Army decided that the Lakota were too powerful an enemy to fight in Montana; they did not have enough military personnel to monitor the entire length of the road. In the fall of 1868, as part of the Fort Laramie Treaty negotiations, the government agreed to close the Bozeman Trail and evacuate its forts along it. After the soldiers left, Lakotas burned the forts to the ground. Their ruins stood a reminder that while migrants, miners, and surveyors might believe these lands were theirs, Indigenous communities stood ready to disabuse them of that notion.

On July 9, Hayden and his team rode down from the mountains and into Bozeman, creating "some little sensation," Robert Adams noted, given that it was Sunday and the residents were all out and about. Passing through the town, they made their way to one of the only military forts left standing in Montana. Built in 1867, Fort Ellis was garrisoned by the Second Cavalry, whose job was to protect American miners still dreaming of a rich strike and farmers planting wheat, corn, potatoes, and turnips in the rich soil of the Gallatin Valley.

"Although considered one of the extreme frontier posts," Hayden mused, "it is a very pleasant station, surrounded with beautiful scenery with a climate that can hardly be surpassed in any country."

The survey team camped just outside of the fort, in a meadow of purple and yellow wildflowers.

The next day, the men climbed a mountain north of the camp. Hayden collected fossils along the way, all of them well-preserved plants. He would pack them up and send them directly to Leo Lesquereux, the scientist he had hired to analyze fossilized flora. After taking in the view of the country from the top of the mountain, Albert Peale reclined on the roots of a large fir tree. The view was wonderful in every direction, he judged, but especially to the southeast.

That way lay Yellowstone, with its "wonderful phenomena of waterfalls, cañon, geysers, mud volcanos, etc., the terminal point of the expedition and the main object of the whole survey."

For George Allen, the view was bittersweet.

"Here and now, doubtless, is my last experience in climbing the Rocky Mountains," the older man mused. "My face will soon be turned southward and homeward. Stage and Rail car will soon remove me from these glorious scenes. I have come far to gaze upon these mountain peaks—their broad swelling foot hills—their beautiful terraces—their pure sparkling mountain streams."

It had cost Allen a great deal to come with

the expedition, but he did not regret it. "I am a thousand times repaid," he concluded.

The next day, Allen bid his fellow adventurers adieu. He would miss them. Their wild behavior and their cursing, he now believed, was evidence not of sin but of "a frank and manly independence, and a kind quality of heart in many of them which serves as a bond of attachment." Yellowstone, the great center of their interest, lay before them, and he wished them well.

Ferdinand Hayden was not there to see Allen's stage disappear along the road. He had said his farewells earlier in the day and then set out to visit Mystic Lake, more than ten miles from Fort Ellis. With several officers from the fort as their guides, Hayden and the others spent a lovely afternoon hiking the shoreline, through "slopey hills covered with pines."

Hayden regretted only that one of the fort's officers, Lieutenant Gustavus Doane, did not accompany them and would not be part of their escort into the Yellowstone. Doane had been with Langford, Washburn, and Everts the previous year, and the report that he wrote of their findings had caused quite a sensation in Washington, D.C. Hayden had been impressed with Doane's writing and wanted to meet him. When they arrived at Fort Ellis, however, Doane was away on another campaign. Hayden had looked forward to comparing notes with this officer whose talents for composition and geological understanding seemed to him unsurpassed.

The limestone along the shores of Mystic Lake, Hayden was delighted to find, was packed with the fossils of ancient bivalves, the ridges of their shells rising in sharp lines from the rock. He secured enough of them to prove that the area was Jurassic, more than 150 million years old. Hayden was delighted that before the team had even entered the Yellowstone Basin, they were already making important discoveries that determined the age of the continent and the nature of its momentous geological changes. He wanted to stay and collect more fossils, but he had more work to do down at the camp. Peale, Jackson, Moran, and some others decided to sleep "in the open air" around the lake that night, so Hayden and the others left them there and returned to Fort Ellis.

As Hayden drew close to camp, he could see that another party had arrived at the fort. It was a U.S. Army's Engineers Corps team led by Colonel John Barlow and Captain David Heap. They had been sent by General Phil Sheridan to accompany Hayden's Expedition. The army, which had so long controlled the production of knowledge through government surveys, wanted to stake their own claim to Yellowstone.

It was irritating to have to share the trail, their Second Cavalry escort, and the glory of scientific discovery with these other explorers. Hayden was in no position to refuse Sheridan, however, when the general wrote to ask if Barlow and Heap could join him. The U.S. military supplied Hayden with food, fodder, horses, guides, and protection. He needed to stay on their good side. Hayden approached their camp to introduce himself. His plan was to be polite and to let Barlow and Heap run their own exploration alongside his. They could camp together occasionally, but otherwise Hayden would leave them to their own devices.

During the next few days, Hayden made his final preparations for the journey into the Yellowstone Basin. He hired a hunter named Joe Clark and a guide named José. The first Hispanos who came to the northern Rockies were there long before Americans ventured into the region, exploring and hunting and trapping on Indigenous lands. By 1871 they were living in many towns and camps across the Northwest, working as farmers, teamsters, wagon drivers, and miners. José and other Hispano guides often visited Fort Ellis looking for work, as did a few Black scouts and hunters like Charles "Smokey" Wilson, who had been born into slavery in St. Louis and came with his former master to Montana after Appomattox. Hayden's expedition was paying particularly good wages, and José and Clark were happy to join the team.

Satisfied with his hires, Hayden then went to

see the fort's quartermaster, from whom he drew the supplies they would need for the most arduous part of their journey into the Yellowstone. The wagon masters fixed and refitted the wagons, preparing them for the rougher roads over high mountain passes to the banks of the Yellowstone River. Presenting plans to the woodworkers, Hayden explained how he wanted boards cut to make a small boat that could be carried in pieces on muleback and then assembled on the shores of Yellowstone Lake, to sail across it and make measurements.

The other men of the expedition busied themselves taking their clothes to the fort's washerwomen to be laundered and tailored and delivering their horses to farriers to be freshly shod. They had time for some fun as well, challenging Fort Ellis's soldiers to a game of baseball.

On July 13, Hayden sat down to write a letter to Spencer Baird. He described his preparations, told Baird of the arrival of Barlow and Heap, and asked that his mentor send notices based on his letters to *Harper's Weekly*. Surely that magazine's educated, middle-class readers would be curious about the scientific discoveries that Hayden's team were about to make in the Yellowstone. They might even find the first weeks of the journey interesting, although they had been devoid of drama.

"Nothing remarkable has occurred," he told Baird, "while everything may be said to be remarkable."

On July 15, Hayden's expedition left Fort Ellis on a narrow mountain trail, bound for the Yellowstone Basin. For two days, the march was a hard slog. They yanked and pushed the wagons through a few miry places, and at one point they had to dig out a wider passage so the wagons could get through. Some of the scientists took the wrong trail. Luckily Chester Dawes and Clifford Negley, two of the political boys, found them and led them back. From the beginning, the engineers of Barlow and Heap's team lagged far behind Hayden's group, and the Second Cavalry had to divide its cohort to act as a rear guard.

When the party coalesced again at Bottler's Ranch, the men bought milk from the owners, three brothers who emigrated from Germany to Montana in the 1860s and had twenty-five dairy cattle grazing on land along the Yellowstone River. Given that the trails that led from Bottler's through the narrow canyons into the Yellowstone Basin would be even rougher and steeper than the path they had come in on, it would be impossible to take the wagons. The men spent several days repacking their supplies into saddlebags that the mules would carry.

On the night before they left, the men sat up after midnight, talking about what lay before them. Hayden leaned back against one of the packs and closed his eyes, listening to José and the other guides and packers describe Yellowstone's marvels. He said nothing about what he had learned reading the reports of Nathaniel Langford, Gustavus Doane, and the other amateur explorers who had come before.

"He was satisfied to let the wonderland tell its own story," William Henry Jackson observed, "to himself as well as to the rest of us."

On July 19, 1871, an "advance party" consisting of Jackson, Thomas Moran, their assistants, and José the guide left Bottler's and disappeared up the trail into Yankee Jim Canyon. Hayden and the others followed the day after. Their travels up to this point had been through a wilderness of people. But now they were actually "jumping off" into the relative unknown. Like the gold miners before them, the men of the Yellowstone Expedition were propelled forward by the not knowing. And by the prospect of making discoveries that would transform their lives.

Yankee Jim Canyon was a narrow thoroughfare carved by rushing waters moving through mountains that hemmed in the Yellowstone Basin. The expedition members rode their horses in single file along a narrow track high above the Yellowstone River. Its waters were bright green, a "roaring torrent" tinted that color by either algae or rock particles suspended in the water.

Emerging from the canyon walls into a valley, they passed by Devil's Slide, which Hayden judged "one of the singular freaks of nature which occur very seldom in the West." The internal forces of the earth had heaved dirt and rock skyward millions of years before. This process created high ridges made of pink sandstone, white limestone, and pale brown quartzites that moved down from the top of the mountain to the bottom in parallel.

"The intervening softer portions [were] washed away," Hayden noted, "leaving the harder layers projecting far above."

Beyond Devil's Slide lay a series of valleys, leading them toward the Basin. At the confluence of the Yellowstone and Gardiner Rivers, Hayden and the men turned their horses up the trail along the Gardiner. A handful of circular basins from six to ten feet in diameter dotted the landscape, steam rising from their placid surfaces. This was the expedition's first encounter with Yellowstone's hot springs, pools of water superheated by the volcanic forces deep beneath the ground, then circulated around the pool so that they never quite reached the boiling point. Around the edges of these hot springs, much to Hayden's surprise, sat several men.

They were men beset by illness, they said. Miners from Virginia City and other diggings who had come to the pools to heal aching muscles and rheumatism. They were living in tents they had pitched farther back from the riverbank.

"Their praises were enthusiastic in favor of the sanitary effects of the springs," Hayden noted.

Seeking to leave this unexpected evidence of civilization behind, Hayden flicked the reins and turned his horse to the right, urging him up a steep hillside. Birds flitted between the pines and cedars along the trail. Between the notes of their songs, another sound reached Hayden's ears: the dull echo of his horse's hooves as they hit the ground, suggesting that it was hollow just below the surface.

The path pitched sharply upward. As the expedition came over the crest the men stopped, one by one. Before them rose a huge complex of hot springs, three hundred feet high and at least half a mile wide. It looked like a frozen waterfall. It was bright white in places because, as the scientists on Hayden's team would determine later, it was made of travertine, a calcium carbonate rock that is the primary compound in limestone. Hot water, forced to the surface at the top of the structure, made its way down through hundreds of oval pools, pausing briefly in one before dropping to the next. The bacteria and algae living within the pools stained them bright pink, yellow, brown, or red. After gazing upon this marvel, the leader of the Second Cavalry escort, Captain George Taylor, reached into his pocket, groping for his diary so he could record his first impressions. He had left it with the pack train, however, so all he could do was stare. After a moment, Hayden turned to Taylor.

"I have traveled all over the world," he told the soldier. "I have been exploring 17 years. I thought I had viewed all the great wonders." Hayden paused. "But all sink into insignificance compared with this."

There had been rumors of this curiosity, hints in the tales of mountain guides and the stories of the Shoshone and Bannock peoples. Taylor himself had heard about it from hunters who roamed the Gallatin Mountains looking for elk and deer to sell to Fort Ellis's quartermaster. Some called it "The White Mountain," and others "The Frozen Cascade." The sick miners taking the waters below clearly knew that it was here. But Langford and his exploration team had passed right by it. No American had ever written a record of it, much less a scientific analysis.

The survey team left their horses on a grassy flat and began to climb up a path along its edge. They passed pool after pool. Their vivid colors Hayden could compare only to aniline dyes, manufactured in the textile mills of the East Coast: scarlet, delicate pink, light rose. Indications of iron in the water, Hayden surmised. Deep yellow and light cream, signaling the presence of sulfur.

As the men climbed upward, they moved

backward in geological time. The bubbling springs were smaller, and the ground was covered with elegant travertine mounds and tall, fragmented chimneys. These were remains of dead hot springs, the ruins of nature. Inspecting them more closely, Hayden could see how the water had precipitated into thousands of thin, delicate layers, like the rings of a tree trunk. How long it had taken the water to build up such a beautiful structure, Hayden could not tell. He broke off a piece of the travertine and placed it carefully in his leather bag.

The men clambered back down the path and returned to their horses. Taking the tents from the pack mules, they stretched the large canvases over poles and tapped the spikes anchoring the ropes into a grassy field below the structure. Barlow, Heap, and their men, along with the Second Cavalry soldiers, camped nearby. When they lay down to sleep that night, they could hear water boiling and bubbling beneath their heads.

The expedition stayed at their camp below the White Mountain for the next two days. Hayden hiked around it, collecting rocks and other specimens. The artist Henry Elliott went with him, stopping periodically to sketch the plant and animal fossils that Hayden found. Anton Schönborn came along as well, making notes regarding the White Mountain's location and elevations.

Several of the scientists lay down on their stomachs next to the pools, reaching out beyond the encrusted edges to dip their vials in the water. They discovered that the water was hottest at the top of the structure and cooled as it tumbled downward. By the time it reached the pools by their camp, the water was the perfect temperature for bathing. At the end of each day, the survey members stripped down and submerged themselves.

William Henry Jackson spent his days leading his mule up and down the steep path along the side of the cascade, unpacking his equipment whenever he found an angle that appealed to him. The hard and soft edges of the White Mountain, in contrast with the dark, forested hills all around, made for striking views.

Thomas Moran went with Jackson, pulling sheets of paper out of his portfolio to capture the scene in pencil sketches, which he would fill in with watercolors. His painting was often interrupted, however, when Jackson sent him to clamber over the calcified structure to pose among the frozen mounds. Humans gave the viewer a sense of scale, and Moran appeared in several of Jackson's photographs, standing or sitting, leaning on a tree or the cascade itself, his dark form a contrast with the white structure. When Albert Peale came by, returning to camp after a day of collecting minerals around the edges of the pools, Jackson pulled him in, too, and he posed with Moran on the top of what would become known as the Pulpit.

On the third morning, the survey members sorted their specimens, sketches, maps, and photographic negatives, packed them in wooden boxes, loaded the mules, and left the White Mountain. On their way back down to the Gardiner River, they passed the convalescent camp once again. Here they found two men named J. C. McCartney and Harry Horr, who told Hayden that they had a ranch in the vicinity.

"We have taken out a claim for 320 acres," they bragged, much of which included the frozen cascade. "We expect to commence the construction of a two-story hotel next week."

Albert Peale was impressed, commending the men for their foresight.

"It requires no stretch of the imagination to see this place in the near future thronged with invalids drinking this water and bathing in it for their health," he wrote to the *Philadelphia Press*. Surely one of the city's wealthiest benefactors, Jay Cooke, would be pleased.

"When the Northern Pacific Railroad runs through the country, this will be one of the places that no tourist will think of neglecting, for it will rank with any natural curiosity that the world can produce."

Hayden was not so sure. Could scientists

continue to study the White Mountain if it were thronged with tourists and health seekers? Would private ownership turn one of the West's grandest sights imaginable into an eyesore, like the commercial hotels crowded around Niagara Falls in New York? Could this place continue to exist if it were full of people?

Hayden did not consider that Yellowstone was already a crossroads of many other people, Natives who had long been stewards of the land and kept its ecosystem in balance. And he did not have time to dwell on his vision of the region's future now. The expedition set off to the north, following the Gardiner River back to its junction with the Yellowstone.

"We must not linger here," Hayden mused, "but wind our way up the valley in search of more wonders."

5

No Middle Ground

Washington, D.C. July 1871.

Throughout the summer, Americans read updates from the Hayden Expedition in the newspapers: their progress northward through Idaho, their turn toward the Yellowstone Basin, the incredible discovery of the White Mountain. Alongside these were articles about crop conditions in the drought-ridden midwestern states, spectacular murders and other acts of villainy across the country, and local news and gossip. The papers in the East also carried news of Jay Cooke's Northern Pacific Railroad and the glorious prospects for the white settlement of the Great Northwest, along with notices announcing that railroad lines like the Denver and Rio Grande were laying down track across the Plains.

There was not much legislative news to report. The Forty-Second Congress had ended their first session in April and would not reconvene until December. Some senators and congressmen stayed in Washington, while others went home to tend to their families, constituents, and other business ventures. The Republican members of Congress were satisfied with all they had done in the first session to exert federal control in the West, including funding the Hayden Expedition. In July, the newspapers were abuzz with the latest news about their efforts in the South, reporting in detail about the work of the "Ku-Klux Committee."

Republicans had been worried about the increasing violence of the Ku Klux Klan since reports of their assaults on Black and white Republican voters poured into Washington, D.C., the previous fall. In February 1871, the Forty-First Congress decided to launch an investigation of conditions in North Carolina. The Senate's published report confirmed that white southerners were carrying out campaigns of violent intimidation there, and that the state government and local militia were doing nothing to protect Black men and women from these assaults. The Forty-Second Congress had decided to continue this work, and President Grant encouraged them.

"The United States is bound," he declared in March 1871, "to protect the peaceable citizens of [any] State against domestic violence."

It was imperative, Grant argued, that Congress pass legislation to enforce the Fourteenth and Fifteenth Amendments where state governments had abandoned their duty to do so. Grant also suggested that a joint committee be formed, to investigate the realities of the situation.

Answering that call, Congress had created the Joint Select Committee on the Condition of Affairs in the Late Insurrectionary States. This decision signaled the seriousness of the Republicans' intention to halt the Klan's violence and protect Black rights. Democrats from both houses agreed to serve, and the committee members remained in the capital into the early summer, interviewing witnesses about racial conflicts in North Carolina, South Carolina, Georgia, Alabama, Mississippi, and Florida.

The formation of a joint select committee was not unusual in congressional history, but it was not commonplace either. Created in response to specific crises for the purposes of investigation, most of these committees in the mid-nineteenth century focused on conditions in the South or the West. The Joint Committee on the Conduct of the War operated from 1861 to 1865, gathering testimony related to the misconduct and corruption of U.S. Army officers, reports of "savage" actions on battlefields, and mistreatment of prisoners of war. News of a U.S. Army company's brutal massacre of Cheyenne and Arapaho men, women, and children at Sand Creek in Colorado Territory in 1864 led to the formation of a separate joint committee, charged with determining the "Condition of Indian Tribes" that controlled territories in the Great Plains, Northwest, and Southwest. Committee members fanned out across the West, interviewing Indigenous peoples, government officials, and U.S. Army officers from Kansas to California, Montana to New Mexico.

"The Indians everywhere," the committee concluded in 1867, "are rapidly decreasing in numbers from various causes," including disease, warfare among themselves and with whites, and the destruction of buffalo and other game because of "the steady and resistless emigration of white men into the territories of the west."

Indigenous peoples were doomed, they determined, "by the irrepressible conflict between a superior and an inferior race."

To bring the states and territories of the West more firmly into the Union, the committee decided, the federal government would have to remove Indigenous peoples to reservations, provide them with provisions and other forms of support, and encourage their "civilization." This embrace of the reservation system would have the added benefit of clearing the way to the rich agricultural lands and mineral deposits of the American West for white settlers.

While they laid plans to control the West in the postwar years, Congress also turned their attention to bringing the South back into the fold. The Joint Committee on Reconstruction, formed in December 1865, ultimately determined that the federal government would have to set strict guidelines for readmission, forcing the rebel states to acknowledge the Thirteenth Amendment and protect Black rights to regain their seats in Congress. The committee's discussions had led to the passage of the Fourteenth Amendment, providing citizenship for all people born or naturalized in the United States—except for "Indians, not taxed." In other words, all Native peoples who remained in their homelands and refused to be removed to reservations.

Although the former Confederate states rejoined the Union by 1870, it was clear to all members of Congress that states across the South were still in turmoil. In South Carolina, the violence directed at Black people that spring and fall became so constant and intense that the state's Republican governor, Robert Scott, requested U.S. soldiers to defend its citizens. President Grant did not hesitate. He diverted several companies of the Seventh Cavalry from their posts in the West to the Palmetto State.

In June 1871, as they spoke to white and Black witnesses in Washington, D.C., the Joint Select Committee on the Condition of Affairs in the Late Insurrectionary States decided to send a subcommittee to South Carolina to interview victims of Klan atrocities there. Its members were John Scott (a Republican Senator from Pennsylvania), Job Stevenson (a Republican representative from Ohio), and Philadelph Van Trump (an Ohio Democrat).

President Grant, who was spending the summer at his beach house in Long Branch, New Jersey, kept tabs on these developments. John Scott came to see the president before he left for South Carolina, and the two discussed the goals of the trip. The subcommittee intended to determine whether there were clandestine organizations with political motives at work in South Carolina, Scott told Grant. If they were armed and numerous enough to change the outcome of elections, these groups were in violation of the Ku Klux Klan Act, which Congress had passed in April.

In this act, Congress gave Grant the power to suspend the writ of habeas corpus in places where the state failed to protect the rights of all citizens and where violence constituted a rebellion against the federal government. Klan members had been taking advantage of the writ (which ensured that authorities could not unlawfully or indefinitely imprison citizens) to avoid arrest and intimidate potential witnesses against them. The suspension of the writ would allow government and military officials to arrest Klan members, put them in jail, and try them immediately. It would be an unprecedented use of executive power in peacetime.

Grant was confident that the Constitution

allowed him to exert his presidential powers in this way. The federal government had expanded considerably during the Civil War, because Congress and the president needed to marshal a tremendous amount of financial and human resources. That growth continued during the first years of Reconstruction as Congress passed amendments that brought an end to slavery, defined what it meant to be a citizen in America, and expanded the vote to all men— all the while confirming the right of the federal government to "enforce [these articles] by appropriate legislation." Grant believed that he and Congress now had the right to enact their expanded authority on behalf of the South's most vulnerable citizens.

John Scott and the other subcommittee members left for South Carolina in late June. They went first to Columbia, the state capital. They took testimony there and stayed through the fourth of July, celebrating the nation's founding in the cradle of secession. The next day they boarded a train bound for the town of Spartanburg, a busy commercial center in the Carolina upcountry and one of the hotbeds of racial violence.

On July 10, a woman named Lucy McMillan appeared before them in the second-floor ballroom of the Palmetto House in central Spartanburg to tell her story.

McMillan had lived on a farm north of

Spartanburg for more than twenty years. Bob McMillan purchased her sometime in the late 1840s, after she ran away from a previous owner and lay out in the countryside for more than three months. She was in her twenties then and a good worker; that's likely why McMillan bought her despite her rebellious past. The farm was tucked between two forks of the Pacolet River, in a region of the South Carolina upcountry that produced some cotton but mostly corn and wheat. It was land that originally belonged to Catawba and eastern Cherokee peoples; several of their communities remained on Spartanburg County's northwestern borderlands in the Great Smoky Mountains. By the 1850s, there were 20,000 whites living in Spartanburg County and 9,000 enslaved people.

As one of several slaves on McMillan's farm, Lucy worked the land and looked after one of the white family's sons, a boy named Kennedy. She had three children of her own, two of them with her husband, an enslaved man whom Bob McMillan sold away from her right before the Civil War began.

After the war McMillan chose to stay on the farm, where she had a small house built of logs with a rock chimney. To leave would have been to abandon lands that McMillan believed were rightfully hers by the labor she had put into them. For more than five years after the war she worked for Bob McMillan, and the crops she planted flourished.

The Ku-Klux came for her on a Monday night in October 1870, a few weeks before the midterm election. She had been going out on Saturday nights to "speakings," political meetings at which Republican party members told Black men and women about the rights and privileges granted to them by the Fourteenth and Fifteenth Amendments. McMillan could not vote (the recently ratified Fifteenth Amendment had reserved the right of franchise to men only), but she and other Black women often attended these gatherings, absorbing information about possible land redistribution efforts and asking questions about land sales in the area.

One Saturday night, after she returned from a speaking, a local woman pulled her aside to warn her that the Ku-Klux knew where she had been.

"They say you were bragging and boasting that you would have the land," she told McMillan. "The Ku-Klux are going to whip you for that."

The mere thought that a Black woman might aspire to be a landowner enraged the white men and women of Spartanburg County, who had built their wealth and sense of themselves on their perceived racial superiority. White identity became even more important to them after the defeat of the Confederacy during the Civil War, and the return of rebel soldiers to a new world of Black freedom and political equality. In Reconstruction South Carolina, a Black woman speaking out about her ambition and her potential in public—that was an unpardonable crime.

McMillan knew the Ku-Klux and what they were about. All the Black women and men in Spartanburg County did. The masked riders first appeared in the area in 1868, adopting a model of action from Klans in Pulaski, Tennessee. They took oaths of loyalty to one another and to the organization. They recruited merchants, clerks, lawyers, and laborers, spreading the word along railroad lines across upcountry South Carolina. They disguised themselves and rode out at night, attacking Black women and men and white Republicans who dared claim spaces and power for themselves. They had stepped up their activities during the 1870 election, riding through the county "drowning people, and whipping people, and killing them."

McMillan spent the next three nights hiding out in the woods with her youngest daughter, Caroline. On the third night, they heard hoofbeats along the river. A group of riders emerged out of the darkness and turned their horses toward her small log house. The moon was shining bright, so she could see them clearly. As they passed by her hiding place, McMillan backed quietly through the underbrush and took Caroline by the hand. The two of them crept through the woods up a small hill. They watched as the men dismounted, their white gowns glowing in the moonlight.

The Ku Kluxers pounded on her front door, yelling for McMillan to come out. A couple of them tipped their heads back and howled into the night, shooting off their pistols. When there was no response, they knocked down the door and rushed into her house, throwing furniture around the small room. When they could not find her, the men came back outside and stood around together. McMillan did not know what they were up to until she started to see the flames licking up through the oak boards of her roof.

The light of the fire illuminated the men's faces. Some were painted red and others black. Several wore horns on their heads, made of rags stuffed with cotton. Despite their disguises, McMillan knew four of them by the sound of their voices as they passed her along the wood edge, and by the way they walked after they jumped off their horses. One of them was Kennedy McMillan.

Once McMillan's house was entirely ablaze, the night riders mounted their horses and galloped off in every direction. In the morning, McMillan walked out of the woods to inspect the ruins of her house. Only the rock chimney remained. It was a devastating loss: for most freed people, establishing a home was their first act of freedom. Homes protected them from the elements and symbolized the strength of their families. This was, of course, why the Ku-Klux targeted Black people in their houses, as well as the houses themselves. It was the white man's way of reasserting the hierarchies of enslavement and control over the bodies and lives of their former slaves.

McMillan took Caroline and her son, who had been away the night of the Ku-Klux attack, to stay with a friend in Spartanburg. She reported the arson to a local official, who upon hearing her story promised to arrest Kennedy McMillan and his co-conspirators. She waited. They were never arrested.

Afraid to return to the farm, Lucy McMillan decided to stay in Spartanburg. She turned her attention to making a new life for herself in town, working as a washerwoman to support herself and her children. For almost nine months, McMillan had gone from house to house to pick up laundry and then return to the yard behind hers to stoke the fire and scrub, rinse, and wring out clothes and linens. This was not the post-emancipation life she had dreamed of. She had wanted to own and tend to her land and raise Caroline in a home of her choosing. But she was surviving.

And now, finally, in this hotel ballroom on a sweltering summer day in 1871, was McMillan's chance to bear witness to what she had lost to the Ku Klux Klan. After she told her story, the committee members questioned her about the details. Philadelph Van Trump accused her of lying.

"I am not going to tell a lie for anybody, because it is no use," she retorted. "I know the consequences will be with me at the day of the resurrection . . . I must be just and He will be just to us all."

Appearing at the Palmetto House that day was a huge risk for Lucy McMillan. The Klan might punish her for speaking up. But the federal government had defined her as a citizen in the Fourteenth Amendment and declared that she had rights that it would protect. These northern congressmen had come to Spartanburg to hear her story. Backed by the power of the president and the U.S. military, perhaps they would bring her some form of justice. The very fact that they were asking about her life was unprecedented, a unique moment in the federal government's history of intervention on behalf of the nation's citizens. Maybe Lucy McMillan's voice—and the hundreds of other voices of Black Americans who bore the marks of Klan attacks—would not be lost in the din and whirl of life in 1870s America. Perhaps they would resound and be heard as a call to action.

The subcommittee spent almost two weeks in Spartanburg, then moved on to Yorkville, another breeding ground of Klan violence. Back in Long Branch, President Grant continued the work of his office and waited for their reports. The subcommittee would return at the end of July, and then write up their findings. Grant was eager to know what the Black residents of upcountry South Carolina had told them, and whether they had enough evidence to justify federal intervention.

Most of the Republicans in Congress supported the president's aggressiveness on this matter. The Democrats, many of them from New York and the midwestern states, did not.

"Grant is a mere military chieftain," scoffed Philadelph Van Trump, the Democrat on the subcommittee, "unlearned in the civil policy of the government," for whom "no violation of the Constitution, however palpable, no assumption of power, however outrageous, is deemed too great a sacrifice in extending and strengthening the executive power in his hands."

Grant knew that these fights about the nature and extent of presidential authority would continue. Democrats did not have the majority in Congress, but they were a vocal minority. Van Trump would likely return from the trip to the Palmetto State with a very different view of the situation there than John Scott and Job Stevenson. Grant would have to wait for their reports, however, before making his decision about declaring martial law in South Carolina.

While Grant's Democratic political rivals

worried about the president's embrace of federal authority to defend equal rights in the South, they had very few qualms about the use of executive power to contain and control Native peoples in the West. This was one belief almost all white Americans shared in 1871: the federal government owned all public lands across the continent, and Congress could do with these lands what they wished. If any of the tribal nations stood in the way of white settlement and development, they would have to be exterminated or removed.

Grant rejected the former option for the latter. He favored a reservation policy based on treaties and a process of "civilization" that might lead to Indigenous political representation in Congress.

"The proper treatment of the original occupants of this land, the Indians, [is a topic] deserving of careful study," he had told the nation in his first inaugural address in 1869.

The reservation system had been in place since the early nineteenth century, and most white Americans believed Natives would have to abandon their Indigenous identities to survive. But Grant's emphasis on Indigenous citizenship struck some of his Republican colleagues as too progressive.

One of the president's only allies in this vision of U.S. Indian policy was Ely Parker. The two men first met in Galena, Illinois, in 1860, where

Parker was working as a civil engineer and the future president was clerking in a leather store. Parker was six years younger than Grant, a stocky block of a man with a large head, sweeping black hair, and a wispy goatee. At first glance, the two men had almost nothing in common. Grant was the child of hardscrabble tanners and Parker was a descendent of the eminent Seneca leaders Red Jacket and Cornplanter. Grant had washed out of the military and cast about for a career for a year, while Parker was driven and focused, mastering English at several different academies and reading the law. When American citizenship requirements prevented him from taking the bar exam in the state of New York, Parker switched fields to engineering. He took a job with the treasury department, inspecting and building lighthouses in the upper Great Lakes. Then he was transferred to Galena to supervise the construction of federal buildings there.

When the Civil War began, Parker was eager to serve in the U.S. Army, but Illinois state officials denied him a commission as an officer because, they argued, only citizens could become officers. He could have enlisted in the war as a private or an auxiliary (a scout or spy)—around 20,000 Indigenous men served in this capacity, in both the U.S. and the rebel armies—but he believed his talents lay in command, not fighting. Parker watched as many of the white men he knew in Illinois went off to war without him.

Grant, who had come to appreciate Parker's prodigious talents and trusted his assessments of the world around him, used his leverage as a major general in the U.S. Army to lobby for Parker's appointment to his staff. Parker joined Grant at the Battle of Vicksburg in 1863 and began his work as the general's secretary; the two men spent the rest of the war together. It was Parker who, in his meticulous handwriting, wrote Grant's letter to Robert E. Lee at Appomattox on April 9, 1865, laying out the terms of the rebel army's surrender.

When Grant became General of the Armies during Andrew Johnson's administration, he found more work for Parker, sending him to Louisiana, Mississippi, and Texas to determine how Black and white southerners were negotiating their new realities. His reports to Grant were prescient.

"Time alone will change the long-settled convictions of the Southerner into the necessity of granting the negro all the rights demanded for him by the General Government," Parker advised Grant, "and I fear that until that event takes place the presence of troops in the South will be an absolute necessity."

During his travels, Parker saw the parallels between the situation of freed people like Lucy

McMillan and Native peoples in Reconstruction America. White people across the nation assumed their racial superiority over both groups and clearly intended to do all they could to take freedom and means of subsistence from them. In Parker's view, the federal government must protect both Black Americans *and* Native peoples, to gradually bring them into the body politic as full citizens.

Like the members of the 1865–67 joint committee who were sent to investigate the condition of Indigenous peoples across the West, Parker believed that Indian removal to reservations was the key to a peaceful future. Although many Indigenous peoples across the nation and chiefs like Sitting Bull disagreed with this vision, Parker steadfastly argued that all Native peoples should be guaranteed residency and ownership of their reservation lands, be taught English and farming, and eventually become "civilized." Then perhaps their reservations could be admitted into the Union as territories or even states. Parker's plan appealed to Grant, and he made it the centerpiece of his Indian policy as president.

"A system which looks to the extinction of a race is too abhorant [*sic*] for a Nation to indulge in," Grant told Congress in his first message to them in 1869, "without entailing upon the wrath of all Christendom . . . I see no remedy to this except in placing all Indians on large reservations . . . and giving them absolute protection there."

Grant wanted to see this policy through, and he thought that Ely Parker was the man to do it. In April 1869 he nominated his friend and former secretary to be the commissioner of the Office of Indian Affairs. Grant argued that Parker could serve in this position because, according to the recently ratified Fourteenth Amendment, Parker was in fact a citizen. The amendment excluded "Indians, not taxed" from citizenship, and Parker had paid taxes to the U.S. government for years. Congress was persuaded, and Parker became the first Indigenous person to hold this important position.

The job was strenuous, requiring regular contact with hundreds of Native nations (many of them in the West), oversight of annuity distributions, and the hiring and firing of Indian agents housed at federal agencies across the country. Parker worked hard, hoping to bring his and Grant's vision of a peaceable future with Native peoples to fruition.

Very few congressmen of either party supported Grant's and Parker's plans. A concerted effort to oust Parker from his post began only a year after his appointment. That spring Congress had debated the annual Indian Appropriations Act for so long that the annuities usually distributed to

Native nations in the early summer were delayed. Parker was forced to forgo the open call for bids to provide food and other provisions to Indian agencies. Instead, he decided to hire one merchant to ship annuity goods to several agencies along the upper Missouri River, including those that served Lakota bands. This single decision, made for the benefit of Native peoples, initiated a power struggle between Parker, Congress, and a newly created oversight committee called the Board of Indian Commissioners.

During the next year, Congress launched investigative hearings to decide if Parker's hiring of the one contractor was illegal. Although they ultimately found that it was not, the board continued to criticize Parker's leadership and Grant's policy vision in Indian Affairs. When Congress passed the 1871 Indian Appropriations Act—at the same time they gave $40,000 to Ferdinand Hayden to explore the Yellowstone—they inserted a rider at the end of the measure.

"Hereafter no Indian nation or tribe within the territory of the United States shall be acknowledged or recognized as an independent nation, tribe, or power," it stated, "with whom the United States may contract by treaty."

Although the rider kept existing treaties in place, it constituted a meaningful shift in U.S. Indian policy. It meant the government no longer recognized Indigenous sovereignty, and that officials would increasingly choose warfare rather than diplomacy as a method of "negotiating" with Native nations. The rider also undercut Ely Parker's ability to implement his and Grant's plans.

Some politicians recognized the potentially catastrophic effects of this rider for Indigenous peoples and for the development of the West.

"I greatly fear the adoption of this provision," Eugene Casserly, a Democrat and senator from California, declared, "is the first step in a great scheme of spoliation, in which the Indians will be plundered, corporations and individuals enriched, and the American name dishonored in history."

Ely Parker knew this to be true. The rider would change the trajectory of Indian Affairs. Because it was an appropriations bill, Grant was forced to sign it. If he did not, Native peoples living on reservations would go without their annuities for at least six months, possibly a year. With buffalo herds declining and a drought spreading across the Great Northwest, this lack of federal provisioning meant that tens of thousands of Indigenous people in the region would starve. While Grant and Parker had been optimistic that they could help reorient Congress toward a new vision of federal Indian policy, it was clear now that Congress would continue to dispossess and disempower Native peoples to promote white settlement in the West.

Grant had hoped for a better outcome. But even he had doubts about the efficacy of treaties as the primary method of dealing with Native peoples. Several Indigenous nations, including the Lakota, had launched effective campaigns against Indian agencies and U.S. forts in the Yellowstone River Valley since the early 1860s. Grant's time in the U.S. Army had conditioned him to see the military as the most useful tool in Indian diplomacy. And as much as he liked Ely Parker, he considered him to be exceptional. Most Native peoples, the president believed, were "savages."

In the summer of 1871, Parker decided to resign.

"The effect of Congressional legislation, had since I have had the honor to be Commissioner of Indian Affairs," Parker wrote to Grant in his resignation letter in late June, "has been to almost wholly divest the Indian Bureau of all its original importance, duties, and proper responsibilities."

Parker had tried to promote Grant's "wise and beneficent Indian policy," he went on, "but I cannot in justice to myself . . . continue to hold the ambiguous position I now occupy as Commissioner of Indian Affairs."

Sitting in his oceanside office in Long Branch, Grant regretted that this moment would bring an end to his and Parker's time together. To him, Parker exemplified everything that Indigenous peoples could become if only they abandoned their traditional ways and embraced American identity. Parker had served his country ably in the war and had always acted honorably in his position as commissioner of Indian Affairs. He was also a loyal colleague.

"Your management of the Indian Bureau has been in entire harmony with my policy, which I hope will tend to the civilization of the Indian race," Grant wrote in his reply to Parker. "It has also been able and discreet. In leaving the public service to pursue a more independent course of life, you take with you my sincere wishes for your prosperity."

Grant folded and sealed the letter and added it to his pile of outgoing mail. He had several other reports to read and letters to write, including one concerning the future of the Chiricahua Apaches in New Mexico and Arizona. Their agent had written to say that that tribe, under the leadership of Cochise and Geronimo, might be willing to go to a reservation if it were in their homelands. If the agents and military commanders could bring this about, such a move would end a ten-year struggle in the Southwest, which had begun as part of the Civil War in that region.

Grant hoped that this would happen. When he had said "let us have peace" during his presidential campaign, he had meant it. He wanted an end to the turmoil in the South and in the West. In South Carolina *and* in Lakota

Territory. If he had to use force, he would. But he did not want to.

"I don't like riding over and shooting these poor savages," Grant told a newspaper reporter that summer, revealing that his approach to Indian policy rested firmly on his belief in white racial superiority. "I want to conciliate them and make them peaceful citizens. The policy of peace, sir, is much preferable to the policy of war."

6

The Most Remarkable Scenery in the World

Mount Washburn, Yellowstone Basin.
Late July 1871.

T here is nothing like standing on a mountain-
top for seeing how everything fits together.
Ferdinand Hayden stepped carefully among the
broken piles of brown and black volcanic rock
near the summit of a peak named after Henry
D. Washburn, the surveyor-general of Montana
Territory who was a member of Langford's
1870 expedition. Hayden moved to the edge
and took in the landscape spread out below him.
Along the horizon in every direction were sharp
peaks rising, their summits covered in everlasting snow: the Gallatin Range, named for
Thomas Jefferson's secretary of the treasury; the
Absarokas, named for the Crow people's term
for themselves; and the Tetons, another name for
the Lakota. To the south, the broad blue sheet
of Yellowstone Lake, which Hayden believed to
be the highest freshwater lake on the continent,
glinted in the sun. And to the southwest, the
jagged chasm of the Yellowstone River plunged
into the earth, its depths obscured in darkness.

The wind blew in powerful gusts. Hayden backed away from the edge and took barometric measurements of air pressure to determine the summit's elevation, while Albert Peale and Henry Elliott lay prone on the rocks, holding down Elliott's paper as he sketched the peaks in the distance. It was a struggle, but the artist was able to produce an accurate rendering of all the surrounding ranges in the short time they had available to them at the summit. It was the expedition members' first glimpse of the great Basin from above, and Elliott's sketch would provide Anton Schönborn with the landmarks he needed for his topographical maps. It would also help Hayden prove his theory of the geological origins of Yellowstone.

The Basin was "one vast crater, made up of thousands of smaller volcanic vents and fissures," Hayden believed, a caldera "out of which the fluid interior of the earth, fragments of rock, and volcanic dust, were poured in unlimited quantities" during the final years of the Pliocene epoch, more than two million years before. This meant that, in the broad sweep of geological time, Yellowstone was a comparatively young landscape. In many millennia since its creation, driving wind and rain carved the cooling lava rocks into valleys, gullies, canyons, and steppes.

For years, geologists had argued about the processes of geological change. Some advocated the "vulcanist" theory, the idea that the earth's molten core was under constant pressure and at times broke forth in massive cataclysms that elevated new mountain ranges, spewed lava, and caused earthquakes that changed the earth's surface. Others argued that long periods of slow erosion transformed the continent. The Yellowstone Basin proved for Hayden that it was *both* eruption and erosion that explained America's geohistory.

Mindful of the miles they still had to ride, Hayden led his horse down the steep slopes of Mount Washburn, heading southwest toward the canyon. It had become clear to him that the mountain range over which Washburn loomed constituted the northern rim of the caldera. Here was a zone of transformation, in which the basaltic rocks of the rim gave way to the breccia of the crater. The latter were softer and more vulnerable to erosion. As the Yellowstone River carved its way through both rim and crater, it wore away the rocks downstream and formed a series of ledges.

"It is through this portion of the rim that the river has cut its channel," he concluded, "forming the remarkable falls and the still more wonderful cañon."

Peale and Elliott joined Hayden on the descent and, near the foot of the mountain, they ran into members of the Barlow-Heap party. They walked together through seven miles of thick forest, guiding their horses carefully through a maze of fallen fir and pine trees, to the expedition's camp along Cascade Creek. It was a lovely place, perched on the edge of the creek before it entered the Yellowstone between that river's Lower and Upper Falls. From their tents the men could hear the "thunder and thud" of the cataracts. They took only a moment to bolt some bacon before heading to various points along the canyon's edge.

They crossed the creek and moved south, and the Upper Falls came into view. George Tyler, the commander of the expedition's military escort, was amazed by the power of the water moving through its narrow channel.

The water "projected like a broad fan into the air with a hissing sound to the distance of 60 feet," he wrote in his diary, arcing out and falling more than one hundred feet, "dissolving into clouds of spray."

The river below the Upper Falls seemed to slow and then regather its energies for a quarter mile before arriving at the next precipice. The Lower Falls was almost three times the height of the Upper, plunging down in one broad sheet more than 350 feet into the canyon floor below. Tyler scrambled down the slope to a rock that jutted out over the water just as it fell over the ledge.

"[I] took but a very slight glance at the scene

below," he reported. "It was fearful, appalling. I quickly hurried back."

Robert Adams and a few others took Tyler's place on the ledge, gazing over the brink until they were too dizzy to look any longer.

"There, looking down the great divide, with its mountain sides shutting out all other view," Adams observed, "and seeing the water which passed but a moment ago flowing hundreds of feet beneath us. Oh! it was grand! Sublime! A sight never to be forgotten."

The rest of the men expressed similar sentiments upon seeing the falls of the Yellowstone. They were responding to what the painter Thomas Cole identified as the most pleasing features of a waterfall.

"[It] at once presents to the mind the beautiful, but apparently incongruous idea," Cole wrote in 1836, "of [both] fixedness and motion—a single existence in which we perceive unceasing change and everlasting duration."

Such contrasts were pleasing to both the eye and the intellect, Cole believed, and gazing upon them produced powerful emotions. The waterfall's immensity and uncontrollable power revealed the sublimity of nature: its ability to inspire but also to terrify, and to overwhelm.

From the Lower Falls' edge, Tyler and Adams could see the tiny silver ribbon of the river, rushing through a deep and jagged canyon whose depths extended into the distance. The canyon shaded from red to brown to white to yellow, evidence that the sulfuric waters that flowed through the Yellowstone Basin had seeped through the rocks. Erosion had carved tall pinnacles and columns out of the canyon walls; they stood like sentinels guarding the banks of the rushing river. Vivid green pine trees sent their roots into clefts in the canyon sides, "as if struggling with a sort of uncertain success to maintain [their] existence." It was an impressive sight, full of pleasing contrasts.

"In some respects this cañon is the greatest wonder of all," Hayden concluded.

That evening and the next day, the expedition teams got to work. Hayden roamed the edge of the canyon with Schönborn, collecting rock samples and taking measurements to determine the width and depth of the waterfalls and the canyon.

After rendering the scene along the rim of the canyon, Henry Elliott decided he would attempt a descent to sketch the Lower Falls from the riverbed and obtain an accurate measurement of the canyon's depth. Ignoring the advice of the hunters Joe Clark and José, who said that such a feat could not be accomplished, he set out with Albert Peale by his side. Their first attempt came to nothing when they reached a cliff that dropped straight down to the river. They climbed back up, got on their horses, and rode a bit farther downriver. Here, the walls plunged downward at only an eighty-degree angle, so they descended. At one point, Peale saved himself from ricocheting down the entire canyon side by catching his foot against a rock. After more than an hour, they made it to the bottom.

"All was silent," Peale reported, "except the roaring of the water as its waves dashed upon the solid rock at our feet."

After taking measurements with the barometer, Peale collected samples of chunky, dark gray trachyte, embedded with pieces of obsidian, and rocks tinted yellow by sulfur. A few hours later, Peale and Elliott began to climb back up the canyon wall. Peale was forced to abandon several of his largest mineral specimens on the way.

"Along some of the edges," he later reported to the readers of the *Philadelphia Press*, "both hands and feet were needed to hold on."

Hayden would have loved to linger at the canyon for several more days, but the expedition members had to keep moving. It was already late July and there were more wonders to explore, measure, map, and sketch. The team set out, moving southeast toward Yellowstone Lake.

They left a few men behind. William Henry Jackson, Thomas Moran, and their assistants had been working their way up and down the canyon edge, assessing the views, and they needed more time with their subject. They remained with Joshua Crissman, a photographer from Bozeman, who had joined the expedition at Fort Ellis. Jackson set up his dark box and other equipment in tents under the trees along the rim.

"Plate after plate was made from every available point of view," Jackson noted.

In one, Jackson centered the froth and the foam of the waterfall in motion, the canyon walls looming up around it, and pine trees framing the scene below and above. For another plate, Jackson placed his camera above the Lower Falls on the canyon rim, tracing the river below the cataract, winding through the canyon from foreground to background. To gain yet more views, Jackson followed Elliott's and Peale's example and descended to the canyon floor with his camera strapped to his back. From that vantage point, the walls shut out the sky and he could barely see the waterfall itself through all the spray. The photographer's position was precarious. There was not much flat land even on the riverbank, which was strewn with rocks and slick with spray. It was a dangerous place to be, with the river rushing along the canyon floor.

"Were one to fall in," Peale had warned, "he could be dashed to pieces among the rocks at the bottom."

There were other dangers as well. Crissman

left his camera unguarded at the edge and it was "blown over into the depths of the canyon, never to be recovered." Jackson felt sorry for the man. They had met two years before in Utah, where Crissman had allowed Jackson to use his darkroom in Corinne, to develop his Union Pacific railroad images. Repaying that debt now, Jackson gave him one of his cameras to use for the remainder of the trip.

Meanwhile, Thomas Moran wandered along the canyon's edge with his portfolio tucked under his arm, stopping at various vantage points to pull out his paper and paints. He made sketch after sketch of the canyon and the falls, using all the watercolors available to him in his palette. Moran wanted to represent the vivid coloration of the canyon walls with accuracy, but he was not sure it was possible.

"These beautiful tints," the painter confessed with regret, "were beyond the reach of human art."

This was a scene that every ambitious landscape painter dreamed of. The only artist to have depicted it before was Moran himself, in a woodcut illustration based on Nathaniel Langford's descriptions, in his article for *Scribner's Monthly*. Now he had the opportunity to render "the Grand Cañon of the Yellowstone" (as the men began to call it) in color, a much more effective way to astonish the viewer than magazine illustrations or even Jackson's photographs.

"Moran's enthusiasm was greater here than anywhere else among Yellowstone's wonderful features," Jackson attested. "It would seem, that here was something peculiarly adapted to his own remarkable technique as a painter and fit subject for a masterpiece."

While Moran, Jackson, and Crissman were capturing the sublimity of the falls and the Grand Cañon, the rest of the expedition members moved south along the western bank of the Yellowstone River and entered the brimstone region of the Basin.

Here Yellowstone revealed its geothermal nature. As the men crossed a wide valley (that would later bear Hayden's name), a series of thuds and hisses grew louder until they reached a group of mud volcanoes. They were hot springs like those they had seen along the Gardiner River but coming through clay instead of limestone. The boiling water and steam melted the clay into a thick sludge. The pressure of gases below the surface resulted in the periodic creation of mud "puffs" or, in more dramatic moments, an eruption that coated the limbs of pine trees in the vicinity with brown clay, which when dried turned a pure white.

The botanist Robert Adams found the mud geysers "more curious than beautiful," and all agreed that both little children and artisans would be delighted to have its contents at their disposal.

"This mud, which has been wrought in these caldrons for perhaps hundreds of years," Hayden declared, "is so fine and pure that the manufacture of porcelain-ware would go into ecstacy [*sic*] at the site."

At a safe distance from the mud volcanoes, the ground was surprisingly lush, Hayden observed, crowded with "green grasses, rushes, mosses, and other plants." But closer to the springs it was bare of vegetation, and hot and perforated like a sieve. As he approached one of these "volcanoes," Hayden felt the ground yield to the pressure of his boots.

"I broke through to my knees," he reported later, "covering myself with the hot mud." Hayden managed to pull himself out onto safer ground before sinking any farther, but in that short time, the heat and the acid of the mud spring had already saturated his pants and boots, scalding his legs. They also dissolved the sinew holding together the leather uppers and soles of his boots. He walked back to the others barefoot, holding the pieces of his boots in his hands. It was a narrow escape, one that gave him "great pain and subsequent inconvenience."

The mud geysers were clear proof of the German scientist Alexander von Humboldt's theory that the molten interior of the earth and its surface were in constant communication. The threat of violence suggested by this connection was continuous. Hayden and the other scientists on the expedition did not know many specifics about how these thermal features operated. They could witness the eruptions and even crack open the edges of the mud pots to reveal the beautiful "lacework" hidden underneath, but they could only guess at what was happening beneath the surface of the earth. It was frustrating to Hayden that he would likely never be able to observe or measure these subterranean forces. But the mystery of it all also intrigued him.

As the team gathered at their camp, pitched far enough away from the mud geysers to sit on stable ground but near enough to hear their hissing and bubbling, the men discussed what they had seen.

"What wonder will this country produce next?" Peale asked.

The next morning, after another struggle through six miles of fallen timber, Hayden and his team arrived at the northwestern shore of Yellowstone Lake.

"[It] lay before us," Hayden marveled, "a vast sheet of quiet water, of a most delicate ultramarine hue, one of the most beautiful scenes I have ever beheld."

This was water in a different form than the cataracts they had gazed upon just two days earlier. Instead of propulsive energy, here was tranquility, stillness. The water extended out toward the horizon, its surface reflecting the green trees lining its shores, the snow-tipped mountain ranges in the distance, and the white clouds moving over it.

"A more enchanting view of water and land I never witnessed," Henry Elliott mused. It seemed "a water picture too perfect for pen or pencil; it must be seen, not described."

As they pitched their tents, unloaded their supplies, and turned out their horses to graze in a nearby meadow, the men were happy to look upon such a refreshing scene after the toil of the morning. They needed a break from Yellowstone's strange sights. The lake looked much like bodies of water back home and was pleasing to the mind rather than overwhelming.

For Hayden, Yellowstone Lake was also an important site for the survey, one that would prove that the Basin was the "watershed of the continent." The explorations of the next week, he hoped, would confirm another of his theories that the lake was the source of the Yellowstone River. This waterway, along with the Bighorn, the Madison, and the Gallatin, flowed from the Basin and its rim to the Missouri, ultimately merging with the Mississippi and then dispersing into the Gulf of Mexico. The Basin most likely also gave rise to the Snake River, which flowed north to the

Columbia and then on to the Pacific. If Hayden could confirm and map these riverine routes, he would prove that the Yellowstone Basin was the principal source of the nation's greatest rivers, the heart of the continent.

While most of the expedition members busied themselves in camp—which they named "Lake View"—several unpacked the mule that had carried the deconstructed boat on its back all the way from Bottler's Ranch. After putting the wooden slats together, they covered it with canvas to prevent leaking and stretched a blanket between two poles for a sail. Making two oars out of tree branches, the men considered the little skiff seaworthy and christened it the *Annie*.

The next morning, July 29, Jim Stevenson and Henry Elliott pushed off from the shore in the *Annie*. There was no bottle of champagne, "no ceremony [to attend] this, the first entrance of any craft upon the waters of this unexplored lake." But the team gathered to witness this historical event and to watch the two men row off toward one of the lake's major islands, which Hayden wanted them to explore and measure. There was some anxiety about their safety, as the wind tended to rise in the afternoons, and large waves disturbed the tranquility of the lake's surface. The boat was small and might be swamped in such rough weather, and the water was so cold that Hayden was sure that even the most accomplished swimmer could not survive in it for long. Luckily, the day remained calm.

"The adventurers returned in safety" from what they decided to name Stevenson Island, Robert Adams noted with relief, "bringing specimens of minerals, flowers, &c."

The next day, the men built a framework with a weighted line, which they attached to the *Annie*'s bow. They would use this to measure the depth of the lake. Coordinating with a man standing on the shore with a prismatic compass and using Elliott's sketches of the shoreline and Schönborn's elevations, they produced what Elliott called a "hydrographical survey" of Yellowstone Lake. This three-dimensional map revealed the exact shape and size of the lake and what lay beneath the water's glittering surface, making it known to all Americans.

Hayden intended to stay at the lake for more than a week and then take some short trips southward to explore the Upper Yellowstone Valley. On July 30, his plans changed. The expedition had visitors at Lake View, a party of miners crossing through the Basin on their way to rumored gold diggings on the Snake River.

"They bring the report," Captain Tyler wrote in his diary, "that a party of Indians ran off a lot of stock from near Bozeman, killing three men, also having killed 12 men in the Gallatin Valley."

It was possible that the raiders, whom the

miners believed to be Crow and Nez Perce, were merely setting out early for their fall hunts among the buffalo herds of the Great Plains to the southeast. But it was also possible that they might move through the Basin, hoping to stampede and siphon off the expedition's large horse herd. According to a note the miners brought to Tyler from Bottler's Ranch, these Native raiders were not the only threat. A band of horse thieves were also rumored to be on the move toward the Basin. Tyler was skeptical, but in the event this news was even partly true, he ordered his men to tether all 130 of the expedition's horses and mules, and posted six soldiers to guard the animals.

The report of Native raiders startled Hayden. When they entered the Basin, he had ceased to worry about this threat. They had heard that the Sheepeaters were the only Indians living in the Basin. In the summer they stayed high in the mountains to hunt elk and were widely known to be peaceable. If the threat of a conflict with other tribes in the region was real, this might curtail his time in the Basin.

Hayden abandoned his plan to stay at the lake and instead organized a party to head west, into the Firehole Valley. The rest of the men would move the base camp to a second location, more than twenty miles south along the lakeshore, and Hayden's party would meet them there in a week. This geyser basin was the most storied region of Yellowstone, the site of many geothermal marvels of beauty and power. Hayden could not, and would not, miss seeing it.

Scientists had known about geysers for some time, although until the mid-nineteenth century, Iceland was the only well-known geothermal field in the world. In these areas, water sank deep below the earth's surface and was then heated to far above its normal boiling point. As a result, water began to rise, releasing air pressure. If that release was gradual, this process created hot springs on the surface. If it was sudden, the boiling water violently exploded into steam, forcing its way to the surface and creating a geyser.

What lay before them in the Firehole Valley might be the largest and most dynamic system of geysers in the world, far surpassing Iceland's and the recently discovered thermal fields in New Zealand. Such topographical wonders would prove the exceptional nature of America's geology, further demonstrating to white settlers the singularity of the land they claimed as their own.

The morning of July 31, Hayden, Peale, Schönborn, Elliott, José, and Potato John departed, along with a packer who oversaw the odometer and an escort of nine soldiers. Barlow and Heap's party would follow them a few hours later. The rest of the men would wait at the Lake View camp for Jackson and Moran to arrive from the canyon of the Yellowstone. Almost immediately upon moving west from the lake, Hayden's team found themselves in a thick green forest, which looked to Captain Tyler like "a badly tangled skein of thread."

This was the wood in which Truman Everts had been lost.

"Now and then we would come out into an open glade," Hayden remarked, "and start on at a brisk pace with fresh hope, when we would come again to a belt of this remarkable net-work of fallen pines."

The men were relieved to stumble their way out of it two days later, after an exhausting trek. Their meandering sent them farther north than they intended, and when they emerged from the forest, they entered what looked like a large alkali flat, filled with hot springs both living and dead. They struck Nez Perce Creek and began to follow it west, toward the Firehole River.

The river led them into a large basin, over six square miles covered in hundreds of geysers. Hayden's party spent the next week making their way through this enormous geothermal field. They approached the craters carefully, listening intently to the sound of boiling water under their feet. As Hayden gathered specimens of each crater's crust, Schönborn marked them on the map he was drawing. Peale crawled to the lip of each geyser, dipping small bottles in the water to gather enough to analyze, before affixing stoppers and placing them in his specimen bag. When the geysers erupted, the scientists positioned themselves at a safe distance, calculating the height of the spouts through mathematical triangulation. Elliott wandered throughout the valley, making more than fifty sketches of water and steam exploding from the ground.

Native peoples who had made the trails leading to and from this remarkable area may have already given these features names, but the men of the Yellowstone Expedition did not know them. This meant, Hayden believed, that they had the right of priority, the prerogative as the first white men to explore and evaluate this area, to bestow names on the most spectacular of the geysers, the ones that jettisoned water the highest into the air or erupted with the greatest ferocity: Giant, Grand, Grotto, Soda, Castle.

One of the most remarkable of the Firehole's features was not a geyser but a hot spring from which masses of vapor were constantly rising. Reverberating out from its vivid blue center were concentric rings in "all the colors of the prism": green, yellow, red, and an outer ring of orange that ran in rivulets through the surrounding field of snow-white siliceous sinter.

"Nothing ever conceived by human art,"

Hayden determined, "could equal the peculiar vividness and delicacy of coloring of these remarkable prismatic springs."

On their way from feature to feature, they passed hot springs into which trees had fallen. Colonel Barlow, whose team had followed Hayden's into the Basin, was transfixed.

"Their branches, cones, and needles were all completely incrusted," he wrote admiringly, "with a rich coating of mineral, like frosted silver." Both he and Hayden's men were able to obtain several of these encrusted pine cones, which Peale packed away in specimen boxes to be sent east.

Every morning, the men awoke to the sight of columns of steam ascending from what Hayden estimated to be more than one thousand vents. He grasped for some way to understand the sheer number of thermal features.

"I can compare the view to nothing but that of some manufacturing city like Pittsburgh," he wrote, "as seen from a high point, except that instead of the black coal smoke, there are here the white delicate clouds of steam."

Remarkably, though the geysers resembled one another, most were individually contained. Almost every geyser and hot spring had its own water source, its own chemical makeup, and its own timetable for building up pressure. It was this individuality that made each geyser wondrous, and so suited to the American imagination of itself.

The realities of traveling through the Basin, however, began to hit them a few days in. They were running out of flour and bacon, and it became increasingly difficult to find game. Elk and deer were scarce, for the Firehole did not have any vegetation to lure them. José came into camp every evening empty-handed, and by the end of their exploration, Hayden's team were eating squirrels and partridges, cooked up in the waters of the hot springs in what Potato John called "Hell-Fire Stew."

Their supplies of fresh water were also few and far between. "Though there were hundreds of the most beautiful springs around us," Hayden wrote, "we were like Coleridge's mariner in the great ocean, 'Water, water everywhere, but not a drop to drink.'"

By August 5, Hayden knew he was running out of time. His party needed provisions, and the threat of a horse raid remained. There was one thermal feature he still needed to see, and then they would return to Yellowstone Lake. Hayden, Schönborn, Peale, and Elliott approached a single geyser atop a large crater on a low hill, which sat at the head of the Upper Basin. Its waters were calm when they arrived, and they sat down to wait. Soon steam began to billow out of its center, and the surface of the water began to roil. Small eruptions of water began, and then suddenly the geyser threw up a massive column of water—6 feet in diameter and 150 feet high, Hayden believed—with seemingly no effort. The men scrambled to avoid the steam billowing out from its sides. Several minutes later, the plume of water lessened, and then the eruption ceased entirely. They did not have to wait long for the next eruption. It came little more than an hour later. When the Washburn Expedition had encountered this geyser, Gustavus Doane had named it "Old Faithful."

It well deserved its memorable name, the survey team members believed. They had not yet encountered such an accommodating geyser, one so reliable in its eruptions. The next day, Hayden went to see Old Faithful before his team left the Firehole Valley. "[That] grand old geyser," he reported to the others, "gave [me] a magnificent parting display."

The men, in turn, bid farewell to the geyser region, packed up their specimens, mounted their horses, and rode east.

Their way led through the same forest of fallen timber they had come through a week before. Schönborn was at the head of the party, but soon José rode up to Hayden and told him they were moving too far south. Hayden ignored him, and they carried on. Around sunset, Schönborn pulled out his instruments and concluded that it was as

José had said, and they were lost. Elliott went off in disgust but did not go far, lest he meet the same fate as Everts. They tied the horses and set up camp, wedging their belongings in the narrow spaces between the pines.

The next morning, they started early, José now leading the way. In just a few hours they broke free of the timber and found themselves on the shore of Yellowstone Lake, three miles south of the expedition's second camp. When they arrived and began to unpack their horses, Campbell Carrington, the zoologist, walked up from the beach.

"Lieutenant Doane [came] up" from Fort Ellis, he told Hayden, "and ordered most of our escort back to fight the Indians."

Apparently, the attack on the Gallatin Valley had worried Major Eugene Baker enough that he wanted to send out a large contingent of soldiers from the fort in pursuit of the raiders. It seemed clear now that the band was not Crow or Nez Perce, but Húŋkpapȟa Lakota under the leadership of Sitting Bull. What was more, Carrington told them, Baker had orders to "hold all the Cavalry in readiness" at Fort Ellis to escort a surveying party of engineers, sent to scout a route from Bozeman to the Yellowstone River for the Northern Pacific Railroad.

Captain Tyler had already left, with Doane himself as a guide, and was heading west toward the geyser basin to follow the Firehole, Madison, and Gardiner Rivers north to Fort Ellis. His party and Hayden's must have crossed within a few miles of each other in the tangled wood without knowing it. Tyler had taken most of his company with him (twenty-seven soldiers), leaving only six soldiers to escort Hayden's party, and six for Barlow and Heap. Doane would lead him to the Firehole, then return to the camp at Yellowstone Lake and take command of the survey's escort.

William Henry Jackson and Thomas Moran also went with Tyler and Doane. The artists had finally arrived at the lake after taking their time at the canyon and in the region of the mud volcanoes. Jackson took the *Annie* out on the lake several times while Hayden's party was gone, but Moran had seemed ready to return home. He made enough sketches to take back to his studio and was eager to begin work on his oil paintings of Yellowstone. He had decided to travel with Tyler to the fort and then take a stagecoach back to Corrine. Jackson would accompany them as far as the geyser region, then come back to the lake with Doane.

The team members did not know that Captain Tyler left their camp pondering an offer from Harry Horr, the man who had established the convalescent camp at the hot springs below the White Mountain. Horr had told Tyler that he intended to file a claim of preemption on that area, giving him the right to purchase and develop the land around that immense thermal feature. He was anxious for Tyler, and perhaps some other officers at Fort Ellis, to join him in the investment.

"I have not fully decided as yet," Tyler confessed in his journal. "It will certainly be a great resort in a few years."

Hayden's party scrounged the camp for something to eat. Carrington did not have much to offer. He and the political boys had been surviving on three stale biscuits a day, whatever meat they could find, and one cup of tea. The next day, Hayden sent Jim Stevenson with a pack train to get supplies at the expedition's base camp at Bottler's Ranch. Several of the political boys went along, as did Robert Adams, the Bozeman photographer Joshua Crissman, and Potato John. They did not have a military escort, but they were all well armed with pistols and rifles if the Gallatin raiders decided to turn south into the Yellowstone Basin.

Later that afternoon, Gustavus Doane arrived in camp, with Jackson in tow. The army engineers Barlow and Heap were with them; their team had spent a few more days in the geyser basins after Hayden had returned. Hayden was a bit starstruck when he met Doane. He had read the army officer's lengthy, detailed, and eloquent report of the 1870 Washburn expedition.

"He seems to have written under the inspiration of the wonderful physical phenomena around him," Hayden judged.

Unlike many army officers, Doane had an extensive education in the sciences, having gone to college in California and taken classes in geology, botany, and zoology. He was also independent-minded, ambitious, and prone to swearing. Hayden was delighted with him and invited Doane to share his tent until they returned to Fort Ellis.

Soon they moved their camp again, this time to a site on the south side of the lake. From there, the expedition members again divided up into small groups. Elliott took the *Annie* out on the water and made more soundings. Others examined the hot springs that bordered the lakeshore. Barlow and his team made for the Continental Divide, which wound its way through the mountain ranges southwest of the camp.

Hayden, along with Doane and Schönborn, climbed many of the high mountains southeast of the lake and investigated the Upper Yellowstone Valley, tracing what they believed to be the Yellowstone River back up into its mountain source. While they were gone, Albert Peale replaced Moran as Jackson's assistant and enthusiastic subject; Jackson took photographs of the scientist in various places along the shore and in the expedition's camps. Steve Hovey, the wagon master, suggested moving around the eastern arm of the lake to a more central location north of a series of hot springs.

On August 16, Peale was delighted to see Jim Stevenson approaching Camp Hovey with the pack train from Bottler's Ranch.

"Jim was eagerly welcomed," Peale noted, "not only for his own sake, but also for the sake of what he brought with him."

The men ate their fill of freshly made, warm biscuits and read through the letters and magazines that had been delivered to the ranch. Hayden, Doane, and Schönborn arrived from their exploration of the Upper Yellowstone Valley soon after, and the expedition was reunited.

A few days later, everyone was asleep in their tents at a new camp on the northeastern shore when a rumbling noise woke them. Most assumed it was a particularly violent eruption from the nearby Steamboat geyser. But the roar grew louder, and suddenly the earth beneath them shuddered, shaking them out of their bedrolls. The horses leapt to their feet and pulled frantically at their lariats, and the birds and squirrels chattered as the pine limbs to which they clung began to sway back and forth.

It was the first earthquake that many of them had experienced, and it lasted for about twenty seconds. They did not go back to sleep afterward, due to the excitement of the initial jolt—and the five or six aftershocks that followed throughout the night. Only Joe Clark and José were blasé.

"These earthquake shocks are not uncommon," they told Hayden, "and at some seasons of the year are very severe."

Hayden was not surprised at this news. Many of the reports of such events were often connected to volcanic regions, although geologists were not sure why. What was most unsettling about them was their unpredictability, and their mystery. Hayden did not have the scientific instruments to mark or measure such a phenomenon, so in many ways it was unknowable to him. The earthquake suggested, like most of the Yellowstone Basin's features, that this was a landscape in tumult.

The shocks continued for several days as the expedition prepared to leave Yellowstone Lake and return to Bottler's Ranch. After he returned from his trip to the Yellowstone Falls, Jackson took a photograph of what the team now called "Earthquake Camp" from a nearby hill, capturing the array of tents spread out among the pines, with the curve of the lakeshore in the background.

The men continued to explore the area in small groups, collecting specimens and making observations. Colonel Barlow returned from his trip to the southeast, loaded down with specimens and leading several exhausted animals. Hayden, Elliott, and Schönborn left to revisit the Grand Cañon of the Yellowstone one more time. Once the scientists were done with the final soundings, the men dismantled the *Annie*, lauding her for her excellent service to the expedition. Instead of repacking her and forcing the mule to carry her all the way back to Bottler's, they decided to leave her in pieces at the campsite, a remnant of their passage through the Basin.

After they packed the specimens and loaded the mules, the members of the Yellowstone Expedition mounted their horses and rode, single file, out of Earthquake Camp.

"We started bidding farewell to Yellowstone Lake," Peale reported. "The boys all called goodbye as we struck into the woods."

Three days later, after following a route up and over several ridges that then arced west to the Gardiner River, the expedition members were once again at the White Mountain. There they remained for a day, while Hayden and the other scientists collected more specimens and Jackson completed his set of photographs of that remarkable spring.

From there, it was a day's ride out of the Yellowstone to Bottler's Ranch. Although the trail seemed less rough leaving than it had been coming, the men took their time. This was the final day of the expedition, and they wanted to savor it. Jim Stevenson rode ahead, to alert the Bottlers that the entire team would be arriving shortly. After six weeks in the Land of Wonders, the ranch looked crowded to the men of the Yellowstone Expedition. They were glad to sit down to a full meal and glass of fresh milk from the ranch's cows, and to read letters from home.

While Peale continued to wrap and pack specimens and Jackson printed his final plates in his tent, Ferdinand Hayden sat down to write field notes and several letters. "We have completed our survey of the Upper Yellow Stone," he wrote to Spencer Baird at the Smithsonian. "Our success has been complete."

They made maps of the Basin's riverine systems, triangulated every major peak in its mountain ranges, and pinpointed the elevations of its central geographical points. They created beautiful charts of the geysers, mud volcanoes, and hot springs, and Elliott and Jackson thoroughly documented them in their sketches and photographs. These images would serve to authenticate Hayden's written accounts of the survey, and help readers to imagine Yellowstone, feeling like they had been there themselves.

"We think that no portion of the West," Hayden wrote in a separate letter to Secretary of the Interior Columbus Delano, "has been more carefully surveyed than the Yellowstone basin."

Through its scientific data, visual images, and survey narratives, the 1871 Yellowstone Expedition would lay claim to this unique landscape on behalf of the federal government and the American people. Using this information, Congress could wrest Yellowstone's lands and waterways away from Indigenous nations who claimed them as part of their homelands. It was settler colonialism, rooted in science. With Hayden's survey report in hand, Americans could erase Indigenous presence from Yellowstone and point to its geothermal wonders as proof of the country's exceptionalism, which would in turn justify the removal of Native people from this unique and wondrous landscape. And the federal government could establish policies through which white settlers would take up these lands and turn them to productive uses.

The survey team's work in the Basin was over once they returned to Fort Ellis, but there was still much more to be done. Hayden had seen enough of Yellowstone to know that it would take years—decades, even—to explore it fully. But he felt that in this first scientific survey, he and his fellow expedition members "have obtained information enough to convince our readers that the region we have examined is invested with profound interest." They had proven that Yellowstone represented the nation's peculiar combination of the sublime and the terrible.

Three days later, after a side trip to the Crow Mission to see the progress that Indian agents there had made "civilizing" the men and women of that tribe and the Nez Perce, the members of the 1871 Yellowstone Expedition arrived at Fort Ellis. Encamped nearby was a party of engineers with the Northern Pacific. Once the leader of the survey—a man named Milnor Roberts—arrived, the party would set out, following the route that Hayden's men had taken until they reached the Yellowstone River. There they would turn to survey downstream until they met another crew of engineers coming from the U.S. Army forts along the Missouri River. The Second Cavalry were there, and the alarm resulting from the Gallatin Valley raid had abated. Hayden stayed at the fort, enjoying several evenings of conviviality with the officers and their wives, including Gustavus and Amelia Doane.

Jackson took several photographs of them all together, and of the remaining men of the survey. The team members had already begun to disperse, several of them taking the stage southward to Corinne and Ogden. From there, some went to California, and others back east. Barlow was off to Chicago and Heap to St. Paul, Minnesota, where they would sort their specimens and write their reports to their commander, General Phil Sheridan, who had sent them to join Hayden's expedition. Hayden and Peale planned to travel southward together along a different route than they had come up.

Hayden was delighted with everything the

survey had achieved in its short time in the Yellowstone.

"We have had an uninterrupted series of successes, without a single pullback," he wrote to George Allen. "Not an accident has happened to any of our party. . . . Never have we had such success and received such a vast amount of material." Once he returned, he would need to work up his notes and ready them for publication. Only then would the Yellowstone, that "land so rich in wonders," become comprehensible as a landscape, and as part of the nation.

Portrait of Ferdinand
Vandeveer Hayden,
c. 1860s

*Henry Ulke,
Smithsonian
Institution Archives,
Record Unit 95,
Box 27B, Image
No. SIA_000095_
B27B_070*

Portrait of
Sitting Bull, 1885

*David Francis
Barry, Prints
and Photographs
Division, Library of
Congress*

Portrait of
Jay Cooke

*Portrait
Photograph
Collection, Baker
Library, Harvard
Business School*

Portrait of
William Henry
Jackson, 1870

*History Colorado.
Accession #88.189.44*

Portrait of
Thomas Moran,
c. 1890

Napoleon Sarony,
Prints and
Photographs Division,
Library of Congress

Portrait of
Ulysses S. Grant,
c. 1870

Prints and
Photographs
Division, Library of
Congress

Portrait of
Col. Ely Parker,
c. 1860–1865

*Mathew Brady
Photographs of
Civil War–Era
Personalities and
Scenes, 1921–1940,
Record Group 111:
Records of the Office
of the Chief Signal
Officer, 1860–1985,
National Archives*

Portrait of Amos
Tappan Akerman,
May 5, 1871

*Mathew Brady,
National
Portrait Gallery,
Smithsonian
Institution*

Virginia City, M.T.

W. H. Jackson, Image File ZZR700310238,
The Denver Public Library, Special Collections

Bottler's Ranch

W. H. Jackson, Image YELL 02911, Yellowstone Photo
Collection, Yellowstone National Park Archives

Ferdinand Hayden in front of his tent

W. H. Jackson, Image YELL 02935, Yellowstone Photo Collection, Yellowstone National Park Archives

Hot Springs at the Gardiner River
(Mammoth Hot Springs)

W. H. Jackson, Image YELL 03120, Yellowstone Photo Collection, Yellowstone National Park Archives

Earthquake Camp

W. H. Jackson, Image YELL 14860, Yellowstone Photo Collection, Yellowstone National Park Archives

Lower Falls
from the canyon

*W. H. Jackson,
Image YELL 14859,
Yellowstone Photo
Collection,
Yellowstone National
Park Archives*

Old Faithful

W. H. Jackson, Image YELL 14852,
Yellowstone Photo Collection,
Yellowstone National Park Archives

7

If You Do Not Stop Them, We Will

Yellowstone River Valley, Lakota Homelands. July 1871.

I t was early morning when Ťhaťháŋka Íyotake
(Sitting Bull) emerged from his lodge for a
walk. Only a handful of women were already
awake, preparing meat and fruit for the morning
meal. Mostly, the oťhúŋwahe (village) was
still. Sitting Bull threaded his way between
the more than one thousand lodges strung out
along the riverbank. Forty years old and five-
foot-ten, Sitting Bull walked with a slight limp,
the legacy of wounds to his left foot and hip in
battles with Flathead, Crow, and U.S. soldiers.
He wore a slanted red eagle feather in his hair
to commemorate these and other war wounds,
and a vertical white one to signify the first of his
many acts of bravery in battle: when he was just
fourteen years old, he got close enough to a Crow
warrior to tap him with a coup stick.

That fight had been an immensely significant
one for him, and he loved to tell the story to
anyone who would listen. He was young but
eager to prove himself; at the time he still had

his given name, Ȟoká Psíče (Jumping Badger). He had joined the war party in 1845 without telling his parents or his uncle Hé Tópa (Four Horns), a powerful leader in the Itázipa Šíča (Bad Bows) band of the Húŋkpapȟa Lakota oyáte (nation, or people). When his father discovered Jumping Badger in the group, he knew it was useless to try to send him back. Instead, he gave him a peeled stick with a feather tied to the end, an essential weapon for Húŋkpapȟa warriors.

Ride upon the enemy and draw close, his father advised, then strike him with the coup stick. This was the highest form of courage in battle, and all Lakota men measured their achievements in warfare by coups counted, in addition to enemies killed.

"You have a good running horse," he told his son. "Try to do something brave."

When the war party came upon a band of Crow warriors, Jumping Badger followed his father's advice, bolting forward and counting coup on one of them almost immediately. When they returned to their camp, his father painted Jumping Badger's face black, lifted him up onto a bay horse, and paraded him around the lodges. Then he presented his son with a shield, painted in vivid shades of red, green, blue, and brown, with a black thunderbird at the center. To signify Jumping Badger's success in warfare in all cardinal directions, his father had attached four eagle feathers to the frame.

"Today you are a warrior," he said. "You are now a man."

To represent this major transition in Jumping Badger's life, his father made another important announcement. He would give his son his own name—Tȟatȟáŋka Íyotake—and would take another, Tȟatȟáŋka Psíče (Jumping Bull).

Sitting Bull had learned many important lessons in this moment. Perhaps the most important was, as his father told him, "that [the] man is most successful, who is foremost."

As Sitting Bull walked on and the sun rose, the camp began to stir. Children dashed out of their families' tipis, eager to meet their friends for a day of footraces and other games. Women followed, calling to their sons and daughters to go pick up wood and sticks along the river to get the fires going. Sitting Bull felt a keen ache; he was in mourning for Lúta Wíŋ (Red Woman), his wife of five years, who had died in childbirth that winter. After her death he had performed the Naǧí Gluhápi (Keeping of the Soul Ceremony), cutting a lock of her hair to keep in his tipi, to retain her memory and spirit.

He had also lost his first wife, Pȟehíŋ Sáŋ Wíŋ (Light Hair), in childbirth, many years before. The woman he had married after, Awá Wíŋ (Snow On Her), had given him two children but many years of grief, especially after he had taken Red Woman as a second wife. The two had not gotten along, and the discord within his household took a toll on everyone. Finally, he had sent Snow On Her back to her people, although the daughters they had together stayed with him. Sitting Bull's mother, Thatȟíyopa Wakȟáŋ Wíŋ (Her Holy Door), helped to raise them—and his son with Red Woman, who had survived—when she was not offering Sitting Bull her advice on Húŋkpapȟa political matters. Children were the center of the Lakota thióšpaye (extended kinship network). They were wakȟáŋheža: something sacred growing.

Sitting Bull made his way back to his family's lodge and prepared himself for a busy day ahead. He knew the Húŋkpapȟa would face many challenges and enemies this summer, and he had to decide how to help his people endure.

He would not be deciding alone, however. Despite what Americans had come to believe by 1871, Sitting Bull was not the singular chief of the people they called the Sioux. The Húŋkpapȟa were one of seven bands of the Thítȟuŋwaŋ (Lakota), a nation that itself was one of seven "council fires": Očhéthi Šakówiŋ, peoples who had lived in their homelands from the headwaters of the Mississippi River to the northern Rocky Mountains for thousands of years. They had emerged from Wind Cave below Ȟesápa (Black

Mountains—to the whites, Black Hills), an island in a massive sea of undulating prairie, long ago. Its foothills and steep sides were covered in ponderosa pine, birches and spruce, and delicate clusters of quaking aspens. The four bands of the Dakota lived in the eastern part of the homelands, the Iháŋkthuŋwaŋ/na (Yankton/ai) in the southern reaches, and the Lakota ranged throughout the west. Očéthi Šakówiŋ's close kin, Pté Oyáte (Buffalo Nation), came into being at Ȟesápa as well, and now traveled in herds through the great prairies along with elk, deer, and antelope.

The Očéthi Šakówiŋ relied on the buffalo to sustain them. Each fall, after the men brought the carcasses back to the camp from the hunt, the women set to work. They skinned each animal, then sliced away the meat and organs. Cutting the meat into strips, they hung them on wooded racks next to their tipis and let the smoke of their fires cure them. Women reserved the buffalo's blood and tallow for painting their faces, shields, and tipis. Its sinews they saved to make bowstrings and thread, and its bones and horns for spoons, cups, ornaments, and weapons. Pinning the hide to the ground and stretching it with wooden pegs, women used elk horns to scrape away the tissue, and rubbed it with a mixture of brains, liver, and fat. After a week of this difficult work, one buffalo hide would be ready for use as a robe, blanket, or saddle cover. Women kept these for their families or added them to a great pile to be taken to American forts to trade. The work they did ensured that their people would survive.

Buffalo fed Lakota bodies, kept them warm and protected, and helped them prepare for war and ceremonies. Their history as a people was intertwined with Pté Oyáte. Thousands of years before, a spirit being called White Buffalo Calf Woman appeared in a Lakota camp. She presented the Lakota with a pipe, a sacred gift that would help them to become like Buffalo Nation. If they fulfilled their duties to one another as a people and respected the animals of the prairie, they would grow to be as powerful, enduring, and generous as their buffalo kin. This gift had made their lives more meaningful and had directed their actions in defense of their homelands and all its resources ever since.

One of those resources was Mníšoše (Missouri River) and its many tributaries, including the Yellowstone. Since the eighteenth century, English and French traders had used these waters to travel through Očéthi Šakówiŋ lands, bringing devastating diseases like smallpox and cholera and building trading forts on the riverbanks. In the early nineteenth century, American explorers, soldiers, and traders appeared.

Most of the time the Očéthi Šakówiŋ chose to trade with these invaders, and sometimes they attacked them. Other times they opted for a strategy of avoidance. Several Lakota bands, including Sitting Bull's Húŋkpapȟa (Nation at the Head of the Circle), moved farther north and west through their homelands in the nineteenth century. By 1871, they were spending winters between the Yellowstone River (which they called the Elk) and the great curve of Mníšoše to the north. In the summers they moved south of the Yellowstone between the Powder and the Bighorn. When the mornings grew cool, they loaded up their lodges on travois pulled by horses, mules, and dogs and moved toward the great buffalo herds that ranged through the rolling plains between the Ȟesápa and the Platte River in Nebraska.

The location and numbers of Buffalo Nation and the many enemies who competed to control Lakota lands were a central point of discussion for the summer councils along the Yellowstone. Over the next few weeks, Sitting Bull met with his fellow chiefs and band leaders as they determined how best to defend their buffalo kin and their homelands against American invaders.

Although Sitting Bull was not the singular chief of Očéthi Šakówiŋ or even of the Lakota, he was an itȟáŋčhaŋ (leader) of a Lakota omníčiye (council of men). This council was made up of leaders from several Lakota bands, and when they came together at summer gatherings, they made decisions regarding the future of their people.

In the late 1860s, four council elders had come to Sitting Bull's tipi, invited him to sit upon a buffalo robe, then picked it up and carried him to a special lodge they had built for a ceremony. The chiefs of several Lakota bands (Húŋkpapȟa, Mnikȟówožu [Minneconjou], Itázipčho [Sans Arc], Oglála) and their Cheyenne allies were there. As they gathered around the council fire, Sitting Bull's uncle Four Horns lit the sacred pipe. It had a red bowl with a buffalo calf carved on it and twelve feathers hanging from its wooden stem. Four Horns extended its mouthpiece to all four directions, so that the Húŋkpapȟa might see clearly in the days to come, and then offered it to the earth, to make them strong. He then passed it from right to left around the fire, and each chief inhaled and handed the pipe on.

After everyone had smoked, Four Horns laid the pipe aside and began to speak.

Sitting Bull had many times demonstrated his bravery on the battlefield, Four Horns said. He had been a wičháša yatapika (shirt-wearer) for many years, a warrior tasked with protecting the entire nation. Sitting Bull was also a member of the most powerful and prominent Húŋkpapȟa men's societies like the Čhaŋté T'íŋza okȟólakičhiye (Strong Hearts) and the Iníla Wóta okȟólakičhiye (Silent Eaters). These men determined where and when hunting parties should go, and how to protect the people. Sitting

Bull's generosity, a practice admired in all Lakota and especially their leaders, was well known. He gave many of his war trophies and buffalo meat away to Húŋkpapȟa men, women, and children, and often intervened to save the lives of war captives. For these reasons, Four Horns said, the council was appointing him to be a head chief.

"It is your duty to see that the nation is fed," he told Sitting Bull, "that we have plenty. When you say 'fight,' we shall fight; when you say 'make peace,' we shall make peace."

After giving him this charge, the council members gave Sitting Bull a flintlock gun, a bow and ten arrows, and a war bonnet crowned with black and white eagle plumes. The bonnet was so long that when Sitting Bull put it on, it trailed on the ground. The eagle feathers that edged it were contributed by many Lakota chiefs, representing their own accomplishments in warfare. The war bonnet was a symbol of their respect for Sitting Bull as a leader on the battlefield, and an emblem of the collective power of the Lakota as a people. From that point on, Sitting Bull had presided over the summer councils. Once a decision had been made, the akíčita (camp police) enforced it.

Húŋkpapȟa peoples had not encountered Americans in large numbers in Lakota country until the summer of 1862, when thousands of gold miners began streaming toward Crow, Shoshone, and Bannock lands in the northern

Rocky Mountains. Most of them came north and east from mines in Arizona and California, but a good number traveled by boat up Mníšoše and tried to cross Lakota lands on their way west. After surveilling several of these groups and attacking a handful of wagon trains, Sitting Bull and several other Húŋkpapȟa band leaders sent a message to the Indian agent posted at Fort Berthold, a post built on the bend of Mníšoše as it turned southeast toward the Mississippi.

"We wish you to stop the whites from traveling through our country," the message read. "And if you do not stop them, we will."

Since that time, Sitting Bull and his Húŋkpapȟa warriors had engaged in several battles with U.S. soldiers, who were protecting white settlers intent on crossing Lakota lands without permission. Their growing numbers at towns and forts along the banks of Mníšoše and in the mountains to the west were alarming.

"Once [wašíču (white settlers)] arrived," Sitting Bull determined, "they did not leave willingly. Whatever they took, they never gave back; and they did not share."

While several Lakota chiefs—and some of their Dakota and Iháŋkthuŋwaŋ/na kin, who lived farther to the east and were the first to try to counter the pressures of American settler colonialism—signed treaties with the Americans and went into the federal Indian agencies for rations in the 1860s, Sitting Bull and the Húŋkpapȟa had not.

Sitting Bull did not sign the 1868 Treaty of Fort Laramie, either, and refused most invitations to speak with Ely Parker or his Indian agents about removing to reservations. In 1870, Oglála chief Maȟpíya Lúta (Red Cloud) had left the homelands to travel to Washington, D.C., and meet Parker and President Ulysses S. Grant. He returned with stories about giant cities filled with people and the tour he had taken of the Smithsonian Institution. Red Cloud had been impressed but resolute about what the Americans owed to the Lakota.

"All the promises made in treaties had never been fulfilled," he told Grant and the others. "The object of the whites was to crush the Indians down to nothing." He demanded that the Americans remove their forts from Lakota lands and keep white miners and settlers out of Ȟesápa, the lands at the center of Lakota history and culture. They must stop trying to force Lakota to move onto reservations. And they must keep their promises.

"The Great Spirit [will] judge these things hereafter," he reminded them.

Although Red Cloud had been critical of Grant's "Peace Policy" and aggressive in his demands that the government recognize Lakota sovereignty, he remained open to talking with

Indian agents and fort commanders about how to end hostilities. Sitting Bull continued to refuse to negotiate. This disagreement among chiefs was not unusual. Since the 1840s Lakota leaders determined that each band should decide whether their bands should sign treaties, or fight. The seven nations of Očéthi Šakówiŋ were kin and allies, but each band took its own path forward.

In July 1871, in their camp along Rosebud Creek, Sitting Bull and the council discussed where buffalo herds had been seen and how to keep their Indigenous enemies—the Crow, in particular—from beating them there. They noted the continuing decline in the size of the herds, due, it was thought, to increasing numbers of Americans traveling through the West. In 1869, the transcontinental railroad had bisected Lakota homelands, bringing even more white settlers into the region and diverting buffalo herds from their traditional migration routes.

Lakotas had pushed back the road builders before and had been particularly successful in the 1860s, fighting Red Cloud's war against American soldiers and civilians along the Bozeman Trail. But recently, in their visits to the trading forts on Mníšoše, Lakota were hearing of a new railroad, the Northern Pacific, which would span the entirety of the Great Northwest. Its tracks had not yet crossed the river, but agents and traders had told the Lakota that soon they would. Surveyors were coming to their homelands to map out a route.

The council decided to send scouts to see if this was true. One group rode out of the camp to the west, following the Yellowstone upriver toward its source. Lakotas had heard of the steaming geysers and boiling mud pots of that region but rarely ventured that far west in pursuit of buffalo or their Crow enemies. The other group rode east toward Mníšoše.

One month later, the western scouting band returned to Sitting Bull's camp on the Yellowstone, leading a herd of horses. They had ridden as far as the rich farmlands of the Gallatin Valley north of the Yellowstone Basin and found no sign of a railroad survey party. What they did find was stock grazing in the green fields, and they ran off more than fifty horses. They killed two wašíču and easily outrode the company of soldiers and the citizen posse sent to chase them down. They did not turn south into the Yellowstone Basin, where Ferdinand Hayden's surveyors and military escort had a large herd of horses. They had more than enough animals for the moment. And they could always return.

Montana's white citizens were in an uproar. The commander of Fort Ellis, Major Eugene Baker, had promised them "peace." In January 1870, he and a company of cavalry had ridden out after a small band of Piegan Blackfoot warriors who were believed to have killed a merchant south of Helena. The cavalry found a Piegan camp perched on the bluffs above the Marias River more than two hundred miles north of Bozeman. Without determining whether these were the Piegans who killed the Montanans, Baker ordered his men to charge. It was a massacre reminiscent of both Bear River in Utah (1863) and Sand Creek in Colorado (1864). The soldiers killed almost two hundred women and children, none of them responsible for the initial murder.

After Baker's act of "severe chastisement," one Montana civilian reported, there had been no hostile Indians in the area, and the white citizens believed themselves to be safe from further attacks. The Lakota raid in the Gallatin Valley was, therefore, a shock. After thinking it could have been Crow or Gros Ventre raiders, Montanans ultimately discovered that it was "warriors under the command of the getting-to-be-famous Sitting Bull," a man they believed was an "implacable demon" and "Beelzebub of the tribe," hell-bent on menacing towns, murdering white civilians, and preventing the future settlement of Montana.

Citizens and political leaders expected further trouble and called on the War Department to send more soldiers to Fort Ellis. In their view, the arrival of cavalry and infantry companies would signal to the Lakotas—and the Crows and Shoshones as well—that the federal government was dedicated to protecting white settlers on Native lands. They would also purchase meat, vegetables, and grain from the valley's farmers and ranchers.

"Our greatest need here is more troops," Governor Benjamin Potts wrote to the secretary of the interior in August.

To fulfill this request, the U.S. Army would have to redeploy troops currently stationed across the South, who were enforcing the federal government's Reconstruction measures and monitoring the Ku Klux Klan. Would the War Department divert some of them to fight the federal government's major antagonists in the West?

If not, advised one newspaper editor, "the people of Montana must take action. We must hold public meetings. Every man that has access to the columns of an Eastern paper should give an account of the necessities of our situation." If they got the word out about how desperate Montana's white population was for protection, perhaps President Grant, who was at his summer home on the New Jersey shore, would take note. Their clamor for protection might "awaken the heedless lounger at Long Branch to its necessity."

And if the president of the United States did not care about white citizens in the western territories, maybe he would care about railroad companies.

"Who knows but that they are preparing to war on the different working parties along the line of the Northern Pacific Railroad?" asked one Montana official. "Protection is but just to the men who build our railroads, and the government should be awake to any emergency."

As Sitting Bull's camp moved south toward the buffalo herds for the annual hunting season, the riders who had gone east returned.

They had found a railroad survey team, they reported, marching out of Fort Rice and traveling along the Heart River, another one of Mníšóše's tributaries. They were a column of around three hundred soldiers and a handful of surveyors, along with several scouts, including a Black guide named Isaiah Dorman. Married to a Dakota woman and fluent in the language, Dorman was well known around Fort Rice to both whites and Lakotas. He had carried mail between forts for the U.S. Army and sold wood and horses to the soldiers. Dorman had hired onto the expedition as the Northern Pacific's interpreter.

The expedition team had marched very slowly through the expanses of shortgrass prairie, only ten miles per day. Their movements were confusing. The surveyors would start out, with their scouts, in one direction. The soldiers would go in another, and then backtrack. Often the Lakota found the survey team, the escort, the wagon train, and the guides scattered across the plains.

If the Lakota had had larger numbers, they would have been able to attack the survey expedition directly. Instead, they decided to use another tactic of warfare that Plains tribes had been using for hundreds of years to battle their enemies and corral the wild animals of the region. A little more than ten days into their journey, the Americans saw smoke rising in the west.

"Towards night the impressions were strengthened by seeing it gradually coming towards us," the officer in charge of the escort reported, "and by taps the whole heavens were lit up and reflected on the clouds formed by the vast conflagration. The wind coming up soon after nightfall drove the flames toward us with great speed."

The surveyors and soldiers were able to make their way to a hill and light backfires to protect themselves from the flames. For the next few days, the haze made it hard for the Americans to see if any Lakota scouts were following them. The ground, though, suggested to the survey members that they were not alone on the plains. Hoofprints trampled the brown autumn grasses now scorched black by the fires.

"Indian signs were observed in several places today," a soldier wrote in his diary on September 24, "and very fresh."

The scouts continued to track the survey team as they traveled west, left the Heart River, and entered the Dakota badlands in the Little Missouri River Valley. It was a remarkable landscape of "broken bluffs taking on the most fantastic forms imaginable" that ran perpendicular to the planned route of the Northern Pacific.

Jay Cooke's trusted engineer, Milnor Roberts, wanted to know if there was any possible way to span this territory with the iron rails. The soil was soft and silty, and rainfall had eroded the entire area into deep furrows that broke the land into thousands of tiny canyons.

The surveyors looked around them with awe but also in fear.

"We are now assembled in a very dangerous position," one soldier reported. "The space we occupy is very contracted, cut up with ravines and precipitous bluffs hemming us in on front and rear. . . . Should the Indians attack us here, there is some reason to fear disaster."

The surveyors traversed the badlands and emerged up into the plains a few days later, still surveilled by the Lakota. Despite their awareness of potential danger, the soldiers did not bother to send their scouts out ahead or take many precautions, and the entire column was strung out and scattered. On October 3, the survey team reached the Yellowstone River. They stayed only briefly and then turned back to the east. After following them for long enough to make sure that the column was returning to Mníšoše, the Lakota scouts turned their horses toward the southwest, to rejoin Sitting Bull and their people in time for the buffalo hunt.

Sitting Bull was not pleased to learn that the survey had made it so far into the heart of their homelands. He pondered the seriousness of the Northern Pacific's threat to his people and committed himself to work against this latest exertion of federal power, in the interest of his people. Meanwhile, white Montanans braced themselves for further conflict.

"I understand that Sitting Bull, one of the most implacable of the Sioux chiefs, has declared open hostilities against the engineer of the Northern Pacific Railroad Company," Montana's territorial governor wrote to the secretary of the interior.

"I do not know that [he] would make peace on any terms, yet I think the government should attempt to make a treaty of some kind with him. . . . Unless some terms are made, he will certainly give us trouble at no distant day."

8

Order, Chaos

Southern Wyoming Territory. October 1871.

After leaving Fort Ellis in early September, the fourteen remaining members of the 1871 Yellowstone Expedition were "on the lope" for almost three weeks. Their primary survey duties complete, they took their time traveling south, chatting and gathering specimens at their leisure.

"We are moving along pleasantly without accident or interruption," Hayden wrote cheerfully to Baird. "We perform a good day's work every day." He marveled that the expedition had been so little disturbed or delayed. "We have not lost a day from storms or anything else since we left Ogden in June last."

After twenty-four days, the men spotted the tracks of the Union Pacific crossing the valley in front of them, and the handful of buildings that comprised Evanston Station, Wyoming. They left their horses at one of the stage stables and mailed off their last remaining specimen boxes. Climbing aboard the eastbound train, they sank gratefully into the cushioned seats of the passenger car.

Fifty miles later, when the conductor called for the Carter's Station stop, Hayden and Albert Peale got up to disembark. Hayden had business at nearby Fort Bridger, named after the famous trapper who first told him stories about the Yellowstone. From there, the two scientists planned to head west again for another week or two, collecting fossils in the embankments created by the construction of the transcontinental. Modernity, it seemed, was a useful excavator. William Henry Jackson, too, broke off from the group. He wanted to take more photographs in Colorado before heading home to Mollie and his studio. The rest of the men bid them farewell and continued. On October 2, Hayden's 1871 Yellowstone Expedition officially disbanded.

Two days later, the men headed east reached Omaha. After saying goodbye to Jim Stevenson, Potato John, and the rest of them, the topographer Anton Schönborn collected his luggage and went to Omaha House, where he would be boarding for a few weeks. Hayden had asked Schönborn to join him in Washington, D.C., in late October, to prepare the maps and help with the organization of the specimens from the expedition. Schönborn would relish it.

"Severe labor or close accurate work does not frighten me," he had assured Hayden.

He preferred it to reassuming his regular

duties as part of the U.S. Army's Department of the Platte, where he made survey maps and watercolor sketches of military posts across the West. Hayden's expedition had been much more exciting, allowing him to contribute to the creation of scientific knowledge. And he had grown comfortable with the men of the survey. They were not naturally vicious or disagreeable to deal with, like some scientists he knew.

Back in Omaha, that feeling of ease slipped away. Schönborn frequented the city's watering holes, drinking until he was quite drunk, most days. One afternoon ten days after his return, Schönborn went out walking. When he returned to his room in Omaha House, he locked himself in. Taking up a knife, he drew it quickly from his left ear across his windpipe. Blood gushed from the wound, soaking his shirt. Schönborn groaned and collapsed back on the bed, his feet dangling off the edge. Twenty minutes later, his landlord broke open the door to find Schönborn's lifeless body. In his pockets, Schönborn had $116 and a train ticket to Washington, D.C. He was supposed to leave the next day.

When the members of the Yellowstone Expedition heard about Schönborn's suicide, they could not believe it. The survey had been so free of bad luck and tragedy, and now this.

The news "cast a gloom over the party," Robert Adams lamented. "Scattered though we be, there is that bond between us only to be formed by camp life and the sharing of hardship and danger."

Schönborn had always appeared so genial. It seemed unaccountable that he would take his own life.

"What was the cause of Schönborn's suicide?" David Heap wondered in a letter to Hayden. The military engineer, who had traveled with John Barlow's team, had seen little of the topographer given their differing routes and schedules. But "I should never have imagined that he would have terminated his career so tragically."

Even when Schönborn seemed happy and content in Yellowstone, he must have been keeping his dark thoughts at bay. Or maybe he had just become "weary of life," as the *Omaha Daily Herald* surmised. Schönborn did not leave a note. His friends and colleagues were left without any answers.

When Ferdinand Hayden came through Omaha a few days later, he went directly to Omaha House. Schönborn's death was shocking and distressing. He had been a dear friend of Hayden's; they first met at the Smithsonian and had embarked on the 1860 Raynolds Expedition together. Hayden trusted him and believed in his talent. Schönborn's expertise was vital to the success of the expedition's next phase, which was to work up reports of its findings, gather all the data, and shape it into a coherent assessment of the region. To bring order out of chaos.

Schönborn had returned to Omaha with two field notebooks crammed with atmospheric statistics and elevation notes for sites from northern Utah to the Yellowstone Basin. There were also several pages filled with the sounding measurements of Yellowstone Lake. When Hayden arrived at Omaha House, he was relieved to find that the landlord had kept the topographer's belongings, which included the notebooks. If his friend had destroyed his field notes along with himself, the loss—for Hayden—would have been irreparable.

His sense of panic lessened, Hayden tucked the books into his bags and set out for the ferry to take him across the Missouri River. From there he boarded a train to Chicago. How would he manage the preparation of the maps without Schönborn? Henry Elliott had a notebook of his own, he knew. Perhaps Heap and Barlow also had maps of the region that he could use in conjunction with Schönborn's notes. It was important that the expedition report he produced for Congress include maps and other visual images. Politicians may not be able to understand the scientific data that the expedition produced, but they would be able to look at a map of the Yellowstone Basin and comprehend its scale, features, and unique nature.

It turned out that Heap could help him. The engineer had returned from the Yellowstone to his army post in St. Paul, Minnesota, with their survey's astronomic and topographic notes.

"I will gladly do what I can to aid you," Heap assured Hayden. He asked that, in return, Hayden send him any data he had gleaned from Schönborn's notebooks. In cooperation, they could "make a better map than either could separately."

Heap could not provide much more than that, however. He and Barlow had experienced their own terrible loss—"tho' yours is the most serious of the two," Heap acknowledged—after returning from the Yellowstone. In mid-September, Barlow had arrived at his head-quarters in Chicago, bringing all of his survey's meteorological records, mineralogical and fossil specimens, and most of his survey photographer J. T. Hines's negatives to his office in the business district.

A few weeks later, on the night of October 8, a fire broke out in a barn on the southwestern side of the city. Such incidents were not unusual. Most American city buildings were constructed of wood, and open fires in homes and businesses were common. But a confluence of factors, including a months-long drought and mistakes made by fire spotters in the first hour of the blaze, meant that the fire spread quickly through the city, moving north and east toward Lake Michigan.

While the fire raged, "the air was filled with flaming brands," a *Harper's Weekly* correspondent reported, and strong winds blew them through the streets, "kindling new fires wherever they fell."

Streets and sidewalks made of wood seemed to explode into flame almost instantly, while the heat of the inferno melted both brick and metal. Residents fleeing from their homes stopped to watch in horror as buildings disintegrated into ash within minutes. Those lucky enough to board eastbound trains and escape the conflagration could still see the flames looming above the city from forty miles away.

The destruction from the Great Chicago Fire was tremendous. The fire consumed more than 17,000 buildings, causing $200 million in damage. Three hundred people died in the flames, and 100,000 people (one third of the city's residents) were left homeless. John Barlow was lucky to escape with his life, but his professional losses were immense.

"Not one single paper or other property was saved from my office," he told Hayden. "All my instruments, maps, books, & everything brought back from the Yellowstone, including specimens, etc. were consumed."

Luckily, Barlow had kept his journal of the

expedition in his rooms at his boarding house, so he was able to start writing his report of the Army Corps of Engineers expedition. He also had Heap's data and maps, which his colleague would be sending from Minnesota. But he had no specimens and very few photographs to work with and would need Hayden's help in that respect.

"I shall have to trust to our old friendship & your generosity," Barlow wrote hopefully.

Hayden was annoyed to be burdened with this new responsibility, but it was his duty to oblige. The field of scientific inquiry had always depended on the exchange of specimens and the sharing of data. Hayden and Barlow were not in competition for congressional funding or public renown. The military engineer was writing his report only for his superiors in the War Department. Hayden could afford to be generous.

He would send Barlow his data and photographic negatives once he returned to Washington, D.C. He had other, more personal matters to attend to as well. After getting things in order at his offices at the Smithsonian, he would be returning to Philadelphia and to Emma. They would be married on November 9.

To catch his train to Washington, Hayden disembarked at a station on the western edge of the Burnt District and made his way through it to the southeast. Chicago's streets were lined with masses of blackened ruins, and he had to pick his way through heaps of brick, stone, and ashes. The city buzzed with activity as workers cleared the rubble and built temporary structures in every direction. Some families were living in shanties, others out in the open air. Still others had pitched canvas tents, sent by the War Department. President Grant had instructed his military commanders in the region, William Tecumseh Sherman and Phil Sheridan, to send supplies and rations.

"Render all the aid you can," he ordered them, "to relieve sufferings from [this] great calamity."

The train stations on the southeast side of the city, which had escaped destruction, were clogged with passengers, wagons, and boxes of clothing, food, and other supplies. Charity organizations, wealthy businessmen including Jay Cooke, and state governments across the nation had sent more than four million dollars' worth of supplies to help the city of Chicago recover and rebuild. The Great Fire was, in a way, the first truly national event since the Civil War. It was an opportunity for all Americans to express a shared sense of patriotism in a nation otherwise riven by discord.

When Hayden arrived at the Smithsonian a few days later, there was a pile of correspondence waiting for him. Some letters were from well-wishers, congratulating him on the successful completion of the survey. Others were from his colleagues in the scientific community, whom he had recruited to analyze the Yellowstone specimens for his government reports.

While the expedition was still out in the field, Hayden had sent them boxes of plants, animal skins and bones, and fossils of plants and vertebrates. Over the next three months, Hayden would be in constant correspondence with these men, urging them to finish their analyses and send them in. The preliminary report had to be completed by February 1872 so it could be printed and distributed to the congressmen voting to appropriate money for the summer's expedition. Hayden was thinking of returning to Yellowstone with a larger team of scientists to continue the work they had started.

There was also a letter from Richard Watson Gilder, the managing editor of *Scribner's Monthly*. Gilder wanted Hayden to write an article for an upcoming issue of the magazine. *Scribner's* had already published Nathaniel Langford's accounts of his team's exploration of Yellowstone in May and June. Truman Everts's searing account of his thirty-seven days lost in the wilderness would be published in the November 1871 issue.

Gilder believed that Yellowstone's features and tales of its exploration and discovery were topics of immense interest to the magazine's white, middle-class readers. Such stories were uplifting, morally righteous, and devoted to American exceptionalism—just the kind of material that *Scribner's Monthly* wanted to provide for Americans casting about for a new sense of themselves and their country after the Civil War.

The magazine, founded by the poet and novelist J. G. Holland and his friend Roswell Smith in partnership with the book publisher Charles Scribner & Sons, was already distinguishing itself as a worthy rival to *Harper's Weekly* after only a year in print. The early 1870s was a period of "magazine mania" in the United States, when hundreds of periodicals competed for the attention of middle-class readers across the country.

Holland had hired Gilder after working with him briefly at another of Charles Scribner's magazines, *Hours at Home.* A slight man with flashing, dark eyes, Gilder was charming, with an easy way about him and abundant connections among the literati of Philadelphia and New York City. Although the magazine's art director oversaw the illustrations, it was Gilder who first brought Thomas Moran into the fold as an illustrator for *Scribner's Monthly.* The two men had known each other during their boyhoods in Philadelphia, and Gilder had hired Moran to create woodcut illustrations for several essays and for Nathaniel Langford's Yellowstone pieces.

In Gilder's letter to Ferdinand Hayden, he promised that *Scribner's* would feature his Yellowstone article and illustrate it handsomely. In his view, the piece (and any others that Hayden might want to write on his trips to the far West) would benefit readers. It would also help promote the geologist's work for the Department of the Interior.

"I think the Department will look upon such articles as a part of the good work it is doing in exploring the far away & peculiar regions of our country," Gilder wrote. "The object of these explorations is knowledge—and the people will the more highly appreciate the work the Department is doing, if its results are presented in a popular form."

Gilder could not have made a more compelling argument to a more willing writer. Although Hayden understood the utility of scientific writing meant for his colleagues, which was often published in the proceedings of learned societies, he had always believed in the power of popular writing to convey scientific knowledge. While the expedition was in the Yellowstone, he had taken to reading and correcting Albert Peale's letters to the *Philadelphia Press*, reprimanding him for writing prose that was "too scientific" for newspaper readers.

Although he saw the merits of "stripping the

romance" from Yellowstone through scientific discovery, Hayden found that a more descriptive writing style, based on the popular genre of the travelogue, suited his purposes better. It enabled him to reveal the wonders of the landscape to readers just as he and his fellow expedition members had encountered them, combining the realism of geological facts with more romantic stories of the "adventure of fieldwork." This style merged pleasure with instruction, combining science with the aesthetics of landscape description.

Scribner's seemed eager to publish the article as soon as possible, so Hayden began to write it. During the next few weeks, he was joined in his labors by expedition team members who came to unpack and organize the boxes they had sent from the field. They took up an office at the Smithsonian and got to work. Although William Henry Jackson was not supposed to come to D.C. until the end of the year, Hayden wrote and asked him to come immediately. He needed help assembling the photographs for the reports and choosing which images to send to Moran for his *Scribner's* engravings.

Hayden needed Jackson for another task as well. One of the letters waiting for Hayden upon his return had suggested an important undertaking for the survey. It was from A. B. Nettleton, Jay Cooke's public relations man.

"[Pig Iron] Kelley has made a suggestion which strikes me as being an excellent one," Nettleton wrote, "viz.: Let Congress pass a bill reserving the Great Geyser Basin as a public park for ever."

That Kelley, a booster for the Great Northwest, would make such a suggestion was not a surprise. A national park would bring tourists, who would report on the potential of the region to other white Americans.

Hayden immediately saw the benefit of this suggestion to preserve Yellowstone for his own career. It would enable him to return again and again to that marvelous region, to examine it in more detail and solve more of its scientific mysteries. In his letter, Nettleton asked that Hayden make a case for this legislative action in his Yellowstone report. Hayden agreed. He also decided to use the skills he had honed throughout his career to lobby members of Congress directly.

Jay Cooke received Ferdinand Hayden's enthusiastic reply to Nettleton's letter just as he returned to Philadelphia from Gibraltar, where he had spent the month of October fishing and hunting with friends. Several of his children and their spouses and babies had joined them. It was a joy to have his family all together again on the island, if only for a short time. Their company helped to lighten the darkness that had fallen on his heart: they were at Gibraltar without Libby. The doctors in Philadelphia could do nothing for her, and she had died on July 21.

It was a difficult adjustment, living without her. Every day since they were married, he had come home from the office to take a carriage ride with her, and she traveled with him on most of his trips to New York City or Washington, D.C. But Cooke did not sorrow without solace. He knew that the Lord had called her to a better life.

"Trust in God was never more beautifully illustrated than in this case," his brother Henry said about him in the wake of Libby's death. "Jay bears his loss with the calm fortitude of a Christian hero."

Cooke tried to manage his mourning by throwing himself into his work, but that did not provide much in the way of comfort. The situation with the Northern Pacific was even more dire than it had been over the summer. The European investors he had sent to tour the Pacific Northwest with Milnor Roberts had come back east and visited him at Gibraltar early in October. They lost their luggage en route due to the confusion the Chicago Fire had created on the rail lines, and they were out of sorts. Cooke gave them the hard sell, but they were not impressed. They left together that evening, on a cutter bound for Cleveland.

Although Cooke still hoped they might invest in

the Northern Pacific and support his emigration schemes to bring German, Austrian, and Dutch farmers to the Great Northwest, he knew the chances were increasingly slim. Europe was still reeling from the economic effects of the Franco-Prussian War (which had lasted for almost a year and ended in May 1871), and investors there remained skittish about putting money in American railroad projects.

The railroad was also taking on debt. Because bond sales had been so meager, Cooke had authorized the Northern Pacific's president, John Gregory Smith, to purchase iron and other supplies by borrowing on credit from Jay Cooke & Co. By November 1871, the Northern Pacific was overdrawn by a significant amount: $600,000. Cooke promised his partners that he would not advance the Northern Pacific any more of the company's funds—money that their customers had deposited with them to invest in other projects—before he sold more railroad bonds.

"I am not an alarmist and have more courage than is good for me," Cooke warned Smith, "but my sober common-sense tells me we are to have a bad, *bad* time."

Cooke knew that the Northern Pacific was in trouble. He was a man with a mediocre poker hand who had already bet most of his money before the final cards were dealt. Cooke could fold, but then he would lose everything. If he stayed in the game, at least he had some chance of winning. If the Northern Pacific failed, it would be a judgment upon him both personally and professionally. His reputation, as the man who saved the Union during the war, as "god's chosen instrument," would be ruined.

This idea about a national park that Pig Iron Kelley suggested cheered him somewhat. Nature had always been a place of solace and contemplation for him, and as a sportsman, he had long been an advocate for the preservation of the wilderness. He saw it as a useful way to keep animal and bird populations plentiful for hunting. But he had some reservations.

"Would this conflict with our land grant, or interfere with us in any way?" he wrote to Milnor Roberts. "Please give me your view on this subject."

If the federal government took control of a large enough parcel of land for Yellowstone National Park, this might obstruct the route of the railroad or restrict the land rights they would gain on either side of the track. But preservation could help the Northern Pacific as well, by preventing competition for future tourism development in the Yellowstone region.

"It is important to do something speedily, or squatters & claimants will go in there," he warned Roberts, "and we can probably deal much better with the government in any improvements we may desire to make for the benefit of our pleasure travel, than with individuals."

If Roberts thought there was potential profit for the Northern Pacific in a national park, Cooke would contact Nathaniel Langford. The booster had proven adept at giving persuasive public lectures about Yellowstone and would make a good lobbyist. Langford had recently returned to Montana, but Cooke felt sure he would jump at the chance at any project that would bring business to that territory, which would be— if both the park and the Northern Pacific succeeded—the gateway to the Yellowstone.

Cooke folded up the letter and posted it to Roberts in Montana. The engineer had gone to Fort Ellis, hoping to complete at least part of the eastbound railroad survey from there before the snow fell. The survey team had started without Roberts in early October, just after Hayden's survey team left for home. They had not made it very far. The surveyor Roberts had hired turned out to be an incompetent and inflexible drunk. Roberts set out after them on November 2, with a military escort that included Major Eugene Baker and George Tyler, who had led Hayden's escort in the Yellowstone Basin.

The route they initially took followed the northern bank of the Yellowstone River, which was cut through with hills and bluffs. Roberts immediately realized that the Northern Pacific's tracks would have to be laid along the southern bank, which fell within the boundaries of the Crow Reservation. He was not worried about this issue. Cooke would lobby Congress to extinguish the Crow land titles along the Yellowstone River and change the boundaries of the reservation. The route, with its adjacent lands freed up for sale, would be theirs.

As for the fertility of the Yellowstone River Valley, Roberts had good news for Cooke.

"The soil is excellent, the side valleys are good, and the uplands are certainly very superior grazing regions," he wrote, "and they are claimed to be good for farming. For sheep, cattle, and horses, this region that we are now in surpasses any that I have ever seen in North and South America." The waters of the Yellowstone, which could be used to irrigate crops, were "clear as crystal, flowing rapidly over clean gravel and boulders."

Roberts was also happy to report that the uplands along the route were covered in pine forests. The railroad builders would have plenty of wood for ties, and the settlers who followed could easily build houses and feed their cookfires for years to come. Huge herds of antelope bounded through the bottomlands, and at one point the survey team even found themselves among a small group of buffalo.

"Such days! Such nights! Such game! Such appetites!" Roberts wrote.

Roberts was similarly pleased with the knowledge he had gained along the way.

"Should the Yellowstone Valley be adopted as the general route," he wrote in his report, "there would be time to examine these next season, without delaying the extension of the road westward of the Missouri River." The Northern Pacific could build the valley section quite easily, he thought, and at a moderate cost.

Cooke was delighted. Finally, there was some good news for the Northern Pacific. The railroad company would continue building the westbound line, cross the Missouri, and then move west into Montana Territory. If Congress passed a measure to preserve the Yellowstone Basin south of the route, it would provide welcome news coverage and hope for the tourist trade. Investors would flock to the project, and Cooke could pay back the money he had borrowed from his own investment bank to keep the Northern Pacific afloat. Buoyed by this vision, Cooke felt confident that 1872 would be the railroad's year.

In late September 1871, Sitting Bull's band moved toward the heart of their homelands between the Yellowstone and the confluence of the Milk River and Mníšoše. He preferred these lands; they were full of game and far away from white settlements, but close enough to the Americans' trading forts to be useful. As a camp of more than two hundred families began to rise out of the grasslands, Sitting Bull and a small party of his best men rode to Fort Peck, sixty miles north. A modest post built of vertical slats of wood, perched on a bluff overlooking Mníšoše as it moved east across northern Montana, Fort Peck was the most convenient place for the Húŋkpapȟa to exchange buffalo robes for American goods that would help them survive the winter. Arriving after nightfall, Sitting Bull called out to the guards at the post.

"I come as a friend for peace," he announced.

The next day, Sitting Bull and his men did brisk and profitable business with the traders at Fort Peck, and then rode back to their winter camp. In early October, Sitting Bull returned and asked to see an Indian agent to discuss the distribution of rations to his people. Sitting Bull and the council had decided to make this rare diplomatic gesture because the buffalo hunt had not been as productive that fall as it had been in years past. The herds were thinning out, overhunted by both Americans and the Lakota's Indigenous enemies. The Húŋkpapȟa would need more food to survive the winter, and a temporary peace agreement with the Americans was the way to procure it. Sitting Bull also promised to restrain any war parties that might move out against white settlements and forts over the winter.

The traders passed this request along to the Indian agent at Milk River Agency, A. J. Simmons, who sent it to Montana's superintendent for Indian Affairs, Jasper Viall.

"If the Indians are subsisted and judiciously managed," Viall excitedly informed Francis Walker, who had replaced Ely Parker as commissioner of Indian Affairs, "they can be brought upon a peace-footing and further hostilities prevented."

Viall wanted to go to Sitting Bull's camp and negotiate with him there. He received permission from the Department of the Interior for this trip, but the war department wrote to say that the soldiers at Fort Ellis were out with the survey teams of the Northern Pacific, so they could not provide an escort.

Viall did not want to let this opportunity pass by, so he tapped Simmons to lead the negotiations at Fort Peck in his stead. Early in November, a messenger arrived at Sitting Bull's camp, bearing a gift of tobacco and an invitation to the Fort Peck council. Although he was more amenable to peace than he had been in recent years, Sitting Bull decided not to go. There had been unrest within his camp that fall. Despite the council's directive that no war parties would go out against the Americans, one day several young men gathered their weapons, painted their bodies and their horses, and rode off to the east. The akičita (camp police, who enforced the council's decisions) discovered their plans. A violent encounter ensued, resulting in the deaths of eight Húŋkpapȟa and twenty horses. The war party was an act of flagrant disobedience, and a sign that the council's decisions and Sitting Bull's leadership were not unquestioned.

Sitting Bull chose to stay in camp to keep an eye on things. But he also wanted to take advantage of this opportunity. He sent a message to Simmons, telling him that he was sending Haŋwí Sápa (Black Moon), a fellow war chief, to represent Húŋkpapȟa interests. When Black Moon and a party of Húŋkpapȟa warriors arrived at Fort Peck, they found that they would not be negotiating a treaty. The rider in the 1871 Indian Appropriations Act had outlawed them. But Simmons had the authority to make a peace agreement with the Húŋkpapȟa, a more informal arrangement that worked more like a contract and did not acknowledge Indigenous tribes as sovereign nations. After signing the agreement, Black Moon and Sitting Bull could then visit Washington, D.C., and discuss a more permanent situation with President Grant.

Simmons began the council by assuring the Húŋkpapȟa that President Grant was anxious to live on friendly terms with them. Quickly, however, his tone became more foreboding.

"Game, upon which you depend for subsistence, is fast disappearing," he said. "If you continue your warfare, you will also disappear—will perish with the buffalo." If the Húŋkpapȟa made peace "and remained faithful to it," however, they would survive, ideally on government reservations.

"I am emphatically in favor of peace," Black Moon responded. "Sitting Bull agrees with me and will stand by me. Most of our headmen and men of sense want peace with the whites." He would do what he could to convince his people that an agreement would benefit them. However, Black Moon and Sitting Bull had their own demands.

"If you wish to have peace with the [Lakota]," Black Moon said, "here is what the President must do." First, he must stop the Northern Pacific. If the railroad project continued, its tracks would cross through Lakota country, destroying the game there, including the buffalo herds.

Second, "the white soldiers and citizens must be kept out." They would not abide any soldiers or settlers on their land. All U.S. Army forts in their territory must be abandoned.

"If the Great White Father would do these things," Black Moon said, "it would satisfy all and they would have peace."

After Black Moon sat down, other members

of the Húŋkpapȟa party spoke, endorsing what Black Moon had said, telling Simmons that the railroad would bring white settlers and as a result their kin, the Buffalo Nation, would disappear. The Húŋkpapȟa would rather die fighting the Northern Pacific than die of starvation because of it. Simmons became impatient.

"The railroad will be built," he said. "You might as well undertake to stop the Missouri River from flowing down stream as to stop the railroad."

As if to confirm Simmons's conviction that the Northern Pacific was an unstoppable force, Lakota runners came into Fort Peck the next day to report that they had seen large groups of soldiers from Fort Ellis, accompanying surveyors working eastward along the Yellowstone River just as the first of the fall's snowstorms came rolling over the Rockies.

"There was much excitement, much talk, and some preparations for fighting," Simmons reported to Viall. "They wanted to know the object of these soldiers—if they were coming to fight them."

"They will not harm you, unless you attack them," Simmons told Black Moon and the Húŋkpapȟa.

Black Moon consulted with the other men in attendance. Then he sent a messenger to Sitting Bull at the camp, advising him to prevent the young men from forming another war party, so as not to undermine the negotiations at Fort Peck. Simmons and Black Moon continued to negotiate. In the end, the Húŋkpapȟa agreed to remain at peace over the winter, while Simmons relayed their demands to President Grant.

As the winter snows blanketed the Húŋkpapȟa camp, Sitting Bull once again pondered his options. They would wait to see if Grant accepted their terms, and if Simmons would send them rations so his people would not suffer. For the moment, Sitting Bull would not declare war against the Americans. But if the whites continued to trespass on their homelands, and if the Northern Pacific encroached on Húŋkpapȟa lands, he would consider no further agreements with Grant or his messengers.

In the fall of 1871, President Grant was still dedicated to the prospect of a peaceable future with the Lakota and every other tribal nation in the West. He was already working on his annual message to Congress and wanted to propose an idea that Ely Parker had advocated: collecting all Indigenous peoples into one large reservation in one territory, which might someday become a state. It was unlikely that Sitting Bull and many of his Lakota kin would accept such a plan, but it would suit Grant's vision of a humane and economical solution to the "Indian Problem" in the West. And it would free up millions of acres of public lands, which the president regarded as the heritage of all Americans.

Grant's hopes for voluntary peace in the South, however, were fading. Testimony from Black southerners like Lucy McMillan and so many others in South Carolina convinced Grant's attorney general, Amos Akerman, that Klan atrocities had become so extensive that they must be exposed and prosecuted. Akerman recommended that the president use the full extent of the powers granted to him as the chief executive to suppress the Ku Klux Klan. Any other course of action would be a disaster.

"Nothing is more idle than to attempt to conciliate by kindness that portion of the southern people who are still malcontent," Akerman believed. "They take all kindness of the part of the Government as evidence of timidity, and hence are emboldened to lawlessness by it. It appears impossible for the Government to win their affection. But it can command their respect by the exercise of its powers."

Akerman, who was the only southerner in Grant's cabinet and the only former Confederate officer, became attorney general in June 1870, a week before the president signed an act creating the Department of Justice. This new department, which consolidated most of the government's lawyers under one roof, was empowered to launch federal prosecutions. In the spring of 1871, Akerman had become absorbed by—his critics would say, obsessed with—the federal government's campaign to eradicate the Ku Klux Klan. He was determined to use the Department of Justice to prosecute Klan members across the South. In early October, the attorney general traveled to South Carolina, consulting with federal lawyers there and with Major Lewis Merrill, a Seventh Cavalry officer posted in Yorkville who had been accumulating evidence of Klan activities in that county since the spring.

It was time to act. A series of high-profile prosecutions would drag the Invisible Empire into the light, expose its prominent leaders and the extent of its reach, and prove its political purpose: to prevent Black Americans from exercising their constitutional rights, in violation of the Fourteenth and Fifteenth Amendments.

Akerman advised Grant to proclaim South Carolina's upcountry counties in a state of insurrection against the federal government. This would enable him to suspend the writ of habeas corpus. Merrill could then send out his troops to arrest suspected Klan members without explaining the charges and keep them in jail indefinitely. The U.S. Army would have the advantage of surprise in the arrests, and protect the prosecution's future witnesses from violence or intimidation.

On October 12, after several days managing military and financial responses to the Great Chicago Fire, Grant sat down to write out his proclamation.

"Unlawful combinations and conspiracies have long existed and still do exist in the State of South Carolina," he began, "for the purpose of depriving certain portions and classes of the people of that State of the rights, privileges, immunities, and protection named in the Constitution of the United States."

South Carolina's state and local governments had been thus far unable or unwilling to protect its citizens. The preservation of public peace and safety had become impossible.

"Therefore, I, Ulysses S. Grant, President of the United States of America," he wrote, "do hereby command all persons composing the unlawful combinations and conspiracies aforesaid to disperse and to retire peaceably to their homes within five days of the date hereof."

Grant ordered the proclamation published. It caused a sensation across the South and even more belligerence from white communities. On October 16, Akerman sent a telegram from South Carolina, reporting that no Klan members had come into any of the army's camps to surrender their weapons. The spirit on the ground continued to be defiant.

The next day, as the period of amnesty he had

extended expired, President Grant was in Boston. He was there to preside over the laying of the cornerstone for a new post office and treasury building in the city, and to visit his son Buck at Harvard. After the ceremony, Grant issued his second proclamation.

"The insurgents" within South Carolina, it said, "have not dispersed and retired peaceably to their respective homes." They had not surrendered their weapons. Grant was suspending the writ of habeas corpus in nine South Carolina counties, "to the end that such rebellion may be overthrown." Any man suspected of being a member of the Ku Klux Klan could now be arrested, "by any soldier or citizen acting under the orders of said marshal, deputy, or such military officer."

As Grant signed the order, he knew there would be an outcry. Democrats would call him a dictator. An enemy of liberty. A military despot. Grant was unconcerned. He was going to battle against the Ku Klux Klan in South Carolina, the former cradle of the Confederacy. This, finally, was the kind of presidential work he liked: pursuing an enemy and bringing him to heel.

The Seventh Cavalry came for the Klan in broad daylight. Across the South Carolina upcountry, they rode to farms and shops and law offices, stately homes, and ramshackle dogtrot cabins, calling out for the men they knew worked and lived there. They arrested them in front of their families, who screamed profanities and insults at the soldiers as they led their fathers, sons, and brothers away. The only disappointment for Major Merrill and for Akerman was that most of the men they arrested, or who subsequently came into headquarters and surrendered, were the rank and file. The moment that President Grant had issued the proclamation suspending the writ, almost fifty of the Klan's leaders in South Carolina, wealthy men who were doctors and lawyers and merchants, fled the state. There were rumors that several had made it to Canada and sought asylum as political refugees.

The Ku Klux Klan trials began in Columbia, South Carolina, in late November. Amos Akerman consulted with the state's U.S. district attorney, David Corbin, on a prosecutorial strategy. It was twofold. First, the government would argue that Klan members had formed a conspiracy to prevent Black men from voting, violating their Fifteenth Amendment rights. Their convictions on these charges would be a potent symbol to Klan members that their crimes would be punished.

Second, the government's lawyers would argue that the judges in the case (a Republican from Baltimore named Hugh Bond and a Democrat from Charleston named George Bryan) should declare that the Constitution gave the federal government power to enforce citizenship rights if individual states did nothing to protect their residents. Affirmation of federal supremacy was necessary if the Grant administration wanted to prosecute future civil rights cases in the South or anywhere else in the country.

The Klan's defense attorneys, on the other hand, planned to attack the notion that the Ku Klux Klan's actions fell under the purview of the federal government. They would contend that only states were constitutionally empowered to bestow and protect the rights of their citizens and that the federal government had no right to intervene. They also hoped to exonerate the white people of the South Carolina upcountry from the charges of rebellion against the U.S. government.

In mid-December, the prosecution of individual Klan members began. Corbin called witnesses, Klan members who described the clandestine nature of the organization, the punishment for revealing its secrets (death), and how their Klans met, donned disguises, and set out together late at night to fulfill their purpose. Such an organization of men, Corbin argued to the jury, bound together in secrecy and intent upon robbing Black men and white Republicans of their right to vote, constituted a conspiracy. The Klan's defense attorneys argued that they had organized not to rob Black and white Republicans of their rights, but to protect themselves and their property.

At the end of the first trial, David Corbin had the last word.

"This organization to defeat the rights of our colored fellow citizens," he argued, *"must and shall be put down*. Gentlemen, I am here, as the representative of the Government, for that purpose. I tell you, and I tell the people of South Carolina, that if this thing is not put down, woe, woe, woe unto them."

The biracial jury was convinced. They found the defendant guilty of conspiracy, and the judges sentenced him to eighteen months in prison. Over the next few months, Corbin went on to prosecute and convict hundreds of Klan members in South Carolina on similar charges. Although the judges declined to rule on the matter of federal supremacy in civil rights matters, Corbin and Akerman considered the trials a success. They were the high-water mark in the history of the federal government's protection of Black rights since the founding of the nation, and it would not reach for this higher ideal again until the middle of the twentieth century.

But Akerman, like Ely Parker, would not last long in the Grant administration. As the Ku Klux Klan trials got underway, President Grant sent him a letter asking him to resign as attorney general. He offered no specific reason, to Akerman or anyone else. To lessen the shock of his firing, the president offered Akerman a new post. Perhaps a judgeship in Florida or Texas.

Akerman suspected that certain congressmen

(he refused to say who) had been working for his ouster for as long as he had been attorney general. Before he had turned so much of his attention to the Ku Klux Klan, he had brought pressure to bear on railroad companies like the Northern Pacific, forcing them to prove that they had built enough track to earn land grants from the government. And at least one member of the president's cabinet had expressed his discontent at Akerman's dogged focus on prosecuting white supremacist violence in the South.

Akerman wrote back to Grant, resigning and declining the judgeships. He would return to his home state of Georgia in January 1872 and resume his work as a country lawyer and farmer. Akerman was satisfied that the prosecutions he spearheaded seemed to have pushed the Klan underground in South Carolina, at least for the time being. During his last days in Washington, D.C., however, Akerman sensed a growing resentment among Republicans regarding Grant's suspension of the writ, along with a flagging interest in punishing the Klan. The party's dedication to protecting Black rights would not last long.

"Such atrocities as Ku Kluxery do not hold their attention," Akerman wrote to a friend. "The Northern mind, being full of what is called progress, runs away from the past."

9

To Consecrate for Public Use

Washington, D.C. December 1871.

Like the state capitol grounds in South Carolina, the National Mall in Washington, D.C., was filled with people in early December. The Forty-Second Congress was back in town to convene its second session, and the city buzzed with journalists, businessmen, and constituents seeking an audience with them. In the early afternoon on December 9, Ferdinand Hayden left the Yellowstone Expedition offices in the Smithsonian Institution and walked across the lawn toward the U.S. Capitol. The massive building was positioned on a small rise, designed to suggest to those approaching it that they were ascending to a place of higher purpose, a site of national significance. This impression was confirmed upon entering the Rotunda, which evoked Rome's Pantheon and situated the United States within a global history of empire and conquest.

Hayden walked through the massive space, past the high, curving sandstone walls and paintings depicting the discoveries of explorers

Hernando de Soto and Christopher Columbus as well as the Revolutionary Era's most consequential moments, including the signing of the Declaration of Independence. Turning left, he moved through the Old Hall of the House of Representatives, with its huge marble columns quarried from the Potomac River. Soon he found the office of the man he was meeting with that day: Henry Dawes, the chairman of the House Committee on Ways and Means, and the most powerful man in the House of Representatives.

Dawes was a generation older than Hayden and a career politician. He entered political life as a Massachusetts state representative, was elected to the House in 1856 and had been serving in that body ever since. A steadfast Republican, he supported many of the Grant administration's initiatives in the South and the West and had used his influence as chairman of Ways and Means to appropriate money for Hayden's 1871 expedition to the Yellowstone.

Dawes rose to greet Hayden, smiling through his bushy beard. The two men were supposed to meet the previous week, but the opening of the session was always a busy time, and Dawes had been detained in one of the first of many committee meetings. They sat down to talk. Dawes's son Chester had been back from the expedition for several months, and Hayden had nothing but praise for the work the young man had done for the survey. At Yellowstone Lake, William Henry Jackson had taken a marvelous photograph of Chester and Jim Stevenson aboard the *Annie*. Hayden thought Dawes might like the photograph for another reason as well: they had named the boat not after a survey team's sweetheart, he claimed, but after Dawes's own daughter, Anna.

"My whole party," Hayden wrote later in his government report, "were glad to manifest, by this slight tribute, their gratitude to the distinguished statesman, whose generous sympathy and aid had contributed so much toward securing the appropriation which enabled them to explore this marvelous region."

Hayden hoped that Dawes would now help with another matter related to Yellowstone. As the congressman likely knew from Chester's stories, the discoveries that the Hayden survey made that summer confirmed all that Nathaniel Langford reported from his 1870 exploration. The geysers, mud pots, thundering waterfalls, and deep canyons were not figments of a frontier trapper's muddled imagination. Hayden had seen them with his own eyes and measured their heights, depths, and elevations with his instruments. He was convinced that the Yellowstone Basin was the most unique landscape on the continent, a place of grandeur and majesty unrivaled in the world.

There was one problem, however. Hayden told Dawes about the health seekers taking the waters at the pools below the White Mountain and the plans that Harry Horr and other local entrepreneurs had to build hotels and resorts in the vicinity. As far as Hayden knew, these men had not yet made their land claims under the Homestead Act or through the process of preemption. Yellowstone must be saved from these squatters, Hayden argued, and from the rampant commercial development that had ruined Niagara Falls. By 1870, the pathways and roads around Niagara were filled with tens of thousands of visitors a year and choked with "a great fungus-growth of museums, curiosity-shops, taverns, and pagodas with shining tin cupolas."

Yellowstone must be protected from this kind of debasement. Congressmen like Dawes, Hayden argued, could make sure that Yellowstone remained a wilderness.

The idea of preserving land for the people was not a new one in American culture. Europeans had come to North America with a tradition of setting aside commons in every town, and in the mid-nineteenth century, a city park movement had taken hold in many urban areas. In the 1840s, the artist George Catlin, who had traveled up the Missouri River painting landscapes and portraits of Plains Indian and Lakota chiefs, had suggested maintaining the entire continent west of that waterway as a pleasure park.

Henry Dawes had been in Congress when it passed the Yosemite Grant Act of 1864, which gave the massive granite domes and waterfalls of Yosemite and the awe-inspiring tall trees of the Mariposa Grove to the state of California to keep them out of private hands. It was the first time in the history of the nation that Congress had acted explicitly to protect lands for recreation and aesthetic enjoyment and to prevent their sale and development.

The Yellowstone legislation would be a slightly different kind of land-taking. Instead of giving public lands to a state, the federal government would take lands from a territory and give it to the Department of the Interior to manage. This was another unprecedented form of federal power exerted on the landscapes and tribal homelands of the West, though put to a higher purpose. Any act granting the Yellowstone Basin to the federal government, Hayden argued, must be passed before white settlers had a chance to file claims.

Before he left Dawes's office, Hayden also asked the congressman to support his proposal to return to Yellowstone for an additional survey that summer. He promised Dawes several of the one hundred complimentary copies of *Scribner's Monthly* that Richard Watson Gilder had just sent him, so that the congressman could read Langford's and Everts's accounts.

Hayden was not the only man in Washington visiting the Capitol that December, lobbying for the creation of Yellowstone National Park. Jay Cooke's brother Henry, who knew everyone worth knowing in Washington and was a particular friend of Ulysses S. Grant's, visited the president and several congressmen, talking up Yellowstone's preservation and what it could mean for prospective white settlers of the Great Northwest. There was also "the Montana Group": Nathaniel Langford, who had heeded Jay Cooke's summons; the newly elected territorial delegate, William Clagett; and Samuel Hauser, a banker with mining interests who had been on the Washburn expedition with Langford.

During the next few weeks, the Montana Group met with as many members of the House and Senate as they could. They made all the same arguments that Hayden had articulated to Dawes. Yellowstone was a wonder of the world. Its lands would be a park worthy of the nation's greatness. It must not fall prey to speculators and schemers. There was already the Yosemite precedent, a national project undertaken during a time of social and political turmoil. What is more, they argued, Hayden's expedition had proven that Yellowstone was useless for agricultural, mining, or manufacturing purposes. Therefore, its highest and best use would be as a place of resort for scientists and tourists.

The Montana Group may have also at this point taken credit, disingenuously, for the origin of the national park idea. According to an account Langford wrote later, one night after his exploration party had given up their search for Truman Everts in the forests around Yellowstone Lake, they had gathered around a campfire at the junction of the Madison and Firehole rivers. At first they mused about taking up lands in the geyser basin or near the falls through preemption and making abundant profits charging tourists for access to Yellowstone's natural wonders. At this point, Langford may have told them, Cornelius Hedges (Montana's U.S. district attorney) spoke up. "There ought to be no private ownership of any portion of that region," Hedges protested, "but that the whole of it ought to be set aside as a great National Park."

According to Langford, the group immediately abandoned their dreams of personal profit and embraced the idea of preservation. If the men of the Forty-Second Congress passed the Yellowstone Act, their action would be the campfire story writ large. This fictitious origin story may have allowed the lobbyists to sidestep the issue of the idea's actual starting point, which lay with Pig Iron Kelley, A. B. Nettleton, and Jay Cooke: men who had every reason to mask their play for railroad profits with a romantic tale of selflessness.

As a result of Hayden's and the Montana Group's efforts at the Capitol, Republican Senator Samuel Pomeroy agreed to join House delegate Clagett in a simultaneous presentation to both houses of a bill to preserve Yellowstone. A railroad entrepreneur who had moved to Kansas as a Free-Soiler in 1854, Pomeroy attained the nickname "Old Subsidy" due to his fondness for enriching himself with land deals spun off from railroad contracts. As the chairman of the Senate's Committee on Public Lands, he was in the perfect position to make such deals and to promote the Yellowstone Act.

On December 18, Pomeroy introduced a bill in the Senate to put the Yellowstone lands "under the direction of the Secretary of the Interior," Pomeroy explained, "keep it from preemptions and homestead entries and from sale, and reserve it from any grants that may be made."

In the House, delegate Clagett introduced a similar bill. Both the Senate and the House referred the bills to their respective committees on public lands for discussion.

That winter at the Smithsonian Institution, Ferdinand Hayden and several survey team members continued their work, sorting through forty-five boxes of specimens and organizing them for the Smithsonian's collections. In late December, William Henry Jackson arrived, ready to help Hayden with another project he had in mind. Jackson was alone; he and Mollie had decided to sell the Omaha studio and move east, but Jackson had left her with his parents in Nyack, New York, for the last few months of her pregnancy.

When Hayden left the Capitol after talking with Dawes, he considered again those portraits of explorers and scenes of discovery that decorated the Rotunda's walls. After he returned to his offices, Hayden had pulled out a sheet of paper and written to Jackson."A bill to establish the Yellowstone as a national park [is] under consideration," he told his friend, "and more prints from [your] negatives [are] required at once."

It was all well and good for Hayden to *tell* the men of the Forty-Second Congress what the expedition team had found in the Yellowstone. Soon they would have his government report, which would include the scientific details. But it would be much more effective if the politicians could *see* the wonders of Yellowstone themselves, in Jackson's photographs, a few of Thomas Moran's watercolor sketches, and several carefully chosen fossils and mineral specimens. These could convey the region's strange, subterranean powers and its unique natural wonders more than words ever could.

Hayden and Jackson carefully arranged a Yellowstone exhibit in the Capitol's Rotunda, below John Trumbull's painting of the signing of the Declaration of Independence and William Powell's *Discovery of the Mississippi*. It was a museum in miniature, a collection that linked the exploration of Yellowstone with America's founding moments and imperial desires. The exhibit argued that America was, in fact, nature's nation. In the chaotic years after the war, people across the nation needed to believe in American exceptionalism. Yellowstone helped them to have faith in this idea that the United States was inherently different from other countries in the world, unique in its politics and its natural features.

Meanwhile, Hayden was also conferring with Samuel Pomeroy and the members of the Senate Committee on Public Lands (all but one were Republicans), and helped draft a report for them on Yellowstone and its wonders. In early January 1872, Pomeroy arose in the Senate to report that the committee recommended to the Senate that they pass Bill 392, to preserve Yellowstone as a national park.

It would be a massive land-taking: more than 1,760 square miles, embracing "those geysers, those great natural curiosities which have attracted so much attention," Pomeroy noted.

He urged his fellow senators to act on the bill immediately, "before individual preemptions or homestead claims attach." Any person found to be living among the park's natural wonders would be considered a trespasser and removed. Yellowstone would come under the control of the secretary of the interior, who would draft rules and regulations for its care and management.

In the Senate debate about the bill, there were objections to the immense size of the proposed park, which, one senator noted, was "several time larger than the District of Columbia."

Pomeroy argued that the geyser basin itself was large—the largest, most likely, in the world—and so the park would need to encompass it. He argued that time was of the essence to keep Yellowstone out of private hands, but several of his colleagues dismissed this worry. They tabled debate until the following week.

As newspapers across the nation began reporting on the Yellowstone bill, it became clear that there was some resistance to the idea. Putting Yellowstone under the control of the Department of the Interior gave that secretary too much power, according to some. With this kind of authorization, what was to stop the secretary of the interior from leasing lands within Yellowstone to enrich himself or other politicians like Old Subsidy Pomeroy?

Others objected to the fact that the park would

take land away from honest settlers, under-mining their preemption rights, which many white Westerners viewed as sacred. The 1862 Homestead Act had affirmed these rights of regular Americans to claim and develop public lands. "The policy of setting apart so large an area of the public domain for the exclusive delights of the rich," one California newspaper argued, "and shutting out actual settlers and cultivators, is un-American and ought not prevail."

Many Americans, however, were enthralled by the idea of preserving Yellowstone. "This is a beautiful idea," one editorial declared. "There is no such grouping anywhere else in the world of the beautiful, the magnificent, the grand, the sublime, and the wonderful in nature as we have them in this marvelous Plutonic region of the Yellowstone."

Yellowstone, with its wild and weird features, would be a park worthy of a great republic. Preserving it, some believed, was an act unique in the world. "That great National Park is such an idea," one of Hayden's fellow geologists wrote to him, "as could originate only in America."

On January 30, when the Senate again discussed the bill, Cornelius Cole, a Republican from California, echoed the objections several newspapers had made. In his view, taking these lands would do much harm to the white people of the West. Allowing settlement in the area would not destroy its wonders.

"The natural curiosities there cannot be interfered with by anything that man can do," he insisted. "The geysers will remain, no matter where the ownership of the land may be, and I do not know why settlers should be excluded from [any] tract of land . . . in the Rocky Mountains or any other place."

Cole and his fellow Californians did not like the idea that the federal government, instead of granting public lands to settlers for production, would withdraw those lands for unproductive uses. As a Republican, Cole believed in using federal power to improve the lives of American citizens. In his view, however, the Yellowstone Act was a misuse of this authority, one that prevented Americans from taking up their natural rights to land ownership and development.

Most of Cole's Republican colleagues disagreed. The question was called, the clerk read out the bill, and the Senate voted without a roll call. A messenger was dispatched to walk across the capitol building to report that Senate Bill 392 had passed. Now it was time for the House to consider the bill.

A few days after the Senate vote, Ferdinand Hayden's article describing the 1871 Yellowstone Expedition was published in *Scribner's Monthly*.

Its contents were widely reported and excerpted in newspapers across the nation. In his final drafts of the piece, Hayden had added a paragraph at the end.

"Why will not Congress at once pass a law setting it apart as a great public park for all time to come," Hayden asked, "as has been done with that not more remarkable wonder, the Yosemite Valley?"

Hayden secured hundreds of copies of the magazine from Richard Watson Gilder and sent them to senators and congressmen. In the first few weeks of February, he also worked feverishly at his Smithsonian offices, finalizing his preliminary government report. He sent off letter after letter to the scientists he had contracted to analyze the specimens, checking on their progress and urging them to submit their reports on the Yellowstone region's paleontology, zoology, botany, and meteorology. Hayden had tasked some of them with writing about the butterflies, reptiles, and fish collected by Chester Dawes and William B. Logan, two of the political boys whose fathers would be voting on the Yellowstone Act in the House of Representatives.

With Jackson's help, Hayden also chose photographic negatives to be included in the report as illustrations. He wrapped them carefully and sent them, along with copies of the maps based on Anton Schönborn's field notebooks, to lithographers in Philadelphia and New York. The lithographers transferred them to plates and mailed these back to Hayden so that illustrations could be printed in every copy of the report, along with several full-page images. Ultimately, Hayden's preliminary report contained sixty-four illustrations and two plates based on Jackson's photographs, Moran's watercolors, Henry Elliott's sketches and cross sections, and specimen illustrations produced by the scientists. It also included five maps, progressing from single features (the White Mountain) to the entirety of what Hayden already called "Yellowstone National Park."

On February 20, 1872, Hayden submitted his preliminary report of the 1871 Yellowstone Expedition to the secretary of the interior. The secretary forwarded it to the Government Printing Office, which began producing the first of more than two thousand copies. Three hundred would go to Congress and the rest would be distributed to federal officials across the nation and to any interested parties who might request a copy.

That same week, the office received the congressional joint select committee's multivolume report of its investigations of the Ku Klux Klan across the South, with thousands of pages of testimony giving voice to Lucy McMillan and other Black southerners who had suffered the violence of their terrorist acts. These thick volumes, circulated to politicians and members of the public, were evidence of the federal government's evolving role as a collector of testimony and producer of knowledge. They were also proof that the members of Congress could act—if they wanted to—to illuminate the nation's terrible and the wondrous aspects.

Hayden wrote up a condensed version of his report to give to the House Committee on Public Lands, describing his discoveries and advocating for the Yellowstone Act. When the House convened on February 27, the committee's chair, Minnesota Republican Mark Dunnell, declared that they were in favor of preserving Yellowstone. The nine members of the committee (six of them Republicans) even suggested saving *more* land than the 1,760 square miles originally proposed in the Senate. Their version of the park would encompass the entire Basin, not just the geysers.

"This whole region was in comparatively modern geological times the scene of the most wonderful volcanic activity of any portion of our country," the report read. "The hot springs and the geysers represent the last stages—the vents or escape pipes—of these remarkable manifestations of the internal forces."

The report also echoed the arguments of the lobbyists and the debates in the Senate, pointing out the fact that withdrawing it from sale or settlement would be no pecuniary loss to the territories of Wyoming and Montana, or the federal government. As a national park, the committee insisted, Yellowstone would instead become a "resort for all classes of people from all portions of the world," a democratic landscape of tourism that would prove the superiority of its features to any other site of sublimity in the world.

If the House acted to preserve Yellowstone as a national park for the people, "it will be regarded by the entire civilized world as a step of progress and an honor to Congress and the nation." After a brief debate about process, the clerk of the House read out the bill in its entirety.

Henry Dawes stood up. In his speech, he mentioned the Yosemite precedent and argued that federal control of Yellowstone would not tread on settler rights. The Yellowstone bill would preserve the remarkable features of this region and protect them from depredations. Dawes was interrupted at this point by John Taffe, a Republican from Nebraska and the chairman of the Committee on Territories.

"I desire to ask the gentleman a question," he said to Dawes, "and it is whether this measure does not interfere with the Sioux [Očéthi Šakówiŋ] reservation."

Taffe's question was surprising. For most Americans and their elected representatives, Native land rights were nonexistent, and such a question would not occur to them. And since Congress had ended treaty-making the year before, Indigenous peoples could no longer negotiate with the government regarding the borders of their reservations. The U.S. government and white citizens, most Americans believed, had the only land rights that mattered.

Taffe went on to argue that if Lakotas laid claim to the Yellowstone Basin under the 1868 Treaty of Fort Laramie, no white settler could go into that country without Lakota permission. And the federal government had no right to interfere there either. Henry Dawes, who would later author the 1887 Severalty Act that took millions of acres of negotiated treaty lands from Indigenous nations to sell to white Americans, had no interest in this argument.

"The Indians can no more live there," he said dismissively, "than they can upon the precipitous sides of the Yosemite valley." To Dawes, the presence of Sheepeater bands in the mountains encircling the Basin and the long-standing use of the region as an Indigenous thoroughfare did not matter. The federal government always reserved the right to take reservation and other Native lands for its own purposes.

At this point, the question was called, the bill was read again, and the House of Representatives voted. Dawes, as expected, voted yes on the Yellowstone National Park Protection Act (known more generally as the Yellowstone Act). As did Pig Iron Kelley, James Negley (whose son Clifford was an assistant on Hayden's expedition team), and Benjamin Turner, one of the newly elected Black representatives from Alabama. John Taffe voted no, along with Philadelph Van Trump and Joseph Rainey, a Black representative from South Carolina. In the end, the vote was bipartisan but fell largely along party lines. Eighty-nine percent of Republicans present voted for the Yellowstone Act, and 70 percent of Democrats voted against it. The Republicans' strong majority in the House meant that the Yellowstone Act passed.

The House messenger sent a note to the Senate informing them of the vote, then sent the bill itself. On March 1, 1872, the Yellowstone Act was placed on President Grant's desk in the executive mansion. Grant signed it, along with several other bills, with no statement or fanfare.

For the next several weeks, Ferdinand Hayden basked in the glow of his achievements. He sent copies of his article in *Scribner's* and his preliminary report to friends, fellow scientists, and admirers across the country. They were unanimous in their praise.

"I am enchanted . . . with your brilliant report of the wonderful Yellowstone," a friend wrote from Cambridge, Massachusetts. "I envy both your enjoyment of such transcendent natural scenery and your achievement of having been so useful to your country and the world—to say nothing of the new fields of scientific inquiry you have offered up." His friend was transfixed by the writing and the imagery in the report. "It does you infinite credit," he crowed, "as a piece of literary effort, and as a piece of magnetic composition prompting one to pack his bag and start for Montana."

Hayden himself was already preparing for another trip to Yellowstone. He wanted to continue the scientific studies the 1871 expedition team had begun. There was so much left to learn about the continent's geology in the Basin, and Hayden wanted to control the collection and scientific analysis effort there, at least for the next few years. Congress had not yet allocated money for the summer's expedition. He was convinced, however, that his lobbying efforts had been successful, and that they would appropriate the money for him at the end of the session in June. He hoped for twice as much funding as the previous year, so he could split his expedition into two teams to cover more ground during the exploration season. He also wanted Emma to join him for the first several weeks of the journey.

In early March, as he was organizing the 1872 survey, Hayden received a letter from Thomas

Moran. The artist had moved from Philadelphia to Newark, New Jersey, and was working on what he called his "Big Picture": an eight-by-twelve-foot scene depicting the massive canyon of the Yellowstone and the Lower Falls. Before he could complete the painting, however, Moran needed to consult with Hayden.

"I cannot feel confident about it until <u>you</u> have seen it," he wrote to the surveyor. "In fact, I cannot finish it until you have seen it." Although it was not necessary (or even ideal) that the painting was an exact "transcript of nature," Moran wanted the painting to reflect accurately Yellowstone's geology. "Your knowledge of Cause & effect in nature," the artist wrote, "would point out to me many facts connected with the place that I may have overlooked."

Now that the Hayden's expedition report and the *Scribner's* piece had been published, and the Yellowstone Act had been signed, Moran hoped that his friend would have some time to visit him in Newark and view the painting. In the meantime, he asked Hayden to send him a set of photographic portraits of himself. Moran wanted to include several figures in the foreground of the painting, including Hayden. Another would be Jim Stevenson, or maybe William Henry Jackson.

"This will make it necessary for me to have a photograph of you, the head to be just the right size," Moran wrote. To demonstrate the size he meant, Hayden saw, Moran had dipped his pen in ink and sketched a tiny man on the right margin of the letter. Bearded and wearing a hat, the mini Hayden was three lines high, and had one hand tucked into a coat pocket.

William Henry Jackson had already visited Moran in Newark, bringing him photographs he had taken of the canyon from different angles. Moran was delighted to have them; he wanted to consult them for detail and depth. The photographs, along with his own watercolor sketches, would help Moran to remember the colors and forms of the canyon and the emotions he felt during his time spent with Jackson and the others along the rim: fear, awe, wonder, fascination.

It was these kinds of feelings Moran hoped to evoke in his Big Picture: a sense of the place that was correct in most details but, most important, *felt* true. To that end he manipulated several elements of the scene. He moved the Lower Falls deeper into the middle ground of the painting and brought the canyon walls into a wider V shape. The basalt pinnacles that rose alongside the canyon wall, formed by erosion over millions of years, were much larger than in reality. The twisted pine tree that dominated the left foreground of the painting was not native to the landscape; Moran had "lifted" it from another painting of his, a scene he had made when visiting Rome.

Jackson tried to be upbeat during his visit to Moran's studio, but he was in mourning. In late February, just as Congress was debating the Yellowstone Act, Mollie had gone into labor with their baby daughter. There were complications and both Mollie and the baby died. Talking about art with Moran always buoyed his spirits, however, and the painting was remarkable.

"So far as I am concerned," Jackson said later, "the great picture of the 1871 expedition was no photograph, but a painting by Moran of Yellowstone Falls. . . . It captured, more than any other painting I know, the color and the atmosphere of spectacular nature."

In mid-April, Hayden found the time to leave his Smithsonian office and travel to Newark to see the Big Picture. Using a magnifying glass, Hayden found himself in the foreground of the painting, a tiny figure standing on a precipice, looking out over the scene with a Native man dressed in bright red cloth and wearing a large war bonnet. The Hayden survey had not employed a Native guide, as Moran well knew. The single Native figure was a common element of American landscape paintings in the mid-nineteenth century, meant to suggest that a vanishing Indigenous past was making way for a white American future in the wilderness.

Hayden studied the rest of the painting and made comments about its geological details. Moran listened intently and noted where he needed to make slight alterations to the canyon walls. It was the tension between these minute particulars—the exact color and texture of the calcareous rocks as opposed to the basalt, the layers in the canyon walls that evidenced the nature of geological time—and Moran's more telescopic "impressions" that would entrance viewers.

Two weeks later, the president, vice president, and members of the board of directors of the Northern Pacific Railroad arrived at Moran's studio to view the painting, wanting to see whether they could use it to promote the railroad."[They] were decidedly enthusiastic over it," Moran wrote to Hayden.

By then, the Big Picture was finished. Hayden sent Moran $200 (an advance on watercolor paintings that Moran had promised the scientist for his offices at the Smithsonian) to help him purchase the frame for the painting. It was a massive gilt structure sixteen inches thick, and in it, Moran told Hayden, the picture "looks stunning."

During the next few weeks, Richard Watson Gilder helped Moran find an appropriate space in the city to exhibit *Grand Cañon of the Yellowstone*. The passage of the Yellowstone

Act and the splash that Hayden's expedition reports and articles had made created a buzz around the painting, and Gilder convinced the owners of *Scribner's Monthly* to pay for the exhibition.

In the spring of 1872, there were few options for Moran's single-painting show. The New York City art season was in full swing, and many of the galleries were already booked with group shows and auctions. While spaces for exhibiting art had proliferated along Broadway below 10th Street in recent years, availability was still limited. The Metropolitan Museum of Art had opened its doors to the public just a few months earlier but was showing only works from its own small collection.

After many negotiations, Gilder finally succeeded in engaging Leavitt's, one of the most important exhibit halls in New York City, for May 2. He could book only one evening, and the show would have to take place in the auction room rather than in one of the galleries. Gilder began to write to his friends in the region, inviting them to come. It was particularly important, he thought, that Hayden attend.

"You <u>must</u> be here," he urged the scientist. "The Northern [Pacific] people— the press— the literati— the artists— the rich people— will all be out in full force. We want to make a big splash and we want you to answer questions & be one of the heroes of the night! Why not bring your wife and make a grand spree of it! Write to me & say yes!"

Late in the afternoon of May 2, Gilder arrived at Leavitt's, which occupied rooms on an upper floor of Clinton Hall, a three-story block-long neoclassical structure on Broadway and 8th Street. He walked to the auction room to check on the painting. The workers had hung it on the bare back wall, between two tables holding piles of miscellaneous books that Leavitt's would be auctioning off the next week. The room was cavernous and dusty.

Gilder thought back on the magnificent scene that had greeted art viewers at the exhibit of Frederic Edwin Church's *Heart of the Andes* in 1859. Church had hung his massive painting on a single wall of his studio, at the end of a long gallery. Gaslights illuminated the picture, which was mounted on a background of rich tapestry and surrounded by foliage. The whole experience was enchanting, and twelve thousand people ultimately paid to see the painting.

This bare space, Gilder thought, simply would not do. In the little time he had before Moran and the guests began arriving, he procured some upholstery and arranged it as best he could around the frame."[But] it was too late," one critic regretted. "[That] quaint bit of stuff, like a blanket in the alarm of fear caught up, made a satire on the usual paraphernalia of such occasions."

And so the premiere of the Thomas Moran's *Grand Cañon of the Yellowstone* had "none of that professional festivity that has come to be the expected thing at all picture exhibitions in New-York."

In the end, however, it did not matter. At around 7:00 p.m., the auction room began to fill with people. The crowd Gilder had promised to Hayden—the railroad magnates, the journalists, the writers and artists and New York's wealthiest residents—appeared. There were some notable absences.

Jay Cooke was not there. His optimism about the Northern Pacific after the passage of the Yellowstone Act had been short-lived. The money market was tightening, and there had been a near panic in April. Jay Cooke & Co. had weathered that storm, but every move Cooke had made to make the railroad bonds more attractive to investors had failed. He had fired John Gregory Smith and was looking to hire a new president of the company. The railroad continued to teeter on the edge of ruin, and Cooke was scrambling to get its finances in order. He continued to mourn for Libby, often visiting the mausoleum he built for her on the grounds of Ogontz. Their family friends sent him letters and memorials about her.

"She was—and is not; — oh, the wondrous space," the hymn composer and writer Josephine Pollard wrote him in the spring of 1872,

That lies between those sentences so brief!
A little world made up of bloom and grace,
Of memory and grief!

Overwhelmed by work and sadness, Cooke sent his brother Pitt to Moran's exhibit opening in his stead.

Gilder and Moran were extremely pleased, however, that Ferdinand Hayden had made it. When the scientist arrived (without Emma) the guests were crowding around the painting, which seemed to glow with a golden light in the shabby room. Some of them were there out of curiosity, others were passionate art lovers. All of them were mesmerized. "The picture kept them there," one critic observed, "by its own intrinsic truth, sublimity, and beauty."

Later in the evening, Hayden gave an impromptu speech. While he described the adventures of the survey team in the summer of 1871 and their geological discoveries, he pointed to different parts of Moran's canvas— the pinnacles, the falls, the yellow rock of the canyon walls—and noted that they were (mostly) accurate. As Hayden talked, he absorbed Moran's *Grand Cañon of the Yellowstone* into the narra-

283

tive of the 1871 Yellowstone Expedition and into a larger story of American exceptionalism.

For many who saw the painting that night, Yellowstone joined Niagara Falls in the pantheon of American landscape icons. Moran revealed the unique grandeur of a place at the heart of the continent, a landscape that evidenced the sublimity of America's long geological history. For those who had not yet seen Jackson's photographs or read Hayden's article in *Scribner's*, Moran's painting opened American eyes to the natural beauty that existed within the nation's borders. And now that beauty belonged to the American people.

"Perhaps, also [the painting] appeals a little to the pleasure we may all have," a reviewer mused, "that this wonderful place is not merely a bit of the continent, but is indeed, the private property of every man, woman, and child of us."

Viewers could look upon Moran's painting and then set out for Yellowstone National Park, to stand upon that ledge and see the mighty canyon for themselves. This was why Congress had preserved this natural wonder. "[It is] for the people of the whole United States to walk abroad and recreate themselves," the reviewer concluded.

Three weeks after the triumphant Leavitt's exhibit, *Grand Cañon of the Yellowstone* was mounted on the wall of Republican James G.

Blaine's office in the Capitol. Blaine, the Speaker of the House, had long been interested in Yellowstone; in January 1871 he had introduced Nathaniel Langford before his speech at Lincoln Hall, which Hayden had attended. He was one of the most powerful government officials in Washington, and his fellow congressmen and lobbyists came to his office on a regular basis. Now they could admire Moran's Big Picture while they waited to talk business.

The painting "has created quite a sensation there," Moran was happy to tell Hayden.

Moran had a reason for wanting the picture to hang in the Capitol: he wanted Congress to buy it. They had passed the Yellowstone Act and now, perhaps, they might purchase Moran's painting of that landscape's most iconic scene as another representation of the federal government's desire to assert its power in the West.

To gauge their interest, Moran went to see a stalwart friend of the Yellowstone. "I asked Dawes what he thought of the chances," Moran wrote to Hayden, "& he made a favorable reply."

Ferdinand Hayden wanted to help his friend—and keep the congressmen thinking about Yellowstone while they debated the appropriation for his 1872 survey—and so he too visited Dawes. He also went to see James Garfield, a congressman from Ohio who had voted for the Yellowstone Act. One of the members of his delegation from Ohio, a Democrat, was serving on the Joint Committee on the Library. Moran had told Hayden that the members of this committee, who could appropriate money to commission artworks for the Capitol, could present a resolution to purchase *Grand Cañon of the Yellowstone*.

For the first six decades of its existence, the members of the library committee did not put much energy into creating a national archive or promoting the cause of arts and letters in the United States. Many of its members viewed any kind of devotion to culture as elitist, in a moment in which the "common man" was exerting his rhetorical and voting power in American politics. Only after the Civil War did the library committee begin to embrace its role in supporting artistic and literary endeavors. In 1866, they oversaw the transfer of the Smithsonian's library holdings to the Capitol. By 1872, the Library of Congress had a large and growing collection of books about and studies of America's natural history, as well as maps and reports of federally funded expeditions to the West.

In the last weeks of May and early June, Moran made it his mission to convince the library committee that buying *Grand Cañon of the Yellowstone* would be a public benefit. It would provide for the American people an enduring image of one of its greatest natural treasures. He did not have much time to lobby them, however. The session was ending. Hayden was already gone, boarding a train west to begin his second exploration of Yellowstone on May 27.

By June 5, there was nothing more Moran could do. Many Republican legislators had already left the Capitol to attend the Republican National Convention in Philadelphia, leaving proxies to vote in their stead. It would be a tumultuous convention, even though the nominee—Ulysses S. Grant, running for a second term—was already determined. Members of the party had to negotiate with a small but insistent movement of "Liberal Republicans," moderates who believed in ensuring civil rights but also wanted an end to the U.S. military occupation of the southern states. The party was fracturing, and its will to use federal power to promote the public good was fading.

Finally, on the last day of the session, Moran received word. On June 10, a line item appeared in an appropriations bill. "To enable the joint committee on the library to purchase Moran's large painting of the Canyon of the Yellowstone," it read, "$10,000."

Hayden was already in Ogden, Utah, when he heard about the purchase and received good news of his own. As was the case in 1871, he had been paying for the first weeks of the 1872 expedition out of his own pocket. Congress had come through with his appropriation, however, and it was an impressive number.

"For the continuation of the geological survey of the territories of the United States by Professor F. V. Hayden," the line item read, "$75,000."

Hayden wanted Moran to join him and the rest of the survey team in Yellowstone, now that he had sold his Big Picture. Jim Stevenson had joined up again, along with Albert Peale and William Henry Jackson. Nathaniel Langford was also with them, touring Yellowstone as its first appointed superintendent. But Moran demurred. He had to finish a series of watercolors he had promised to Jay Cooke in exchange for funding his trip in 1871. Moran had also taken an assignment to draw sketches of the West for a new semi-monthly publication from *Appleton's Journal*, guest-edited by the poet William Cullen Bryant. Bound in 1872 and 1874 as a two-volume set, *Picturesque America; or, the Land We Live In*, gave Americans a full sense of the scenery characteristic of the nation through words and images.

"Art sighs to carry her conquests into new realms," Bryant wrote in the preface to the first volume. "On our continent, and within the limits of our Republic, she finds them . . . mountains and valleys, gorges and rivers, and tracts of sea-coast, which the foot of the artist has never trod;

and glens murmuring with water-falls which his ear has never heard."

Out in the Yellowstone Basin in August, Ferdinand Hayden gathered the sixty men of his 1872 survey and made a speech. He wanted to name one of the Teton peaks after the absent artist. "Mr. Moran, by his good qualities," Hayden said, "and by his great painting of the Yellowstone canyon and falls . . . has immortalized the exploration of [this] region."

Due to the efforts of scientist-explorers and artists, Hayden noted, the thundering, roiling, awe-inspiring landscape of the Yellowstone was "now the property of the nation."

Back in Washington, workmen prepared to hang *Grand Cañon of the Yellowstone* above the grand stairway in the Senate wing of the Capitol. Nearby was Emanuel Leutze's *Westward the Course of Empire Takes Its Way* (1861), a twenty-by-thirty-foot mural installed during the Civil War. Leutze's painting was filled with people walking and riding horses and whipping oxen up and over the Rocky Mountains, a driving force of white conquest of the western lands beyond. There are no Native figures present in the mural; the imperial power of the United States has already swept them from the scene. *Westward the Course* and *Grand Cañon* would work together to erase Native peoples (despite their continuous presence across the nation) and bring the West into the American imagination as a site of scientific knowledge, scenic wonder, and empire building.

10

Bullets Flying All Around

Yellowstone Valley, Lakota Homelands.
Spring 1872.

The winter of 1871–72 had been a hard one. Storm after storm crossed over the rolling plains and deep gullies of the Lakota homelands, piling up snow in towering drifts. If a man dared go out and ride across the bright white expanse, his horse's hoofprints were covered up as fast as he could make them. The Húŋkpapȟa mostly stayed put in their camps that winter, sending men out to hunt elk or deer across the wilderness of snow only when their supplies of dried buffalo meat dwindled.

Sitting Bull had much to occupy his mind and heart. He continued to mull over how best to protect his people, discussing the many options with members of the men's societies. His three children were healthy and growing. As the snow fell in huge flakes on the Húŋkpapȟa camp, it came time for a ceremony to release Red Woman's soul into the afterlife. He burned the lock of her hair and offered dried buffalo meat to Wakȟáŋ Tȟáŋka (the Creator). It was only a temporary leave-taking. Sitting Bull and Red

Woman would be reunited in the spirit world. A few months later, Sitting Bull found joy again in his domestic life. He married, this time to two women, Šiná Tópa Wíŋ (Four Robes) and her older sister Oyáte Tȟáwa Waŋyáŋkapi Wíŋ (Seen by Her Nation). They were both widows, and they brought sons into Sitting Bull's growing family.

When the snow melted and the river ice began to crack and boom across Lakota country, the Húŋkpapȟa packed up their camp, preparing to move to their summer lands along the Yellowstone River to the south. Sitting Bull called a young Itázipčho (Sans Arc Lakota) chief named Waŋblí Gléška (Spotted Eagle) into his lodge. He wanted him to take his band east and deliver a message to the soldiers at Fort Sully on the banks of Mníšoše.

As Spotted Eagle and his people rode off, the women took buffalo robes, tanned elk hides, sacks of dried fruit and meat, and piles of clothing and cooking utensils out of their large tipis and loaded them onto multiple A-shaped travois, to be pulled by their horses, mules, and dogs. They lifted the children onto horses and mounted behind them, turning the animals' noses southward. When the caravan set out, the sharpened points of hundreds of sledges left long dark furrows in the soil.

As they moved toward the Yellowstone Valley,

other bands began to join them. Oglála led by Crazy Horse arrived, compelled by Sitting Bull's continued resistance to American incursions in Lakota homelands. Mnikȟówožu (Minneconjou Lakota) and Sičháŋǧu (Burnt Thighs/Brulé Lakota) followed, choosing to join Sitting Bull in his fight. The Húŋkpapȟa welcomed these kin to the caravan. Cheyenne and Arapaho peoples rode up on their ponies, swelling the camp's numbers into the thousands. They were long-standing allies, their ties grown stronger after the Húŋkpapȟa joined them in the fight against white settlers and U.S. soldiers after the Sand Creek Massacre in the fall of 1864.

Soon they reached the banks of the Yellowstone, fringed with cottonwoods and willows just beginning to bud. It was gushing with the spring snowmelt and growing wider every day. Nearby was its confluence with the Powder River, their waters comingling in a gray slush. The crossing took some time, as riders guided ponies through the frigid river, and men and women maneuvered bullboats, willow branches covered with buffalo hide and loaded with travois, through the snags and eddies. They traveled down the western bank of the Powder for a few more days and then stopped, amidst a landscape of bluffs and ravines, rolling hills covered with prairie grass just greening up, and pinelands nearby to use for their fires.

Women dismounted and began to unload. Within days, a large village of white tipis was strung out along the riverbank. The bands camped together, with the Húŋkpapȟa at the center. They sent their ponies out to graze in the surrounding prairies, the large herds watched over by groups of young boys.

The Húŋkpapȟa and their kin began to prepare for the annual Sun Dance, council meetings, and a war excursion against the Crows far to the west. One day, scouts signaled that Spotted Eagle and his Sans Arcs were approaching. They had traded for goods at the Cheyenne River Indian agency near Fort Sully, Spotted Eagle reported, and he refused to accept any annuities from the agent. There was talk among the other Lakota gathered near the fort. The Northern Pacific's tracks were nearing Mníšoše from the east. With them came hundreds of workers, contractors, traders, and farmers. Claim shanties and houses were proliferating on the prairies, and a new town called Bismarck had sprung up on the east bank, where the company would start building a railroad bridge near its convergence with the Heart River.

Spotted Eagle had also heard that the U.S. Army would be marching westward along that river over the summer, protecting the Northern Pacific's surveyors on their way to the Powder River Valley. He sent word to Colonel David

Stanley, in command of the fort, that he wanted to talk. He and his chiefs sat down for a council with the general and his officers, and Spotted Eagle delivered Sitting Bull's message.

The Húŋkpapȟa leader would not be coming into the forts along Mníšoše this summer or fall, Spotted Eagle told the Americans. Sitting Bull did not intend to fight any white settlers or soldiers; he just wanted to fight the Crows. But President Grant had not acceded to Lakota demands (made by Black Moon at Fort Peck in the fall of 1871) that white settlers and railroad workers withdraw from Lakota lands. Spotted Eagle had seen newly peeled poles with telegraph wire strung along them, terminating at Fort Sully. And then there was the Northern Pacific survey. Neither he nor Sitting Bull had consented to their presence in Lakota country.

"I will not listen to new propositions on this subject," Spotted Eagle insisted. "I will destroy the road and attack any party that tries to build it."

Once the Sans Arc's words had been translated, Stanley spoke. "The railroad will be built despite your opposition," he told him. "If you take this course, there will be fatal consequences to your people."

"I do not care," Spotted Eagle retorted. "It is life or death. I will fight it out."

After Spotted Eagle and his men left the

meeting, Stanley sent for a clerk and wrote a letter to send to Thomas Rosser, the head of the Northern Pacific's 1872 eastern survey team. He described his meeting with Spotted Eagle. "Tis best you should know," he wrote. "There is no danger to small parties east of the river. But there will be constant danger west of it."

Sitting Bull took the information that Spotted Eagle had gleaned to Oglála chief Crazy Horse and the council, and to the men's societies. They agreed to remain where they were for the summer and the fall buffalo hunt. If wašíču and Long Knives (soldiers) came into Lakota lands as promised, they would surveil them and determine their strength in numbers, horses, and guns. If the soldiers did not shoot, then the Lakota would let them be. But if they came shooting, the Lakota would fight the surveyors and the soldiers and kill them.

In midsummer, the Lakota remained in camp. Sitting Bull sent his brother-in-law north to Fort Peck, with a message for the U.S. Indian agents there. He might come in to talk when the snow began to fly, to discuss a lasting peace.

"But only if [you find] a white man there worth talking to," Sitting Bull told him. "One that would tell the truth."

Outside Sitting Bull's lodge, children played games and the young men pitted their fastest horses against one another. Women cut the buckskins from deer carcasses and pinned them to the ground over smoking fire pits, softening them to a rich brown. When this process was finished and the skins were pliable, they cut them up to make leggings, baby caps, dresses, shirts, and moccasins for their families, or to trade at the forts in the fall. Hunters went out regularly to shoot more deer, along with elk, prairie hens, and the pronghorn antelopes that bounded impossibly quickly across the prairie lands.

In June, the young men proved their fortitude and devotion to community in the annual Sun Dance. A few weeks later, in late July, a group of five hundred Lakota painted their bodies with pigment made from prairie plants and gathered their guns, bows and arrows, and lances. Sitting Bull said goodbye to Four Robes, Seen by Her Nation, his mother, and the children. He took two ponies—one for the journey and one for battle—and joined his fellow warriors as they rode westward toward the lands of their traditional enemy, the Crow. A smaller war party of a few dozen men under the leadership of the Húŋkpapȟa war chief Gall set out northward, following the Powder River to the Yellowstone. They would be scouting the badlands between the summer camp and Mníšoše, looking for Native and white enemies.

Sitting Bull, Crazy Horse, and the westbound party had a long journey ahead of them, more than five hundred miles through a landscape of rolling grasslands intercut with wooded, stony hills. The Crow were ensconced on their reservation southeast of Bozeman, and the Lakota hoped to catch their hunting or war parties by surprise. If they should run into any of the other enemy tribes who claimed lands in the region north of Yellowstone (Gros Ventre, Flathead, or Blackfoot), all the better. They rode for three weeks, crossing the rushing waters of the Tongue River, Rosebud Creek, and the Bighorn, sending out scouts ahead to look for enemies in their path. Early in the second week of August, the scouts returned to report a large group of riders making their way slowly through the broken lands on the northern bank of Yellowstone. Not Indigenous enemies, but whites.

The western column of the 1872 Northern Pacific survey, protected again by U.S. Army cavalry from Fort Ellis under the command of Major Eugene Baker, had left their post in late July. On one of the last evenings before their departure, the officers had dinner with a convivial group of guests: a party of U.S. Indian commissioners headed to Fort Peck in hopes of drawing Sitting Bull into peace talks, and Ferdinand Hayden and members of his 1872 expedition to Yellowstone. The peace commissioners had spent the previous two days in the newly created national park.

"They had a most delightful trip," the *Helena Weekly Herald* reported, "and return full of the wonders of the Yellowstone, impressed with the importance of Congress taking immediate action to protect it, and throw it open to the public."

The dinner was a reunion of sorts for two in the group, since Colonel John Barlow had come from his office in Chicago to join the Northern Pacific survey as General Phil Sheridan's representative. It was the first time he and Hayden had seen each other since the previous September. There was another strange coincidence, in that the head of the western railroad survey was named John Haydon. It was surprising that Jay Cooke had allowed Haydon to be hired, given that he was a former Confederate officer who had surrendered to Ulysses S. Grant at Fort Donelson in 1862. But Haydon seemed to get along fine with the fort's officers and soldiers, and his wartime service was rarely mentioned.

The survey party had around five hundred men, Sitting Bull's scouts reported, equaling the Lakota war party in size. Most of them were cavalry, so there were seven hundred horses and seventy wagons of supplies: tempting targets for a raid. The horses were not pulling limbers or caissons. This meant the soldiers did not have any artillery with them, an ideal situation for the Lakota, who had no answer for this weapon in the American arsenal.

On August 12, the Americans set up a camp in a lush green meadow along the Yellowstone River's northern bank. They stayed there through the next day, dismounting and letting their horses graze among the cottonwoods, willows, and rosebushes that grew in a slough that fringed the field. Only a small group of soldiers guarded the animals. The rest were busy erecting their A-frame tents and cooking food on their campfires. As the sun went down on August 13, most of them crawled inside their tents and went to sleep, including Major Baker, who, according to one of his lieutenants, had "overindulged in strong drink" while at dinner. One group of officers stayed up, playing poker in their shirtsleeves.

The Lakota made their own camp south of the river opposite the Americans and behind a ridge. Late into the night of August 13, Sitting Bull, Crazy Horse, and the war chiefs met in council. Attacking the Long Knives directly meant swimming or rafting across the river. It was a dangerous proposition given that the Yellowstone was swollen with snowmelt and summer thunderstorms, rushing in a torrent about two hundred yards wide. There were small silt islands dotting its center, most of which snagged massive trees that had fallen into the water from its eroding banks.

Some of the chiefs preferred to wait, to track the surveyors and soldiers and then send a small band of horse raiders to provoke them into giving chase, luring the Americans into an ambush. This was the Lakota's preferred fighting mode; it made the best use of their fast warhorses and their knowledge of the landscape. But it was not possible here, with the river and the wooded meadow in the way. The chiefs did agree that it was vital to use their greatest advantage—surprise—to best effect. The soldiers were taking no precautions guarding their camp that night, so it was clear that they had not spotted the Lakota scouts who had been surveilling them for the last few days.

In the early hours of the morning of August 14, a young man appeared at the entrance of the council tipi and interrupted their deliberations.

"What has happened?" Sitting Bull asked.

A group of warriors, including Sitting Bull's nephew Tȟatȟáŋka Ská (White Bull), had become impatient with the council's talks. Desirous of making names for themselves by counting coup on the Long Knives, they had taken their weapons and horses and headed for the river in the dark.

Sitting Bull went to his tipi to gather up his shield and lance, and mounted his favorite warhorse. The young men had left the chiefs with no choice.

The river was booming in great waves, obscuring the sounds of the young men swimming through it. They had jumped in upriver, and let the strong current take them down to the leading edge of the American camp as they swam. Pulling themselves out on the bank, they kept close to the ground, crawling through the meadow grass toward a group of tents nestled among the trees. It was the camp of a small group of prospectors and wolf hunters, who had joined the survey for protection as they moved east toward rumored goldfields in Dakota Territory.

Against the trunk of a willow tree, metal gleamed. One of the prospectors had left his rifle leaning up against it. A Lakota warrior crawled toward it and almost had it in his grasp when the owner, awakened by a slight noise, opened his eyes. The prospector had been sleeping with his holster on and his revolver in his hand. Slowly, he brought the gun up and pulled the trigger.

The gunshot reverberated across the camp. Poker-playing officers jumped up from their game, and the guard among the horse herd began to fire wildly into the night. The Lakota, who were now appearing in large numbers within the thickets along the army camp's upriver edge, returned fire. The prospectors and wolfers fell back and joined the soldiers, who were quickly forming to defend themselves against the Lakota attack. One of them shot and killed a young man named Héya Yuğéla (Plenty Lice), and the soldiers dragged his body into their camp.

Sitting Bull arrived at the southern riverbank with a group of warriors and heard the battle unfolding. It was too dark to see much but a few scattered campfires and the flash of the guns as they fired. He knew well enough that the Lakota had lost their advantage of surprise. The young men needed reinforcements, so he led the remainder of his war party across the river, splashing through the strong current.

As soon as they crossed the river, the Lakota fanned out around the meadow, firing into the camp. They did not hit many soldiers, most of whom had taken cover among the trees and underbrush. There was little protection for the Lakota in the meadow, so they got behind the enemy and climbed up to the brow of a high bluff two hundred yards north of the river. Here they had a defensible position and a commanding view of the Northern Pacific camp. Sitting Bull and Crazy Horse moved to the left of their line, and they and the other warriors rained down bullets on the soldiers in the meadow for the next three hours.

When the sky began to lighten, the Lakota could see that the soldiers were entrenched in the meadow. The soldiers, knowing that they were watching, brought out Plenty Lice's body and threw it on one of their fires. Seeing this, the Lakota were enraged, shouting insults and threats at the Americans. Several of the young men "rode the daring line": they galloped back and forth along the brow of the hill in full view of the enemy, challenging the soldiers to shoot them off their horses. Several Lakota were wounded; others lost their mounts.

It became clear to Sitting Bull that the battle was unwinnable. His people had a strong position, but unless they charged the soldiers or the soldiers charged them, they would have no opportunity to fight in their preferred style: hand-to-hand combat, with the counting of coups. The two sides were evenly matched in terms of numbers, so any direct assault would result in massive losses for the Lakota. Sitting Bull did not see the point in such an action and began to spread the word among his men to withdraw.

There was a movement farther down the line. Instead of retreating, several young men— including Sitting Bull's nephew White Bull— directed their horses in the opposite direction and again began to run the daring line. Sitting Bull rode up to the group and found a warrior named Wakȟáŋ Tȟéhaŋ (Long Holy) directing them. Long Holy had had a vision, he told Sitting Bull. "Any warrior who rides with me," he said, "will be cloaked with an invisible blanket and will not be hit by arrows or bullets."

Sitting Bull was enraged. "Enough!" he said. "I do not want the young braves wounded or killed.

Their bravery is evident and the shedding of their blood will not do us any good."

"The great warrior Tȟatȟáŋka Íyotake perhaps has forgotten what it takes to be brave," Long Holy retorted. "Perhaps the great war chief [has] grown old," he added, "and the sight of blood upsets his stomach."

Sitting Bull did not reply. Instead, he dismounted. Leaving his gun and quiver on the grass, he took his pipe bag and tobacco pouch in his hand and turned toward the enemy. The Lakota looked on as Sitting Bull began to make his way down to the bottom of the bluff, where it eased into the grassland. In full view of both his own war party and the wašíču, Sitting Bull sat down.

His voice floated back up to the Lakota on the bluff. "Anyone who wishes to smoke," he called, "join me and share my čhaŋnúŋpa (pipe)!"

Three men stepped forward: White Bull and two Cheyenne warriors. Long Holy and his followers remained on the bluff as the warriors climbed down and sat next to Sitting Bull. He opened his pouch and filled the pipe with tobacco, lighting it with his flint and steel. As bullets from the soldiers' guns flew all around, Sitting Bull took several long leisurely puffs before passing the pipe to White Bull, who was sitting to his left.

"We others wasted no time," White Bull said later. "Our hearts beat rapidly, and we smoked as fast as we could." But his uncle was not afraid. "He just sat there quietly, looking around as if he were at home in his tent, and smoked peacefully."

Each man smoked as gunshots echoed across the field and dirt kicked up at their feet and over their heads. They passed the pipe on until the tobacco was gone. Taking out his tamping stick, Sitting Bull cleaned out the bowl. The young men watched nervously as he buried the ashes and put the pipe back in his pouch. Rising slowly from the ground, Sitting Bull turned back toward the bluff and started to limp toward his horse. He had taken only a few steps when he saw White Bull and the Cheyenne bolt past him and up the hill.

Who had ever seen such an act of bravery? the Lakota wondered. The war party was abuzz with it. When Sitting Bull returned to the Lakota line, he took up his weapons and mounted his horse, and gave the order to withdraw. This time, no one questioned his decision. The war party rode down the back side of the bluff and recrossed the Yellowstone downstream. The Long Knives did not follow.

For the next few days, the Lakota shadowed the Americans. They watched as riders left the camp for the west, bearing dispatches and letters bound for Fort Ellis, the Northern Pacific office in Helena, and the region's newspapers. Major Baker's report to his superiors was matter-of-fact, noting only that "a band of Sioux and Cheyenne" had attacked his command, and his soldiers had acted promptly to repulse them.

The soldiers in the escort, however, seemed to appreciate the real danger they had faced. "We were poorly posted in the open space, surrounded by heavy timber and thick underbrush," one soldier wrote. "The Indian tactics were excellent."

One of his officers agreed. "Captain Ball says the fight was one of the most determined he ever witnessed with the Indians," the *Bozeman Avant Courier* reported, "who fought with dogged determination."

Sitting Bull sent his own dispatches, ordering riders to go east until they found the war chief Gall and his men, and to inform him that they had fought U.S. soldiers in the west. On the fifth day after what became known as the Battle of Arrow Creek, the Northern Pacific expedition, still watched by the Lakota, stopped following the Yellowstone and instead turned north, toward the Musselshell River. To protect his men from another Lakota attack, Baker refused to detach any troops from his command to protect the surveyors, and so John Haydon gave up on surveying a railroad route in the Yellowstone Valley. They would move along the more northern river instead, and then make their way back to Fort Ellis.

Sitting Bull was satisfied. The fight had not

been a battlefield victory. They had not taken any horses or weapons from the soldiers. But the Battle of Arrow Creek had served two purposes. The surveyors would make no headway into the Lakotas' western homelands. And Sitting Bull had reestablished authority within his band. The fact that the Northern Pacific team had come from Fort Ellis suggested, however, that the rumors the Lakota had heard of a similar column coming from Fort Rice in the east were likely true. Sitting Bull divided his war party, sending three hundred of them west to find Crow warriors to fight and horses to steal. Then he galloped off with the rest of his men toward the lands east of the Powder River, where Gall had gone to scout.

Almost three hundred miles away, along O'Fallon Creek, a tributary of the Yellowstone east of the Powder, Gall had already found the second of the two Northern Pacific surveys. This eastern column had left Fort Rice in late July with six hundred soldiers and a large railroad survey team, along with scouts from several Indigenous groups including the Arikara, traditional enemies of the Lakota. They had fewer horses than the western command because many of the troops were infantry. But they had a cannon.

Gall and his men were outnumbered, so they chose the strategy of surveillance. The Lakota followed the column for a few days and were watching as the advance team of surveyors reached O'Fallon Creek and threw themselves down to sleep on August 16.

"I can never think of our recklessness without a shudder," the survey leader, Thomas Rosser, said later.

The Húŋkpapȟa made a dash into the camp the next day, siphoning off a few horses before retreating. Then they watched as the surveyors marched to the nearby confluence of the Powder and the Yellowstone. The Americans cut down a cottonwood limb, peeled it, and wrote some words onto its white surface before planting it in the ground. The Lakota knew this object well. It was a survey marker, a symbol of the Northern Pacific's progress and its purported claim to the land. The surveyors opened two bottles of champagne to toast their achievement.

The next morning, the Húŋkpapȟa caught a surveyor out alone, wandering up and down the ravines of the badlands in search of agates. They chased him back to the camp, and just as he reached it, the expedition's Arikara scouts came galloping out to give them a fight. Afterward, Gall rode down to the bank of the Powder River across from Stanley's troops. He threw down his weapons and his blanket, then dismounted.

"Bring the interpreter!" he shouted across the water. "I wish to speak to the general."

Stanley put down his pistol, and made his way

to the bank with Louis Agard, a Frenchman who married a Lakota woman and often worked as a guide and translator for the U.S. Army. Stanley suggested that the two leaders meet on a sandbar in the middle of the river, but Gall refused.

"I want to know what you are doing," the Húŋkpapȟa chief said. Stanley told him.

"What will you pay," Gall asked, "to build this railroad through our country?"

Stanley suggested that the government could give the Húŋkpapȟa rations if they would come into the agencies, but Gall was not satisfied with this answer.

"You cannot cross the Powder River," he told Stanley.

"What will you do to me if I do?" Stanley asked.

"I will bring all the bands and give you a big fight," Gall promised. "Like Sitting Bull gave Baker at Arrow Creek."

As the two men were talking, an Arikara scout for the survey expedition noticed movement in the hills behind Gall. The Húŋkpapȟa were coming through the juniper shrubs, using the parlay as a distraction to launch a surprise attack. Stanley saw them at the same time and began to back away from the riverbank. Immediately the warriors began to fire, their bullets plowing small furrows into the ground. Stanley ordered his soldiers to pull back, and when they had retreated far enough, Gall and his men crossed the Powder. Pulling the cottonwood survey marker out of the ground, they danced around it and then shouted insults at the wašíču. But they did not pursue. Gall would have to wait for Sitting Bull to arrive if they were going to launch a serious attack on the survey.

It took Sitting Bull and his men a week of hard riding from Arrow Creek to reach Gall's small party. The Húŋkpapȟa were still tracking Stanley's soldiers and surveyors, who had turned back to the east and were trying to find a shortcut back to the Missouri River. The Lakota bands converged just as the Stanley expedition was moving through a valley with a deep canyon ahead. It was a perfect spot for a surprise attack. Sitting Bull sent one contingent of warriors to the canyon entrance to fire down on the soldiers, while another moved behind the column to charge them from the rear.

Lakota fighters in front succeeded in pushing the soldiers back from the canyon's mouth. The Americans quickly closed ranks, circling their wagons and establishing a defensive line. The other group of warriors rode rapidly and boldly at the soldiers in the rear of Stanley's column.

"It appeared certain that they would ride into the guard," the surveyor Thomas Rosser observed. "A collision seemed inevitable, when suddenly, as one man, they broke by the flank and dashed up a ravine and out of sight into the hills."

Again, Sitting Bull had weighed the costs of an open battle with a larger force and opted for a strategy that would save the lives of his men. The frontal attack and the charge in the rear had given his men the opportunity to show their bravery, especially given that the Long Knives had a new kind of weapon with them, in addition to artillery: a Gatling gun, which fired bullets so quickly that there was no time to breathe in between.

Sitting Bull signaled to Gall to retreat, and then rode his horse to the top of a canyon wall. "If the railroad comes through," he shouted down at the Northern Pacific column, "there will be more Indians."

Sitting Bull promised he would call together all seven council fires of the Lakota people. All ten bands of the Húŋkpapȟa would come. Their Cheyenne and Arapaho kin would join them, strengthening the will of the people, their connections to one another, and their collective spirit of resistance. They would come together to fight for one another and for their homelands in the Great Northwest. For their relatives, Buffalo Nation and Mníšoše.

"Oglala! Brulé! Minneconjou!" Sitting Bull yelled.

"Sans Arc! Two Kettles! Blackfeet!"

Together with their allies, the Lakota would

wipe out the soldiers and the railroad workers once and for all. Sitting Bull's voice echoed across the prairie "like a huge bell; loud, clear, and voluminous."

"We will meet you again," Sitting Bull promised before disappearing over the edge of the canyon. "Very soon."

11

A Country Unsettled

Philadelphia. September 18, 1873.

The breakfast room at Ogontz was as sumptuously decorated as the rest of the mansion, with gleaming dark wood furniture and artworks and tapestries hanging on the marble walls. As Jay Cooke and Ulysses S. Grant sat down for their morning meal, they continued their easy conversations from the evening before. Grant had come to Philadelphia to bring his son Jesse to a school nearby that Cooke had recommended. It was not his first visit to the banker's mansion. Cooke had been a generous contributor to the president's campaigns in 1868 and 1872, and often invited him, Julia, and the children to stay at Ogontz whenever they were in town. The two men had much to talk about.

Cooke, as usual, wanted to discuss the Northern Pacific. In the past year, the banker's efforts to sell more of the railroad's bonds had come up short; he had been able to raise only a few million dollars in bond sales. A financial panic in May 1873 rocked American financial markets, and European investors began to liquidate their investments in U.S. stocks and bonds.

Despite these developments, Cooke had continued to send emissaries to the financial houses of Europe, convinced they would ultimately see the benefits of investing in a railroad project of national scope. He was encouraged about the prospects of European immigrants and enterprising Americans coming to Dakota and Montana to take up lands along the Northern Pacific line.

"There is not the slightest probability of there being any cessation in the legitimate demand for lands unless the world comes to an end," he wrote to a potential investor in 1873. "The progress of empire is westward."

His optimism was just for show. The reality was there would be no further European investment. And there would be no help from Congress: a series of corruption scandals involving payoffs to prominent Republicans on behalf of the Union Pacific and other railroads made federal support of the Northern Pacific impossible. Between the summer of 1872 and the summer of 1873 Cooke had advanced more money to the railroad from Jay Cooke & Company's deposits to cover the railroad's costs. By September 1873, the Northern Pacific owed the investment bank more than two million dollars.

Construction had stalled, for these reasons and

one other: Sitting Bull's fights with the Northern Pacific surveyors at Arrow Creek and O'Fallon Creek in 1872 had successfully prevented workers from laying track west of the Missouri River. To meet that threat to development, the U.S. Army (with President Grant's approval) had deployed additional cavalry regiments to the forts along the Missouri River. Several of them were Seventh Cavalry soldiers sent from South Carolina, where they had until recently been posted to protect Black and white Republicans from the violence of the Ku Klux Klan. General George Armstrong Custer came with the Seventh, establishing his headquarters at Fort Abraham Lincoln, on the west side of the Missouri River across from Bismarck.

It was still necessary for the Northern Pacific's surveyors to determine the feasibility of the route from the Missouri to the Yellowstone. Cooke had been confident enough in the size and strength of the U.S. military escorts in the Great Northwest to send out yet another survey team in the summer of 1873. General Custer commanded the escort, and when the expedition once again pushed into the heart of Sitting Bull's territory, Lakota warriors attacked. Custer and his soldiers—and several Dakota scouts, whom Custer had hired as guides—managed to fight them off in two engagements in August. Once again, the Lakota stymied Cooke's plans for the railroad. President Grant had heard about these fights, not only from the local newspapers and military reports but also from his son Fred, who was serving with Custer and had been part of the Northern Pacific's military escort that summer.

Grant understood Cooke's frustration. He had made no headway in diplomatic talks with the Lakota in 1873. He still believed in Ely Parker's vision, that the federal government could do right by Native peoples if the hunting bands across the region would give up their ways, surrender themselves at the government's Indian agencies, and consent to living on reservations. Then they could have peace. But Sitting Bull's Húŋkpapȟa had strong alliances across the Great Northwest and seemed determined to reject the reservation system. Grant, like many of his cabinet members and U.S. Army generals, had come to believe that the Lakotas' successful defense of their homelands would continue unless the U.S. Army took a more aggressive approach.

As the two men talked, the click-click-click of Cooke's private telegraph line reverberated through the large rooms of the mansion. The financier had installed it when he built Ogontz in 1866, to better manage his many business affairs from home. The money market had been turbulent during the past year, and September was a particularly vulnerable time for eastern investment banks. Every autumn, midwestern and western banks that had deposited funds in New York and Philadelphia pulled out their money to finance the harvest and transportation of crops. With money flowing to the West but no investments coming from Europe, banks in the Northeast were in a precarious position.

The clicking became insistent. As the two men finished their breakfast, Cooke glanced at a few of the telegrams, and he and the president prepared to leave Ogontz. They climbed into a carriage, and Cooke dropped Grant off at the railroad station, where he boarded a train to Pittsburgh. The president was planning to attend a meeting of the Society of the Army of the Cumberland there; Fred and Grant's old friend General Phil Sheridan were supposed to join him. Then the carriage driver took Cooke to his office on Third Street.

Cooke walked through the massive walnut-paneled doors of the front entrance and past the clerks, who sat at gleaming wood desks and behind counters. His personal office was in the back, past the giant safe with a large bronze American eagle perched above it on a pedestal. The Brussels carpet, copper-colored leather sofas, and walnut chairs in his office echoed the décor at Ogontz. They were meant to convey Cooke's confidence and success.

A pile of telegrams and letters sat on his desk. Cooke settled into his chair and began to sift through them. The most recent telegram had come in just a few minutes before, from Harris Fahnestock, the Jay Cooke & Co. partner running the New York office. Cooke's relationship with Fahnestock had soured of late. The New York banker had never been fully enthusiastic about the investment company's involvement in fundraising for the Northern Pacific Railroad project and was increasingly alarmed about the amount of money that Cooke was taking from company coffers to pay the railroad's bills.

Fahnestock was also concerned about the U.S. economy, which had been faltering all summer. By the second week of September, two investment firms (which were also heavily involved in financing railroads) suspended their work. The day before Cooke sat down to read Fahnestock's telegram, the stock market had had a wild day, plunging in the morning before regaining value in the afternoon. Fahnestock had discussed the situation at Jay Cooke & Co. with several other New York City bankers. The combination of Cooke's loans to the Northern Pacific and the drawdown on their funds by the western banks meant that if all the company's investors came calling for their money that day, they would not have the funds to pay them.

The telegram from Fahnestock informed Cooke that the New York office of his firm had closed its doors. Cooke looked at the clock. It was almost 11:00 a.m.

Although Cooke had been aware of the gathering storm, this news was a thunderbolt. He had been sure that he had more time, that he could find more money to cover the Northern Pacific's debts and save his investment bank. Fahnestock's action forced his hand. Once word hit the streets in New York that the office had closed, there would be pandemonium. Cooke dropped Fahnestock's telegram on the desk, walked out of his office, and ordered the porter to shut the company's front doors and lock them. After consulting with a lawyer, he had a clerk write out a notice.

"To the public," it read. "We regret to be obliged to announce that, owing to unexpected demands on us, our firm has been obliged to suspend payment."

The company was confident that they would be able to reopen their doors in a few days. "Until which time," the statement went on, "we must ask for their patient consideration. We believe our assets to be largely in excess of our liabilities. JAY COOKE AND COMPANY."

Back at his desk, Cooke began sending telegrams of his own. The first went to his brother Henry, instructing him to close the Washington, D.C., office. Meanwhile, the news spread across Philadelphia with tremendous speed, and soon crowds began to gather outside on Third Street. Police officers arrived next, to control the throng. Newspaper reporters squeezed through the crowd to read the posted notice and knock on the front doors. After they announced themselves to the porter, the doors opened wide enough to let them in before slamming shut again.

Cooke still believed in the power of newspapers, and he used them that day to tell his story of the company's closure. "You can announce that the firm has been temporarily suspended," he told the reporters. "Please state also that I believe this house will speedily be relieved from embarrassment, and that to this end, if need be, every dollar of the means possessed by members of the firm will be applied." None of the firm's investors would lose even a dollar of their investment. He would make sure of it.

"I can say no more now," he said, and waved them away.

As night fell, Jay Cooke left his office by the back door. Although he should have seen this coming by a mile, Cooke was stunned by the events of the day. He ordered his carriage driver to take an unusual and winding route back to Ogontz, lest reporters or unhappy investors were lying in wait for him. His sons and daughters and their families, having heard the news, joined him at the mansion, to comfort him as best they could. The next morning, Cooke telegraphed

Mrs. McMeens and told her to close Gibraltar for the season. He did not know when he would return to that beautiful house or pull a mess of black bass from the waters of Lake Erie.

In the pile of telegrams Cooke received was a note from A. B. Nettleton, who had just arrived from Sandusky. Nettleton expressed his sympathy and informed his boss that he had fired the Northern Pacific's loan agents and the newspaper reporters under his charge and shut down the marketing department.

The failure of Jay Cooke & Co. on September 18, 1873, set off a chain reaction in the U.S. economy. That weekend, dozens of railroads, national and local banks, investment firms, and trust companies closed their doors in America's major cities. For the first time in its history, the New York Stock Exchange halted all trading to try to contain the panic. By the time they reopened ten days later, railroad stocks had fallen between 15 and 40 percent. Hundreds of businesses failed in the weeks afterward, and thousands over the next two years.

Later that fall, Jay Cooke & Co.'s affairs were given over to a trustee, whose job it was to dissolve the company and all of Jay Cooke's assets to pay the company's investors. Cooke moved out of Ogontz and into his daughter's cottage nearby while the trust employees collected all his paintings, sculptures, carpets, tapestries, and furniture to sell at auction. Among the items sold off were the watercolors of Yellowstone that Thomas Moran had finished for him earlier that year.

Jay Cooke never reentered the world of banking or railroads. He did make one good investment—in a Utah silver mine—that paid out in 1880 and made him a wealthy man again. He was able to repurchase Gibraltar the next year and reinstall Mrs. McMeens there as its manager.

The investors who could not or chose not to unload their Northern Pacific stocks during the 1873 panic were ultimately rewarded. The U.S. Army was finally victorious in their fights against the Lakota in the late 1870s. Construction of the Northern Pacific west of the Missouri River resumed in 1879, as the American economy started to recover. It was completed in 1883. Eight years later, in the summer of 1891, Jay Cooke boarded a Northern Pacific passenger car in Minnesota and traveled across the Great Northwest to the railroad's terminus in Washington, then back again. Along the way, he visited Yellowstone National Park. When he returned to Gibraltar afterward, he was elated.

"My sensations as day after day I passed over this road and through this wonderful country, now so rapidly developing," he wrote in the Gibraltar journal, "were such as few have ever experienced. It was in a measure the fulfillment of prophecies which I uttered long ago. I felt that I was justified, and those who were so full of doubts long ago now gladly acknowledge that I was right."

He held firm to these beliefs, and to his conviction that he had played a pivotal role in expanding America's empire on behalf of white Americans, until his death in 1905.

When Ulysses S. Grant parted ways with Jay Cooke on the morning of September 18, 1873, he could not know the chaos that would ensue as he traveled west toward a reunion with fellow U.S. Army veterans. That trip was interrupted, of course, and by Sunday the twentieth he was in New York City, meeting with his Secretary of the Treasury William Richardson in the Fifth Avenue Hotel. The hotel was a hive of activity, its parlors and hallways filled with bankers, speculators, and the members of the stock exchange. Grant summoned the business leaders of the city, including Cornelius Vanderbilt, to confer about how the panic had happened and what the federal government could do about it.

The treasury and Congress enacted short-term fixes, injecting money into circulation to buy stocks at market prices and to stabilize the market. But for Grant and the Republicans, the panic of 1873 was a disaster that further fragmented the party. The president had faced a reelection challenge from the new Liberal Republican wing in 1872, running against their candidate, Horace Greeley. He won handily, but the election had shown how precarious a hold the Republicans had on the nation. To govern effectively, Grant would have to conciliate three different groups: the moderates drifting to the Liberal Republican camp, the Radicals, and the Democrats. And he would have to win over a white population in the North and the West, who were increasingly resistant to using federal power to intervene in local affairs.

"My efforts in the future," Grant informed the American people in his second inaugural in March 1873, "will be directed to the restoration of good feeling between the different sections of our common country."

The president pledged to protect Black rights even before his reelection in 1872, but as Amos Akerman had predicted, the commitment of the Republican party to racial justice waned. Without Akerman there to push him, Grant wavered. In May 1872, he signed the Amnesty Act, restoring civil rights to former Confederates and allowing them to run for public office once again. In the spring of 1873, the Department of Justice campaign against the Ku Klux Klan in South Carolina came to an end. The final federal court session with Ku Klux Klan cases on the docket resulted in only 4 convictions and 540 case dismissals against Klan members. Over the summer, Grant pardoned those South Carolina Klan members still held in jail for their crimes.

Grant hoped that these measures would win over southern whites to the Republican cause, but the economic depression that followed the panic of 1873 dashed any hopes that Grant had of bringing them into the fold. White southerners turned once again to terrorist action, creating White Leagues and rifle clubs that organized violent campaigns against Black Americans daring to assert their civil rights. In 1874, Democrats won state elections across the South and a majority in the House of Representatives, reestablishing their power in local and national politics.

Afterward, the Republican Party abandoned Black southerners in favor of white reunion. In 1876, to retain the influence they had remaining, the Republicans agreed to end Reconstruction in the South during the disputed presidential election. They pulled remaining U.S. troops from the region and ceased government programs promoting Black citizenship in exchange for Rutherford B. Hayes's assumption of the presidency. The American federal government would not again attempt to use its power to achieve a higher goal of equality for Black Americans for almost one hundred years.

In the West, Grant and the Republican members

of Congress had more success winning white voters. The party's continued dedication to removing Native peoples from their homelands pleased the growing numbers of white settlers in the region. In the fall of 1875, President Grant made a long visit to Colorado, wanting to ensure that when "the Centennial State" was admitted to the Union the next year, it would be a Republican stronghold. This came to pass, and Republicans increasingly turned to the states and territories of the West to shore up their political influence. This came at a cost to Native peoples. They did not achieve citizenship until 1924, and the U.S. Congress has only very recently begun to acknowledge the land rights and cultural integrity of Indigenous nations across the country.

George Armstrong Custer's fight against Sitting Bull's Húŋkpapȟa in the summer of 1873— as they resisted the encroachment of another Northern Pacific survey party—had proven that, as William Tecumseh Sherman told Congress, Lakotas were "the most warlike nation of Indians on this continent, who will fight for every foot of the line."

The Lakotas' fierce battle to retain their homelands continued through the 1870s. After their first fight with Custer, Lakota scouts saw something more ominous on the horizon: soldiers moving across the plains in large numbers, but with no migrants or surveyors in tow. In 1874, more than one thousand troops, once again under Custer's command, marched to Ȟesápa (the Black Hills). Lakota scouts tracked them but did not engage, as this army was too large to attack with success.

Custer was looking for a place to build a fort, a symbol of American power in the heartland of Lakota territory. He was also looking for gold. The miners he brought with him on the two-month campaign confirmed for him and for newspaper reporters across the nation that the Black Hills could make a man's fortune.

STRUCK IT AT LAST! one newspaper headline shouted in jubilation. RICH MINES OF GOLD AND SILVER REPORTED FOUND BY CUSTER.

The country was still gripped by a financial depression, and this was welcome news to tens of thousands of unemployed white men. In the spring of 1875, they swarmed into Ȟesápa from every direction, digging into the dirt that Lakota, Cheyenne, Arapaho, and Kiowa peoples deemed sacred. Miners felled trees that provided lodgepoles for Indigenous tipis and travois. The elk, deer, and antelope that had lived in Ȟesápa in huge numbers began to disappear, and the buffalo herds, already dwindling, grew even smaller. The army had promised the Lakota, in treaties and in councils, that they would prevent the encroachment of white railroad workers, farmers, ranchers, and miners on their land. They showed little willingness to do so now, making only sporadic efforts to turn back gold seekers from Hesápa.

In the winter of 1875, Sitting Bull and the Húŋkpapȟa had just established their winter camp along the Powder River when runners came in from the forts on Mníšoše. They bore a message from the American government, which had been sent to all Lakota bands. "Come into an agency by January 31, 1876," it said. "Or the soldiers will march against you."

As the Americans expected, Sitting Bull paid no attention to this latest demand from the U.S. federal government. Moving his winter camp at this point was impossible. He would stay put and look to the survival of his people. As the snow melted and the rivers began to run high and fast, a small band of Cheyenne and Oglála staggered into Sitting Bull's camp from the south. American soldiers, using Sitting Bull's noncompliance with their order as justification for a campaign, had attacked their camp two weeks earlier, driving them from their tipis and destroying their food and clothing.

Sitting Bull was not surprised. "War is inevitable," he declared.

During the spring and summer of 1876, a large camp of several Lakota bands and their Cheyenne and Arapaho allies came together along Rosebud

Creek and then moved near the Little Bighorn River. At the annual meeting of the tribes, Sitting Bull took part in the Sun Dance, his arms bleeding from fifty cuts, and had a vision. He saw Long Knives falling upon their camp.

"They looked like grasshoppers," he told Black Moon, "with their feet above their heads and without ears." There were Lakota among them, falling dead in the same way.

"I give you these Long Knives," a voice had said to him. "They will die, but do not take their belongings."

Over the next week, more bands arrived and Sitting Bull's camp more than doubled in size. In mid-June, they skirmished with U.S. troops under General George Crook, who had more than two hundred Crow and Shoshone auxiliaries with him, riding up from the south. Crook claimed victory, but the Lakota forced him to retreat.

By then, 7,000 Lakota and their allies—men, women, and children—encamped on the Little Bighorn, and 1,800 fighting men prepared themselves and their warhorses for battle. On June 25, 1876, thousands of American soldiers appeared in the hills to the east: three battalions of cavalry led by Major Marcus Reno, Captain Frederick Benteen, and George Armstrong Custer with Arikara and Crow scouts. Among Reno's men was Isaiah Dorman, the Black scout and interpreter who had worked for the Northern

Pacific's westbound survey in the fall of 1871.

All these soldiers were part of a three-pronged offensive, moving from the south (Crook), the west (Colonel John Gibbon, marching from Fort Ellis), and the east in a U.S. Army attack on the entire Lakota camp. As the battle began, women ran from tipi to tipi, gathering up children, elders, and whatever items they thought they could save from destruction. They fled northward, under Sitting Bull's protection.

In the end, the Battle of Greasy Grass (Little Bighorn) was a great Lakota victory, the triumph that Sitting Bull had seen in his vision. Lakota warriors killed Custer, destroyed his battalion, and killed or wounded a considerable number of American soldiers in other fighting units along with Crow, Shoshone, and Arikara scouts (including Isaiah Dorman). They succeeded in defending their families against this latest of U.S. Army attacks on their people. In the midst and the wake of the fight, however, the Lakota stripped the soldiers and scouts of their clothing and weapons, scalped some of them or cut off body parts. Sitting Bull celebrated with his kin during the dances and ceremonies that followed, but he was not filled with joy. By taking the spoils of battle, as his vision had foretold, his people had been cursed.

In the wake of the Battle of Greasy Grass, President Grant approved the escalation of "hard war" strategies against the Lakota in their homelands. American soldiers attacked camps in winter, when families were most vulnerable to weather conditions, destroying Lakota tipis and food supplies. Congress prohibited the Indian agencies along Mníšoše from distributing rations to Lakota until they sold Ȟesápa to the United States and until the bands under Sitting Bull came in to surrender.

These strategies put significant pressure on the Lakota. When the winter snows began to melt in 1877, Sitting Bull met in council again with fellow Húŋkpapȟa chiefs to discuss the way forward. Their strategies of resistance were no longer working. The buffalo herds continued to decline. It was becoming almost impossible to survive in their homelands. In March 1877, Sitting Bull, his family, and his Húŋkpapȟa band began to make their way to Canada. In his people's absence, Northern Pacific workers began to lay track across Lakota homelands, along the lines that Cooke's surveyors had marked in the early 1870s.

For the next four years, Sitting Bull and the Húŋkpapȟa lived in the borderlands between countries, moving back and forth to hunt buffalo wherever they could find herds and trade at U.S. forts along the upper Mníšoše. In that time, Sitting Bull's family grew, as his wives gave birth to three more children. By July 1881, the buffalo had almost entirely disappeared, and Canadian officials made it known they did not welcome the Lakota bands camped along their southern border. Sitting Bull decided that he wanted to go back to his homelands. The only way to do this was to surrender himself at one of the U.S. forts. It would infuriate him to do so, but Sitting Bull felt he had no other choice. He and his family crossed the border and gave themselves up to U.S. authorities at Fort Buford, a U.S. Army post at the confluence of Mníšoše and the Yellowstone River.

The federal government still considered Sitting Bull a dangerous enemy, so authorities separated him from his family and sent him southward to Fort Randall in Dakota Territory, where he was incarcerated as a prisoner of war. After two years, the government released him and sent him to live with his people at Standing Rock, on the Great Sioux Reservation. Three months after his return, in September of 1883, the eastern and western crews of the Northern Pacific Railroad met in a canyon west of Helena, Montana. The railroad that connected the Great Lakes to the Pacific had finally been completed.

Over the next several years, Sitting Bull adjusted to life on the reservation but continued to resist government policies that sought to assimilate Húŋkpapȟa and take more of their lands. In 1887, Congress passed the Dawes

Severalty Act, which allowed the president to subvert treaties signed before 1871 and to allot small sections of reservation lands only to individual landowners. The act was named after its primary author, Henry Dawes, the Republican congressman from Massachusetts who had advocated so vociferously for Ferdinand Hayden's expeditions and for the creation of Yellowstone National Park. In 1889, Congress used this precedent to divide the Great Sioux Reservation, whose boundaries had been negotiated in 1868—a treaty the U.S. government had previously recognized—into six smaller reservations. The government parceled Lakota lands into 80- to 320-acre lots that only individuals could claim, undermining the Lakota tradition of collective land ownership. Congress then put millions of acres of Lakota land up for sale to white settlers.

Lakota were not the only Indigenous peoples to experience massive land loss at this moment. Resistance to this and related policies designed to destroy Indigenous livelihoods and ways of life was widespread. In 1889, a Northern Paiute holy man in Nevada named Wovoka had a vision that would bring Indigenous peoples together and help them escape the adversity that had befallen them. He communicated this vision in "the Ghost Dance"; Indigenous peoples took trains to visit him in Nevada to learn the dance, then informed their kin about it through letters and personal visits. In 1890, Sitting Bull, who maintained his role as a political leader of the Húŋkpapȟa at Standing Rock, welcomed the performance of the Ghost Dance at the reservation. The federal government and its Indian agents, alarmed at this spirit of resistance to U.S. government control, enabled by a strong and growing communication network across reservations, moved to occupy Standing Rock and other Lakota lands. They sent out orders to arrest Lakota leaders, including Sitting Bull.

On December 14, 1890, Sitting Bull met with his fellow Húŋkpapȟa chiefs and the men's societies and told them he was going to Pine Ridge Reservation to confer with Oglála chief Red Cloud about the Ghost Dance. Word of his decision reached James McLaughlin, the Indian agent at Standing Rock. Early the next morning, McLaughlin sent a large group of Metal Breasts (Lakota police officers) to arrest him for allowing the Ghost Dance and for attempting to cooperate with fellow Lakota leaders in its promotion.

The police gathered outside Sitting Bull's cabin in the bitter cold, knocked on the door, and asked him to come outside. When he stepped out into the chill air with his teenage son Crow Foot, the police opened fire, killing both father and son. It was a bitter end, to be killed by his own people. But Sitting Bull died as he had lived, standing in defense of his kin and his homelands. The Lakota, along with other Indigenous peoples across the West, the South, and the East, have continued to claim their lands for themselves, and in defiance of U.S. government policies.

Just as Sitting Bull was returning to his people at Standing Rock in 1883, Ferdinand Hayden was aboard a Northern Pacific train in Bismarck, Dakota. He was with the mineralogist Albert Peale, and they were bound for Helena, Montana. Anyone who had known Hayden during the height of his powers, during the 1871 scientific survey and the 1872 lobbying effort for the Yellowstone Act, would have been shocked by his appearance. He walked slowly through the hills and floodplains around Helena, his hip joints inflamed and aching. His eyesight was failing but still sharp enough that he could point out fossils to Peale, who did the work of collecting them.

Hayden did not know he had syphilis until he began to experience serious symptoms in 1878. It is unclear whether he contracted it during one of his dalliances with women in Philadelphia and Washington, D.C., or in one of the many western towns he visited in a twenty-year career as a scientist-explorer. The disease had remained latent in Hayden's body for many years before revealing itself. It had almost destroyed his marriage to Emma and prevented them from having children. But they reconciled, and in 1885 she joined him and the Peales (Albert had married in 1875, and his wife, Emilie, was good friends with Emma) for another trip to the Great Northwest. While the men gathered more specimens around Bozeman as evidence of the geological age of the continent, Emma and Emilie spent several days touring Yellowstone National Park.

"I cannot get about much," Hayden wrote to a friend about his trip to Montana, "but I am thankful to be able to be here and see these old mountain peaks again. The old spirit comes over me to work but I am chained down by disease."

Hayden had spent the most productive years of his career in the Rocky Mountain West, after the passage of the Yellowstone Act. The survey team he led to the Basin in 1872 had produced even more accurate knowledge of the region's geothermal curiosities, and proof that the continent had taken shape because of periodic violent action, long periods of slow change, and powerful forces of water and wind erosion.

Hayden had not returned to Yellowstone in 1873, however.

"The expenses of transportation, subsistence and labor are so great that it seems desirable to delay the further prosecution of the work in the Northwest until railroad communication shall be established," Hayden wrote to the Secretary of the Interior. "The Indians, also, are in a state of hostility over the greater portion of the country which remains to be explored."

He opted for Colorado Territory instead, sending several survey teams across the territory in the summer of 1873 to collect data for mapping and specimens for analysis. William Henry Jackson led his own team of photography assistants, including the son of Cornelius Cole, the congressman from California who had objected to the passage of the Yellowstone Act.

Thomas Moran was not with him. He had opted to go with another survey team in the field, John Wesley Powell's expedition to the Grand Canyon. The painting he produced after that trip, *The Chasm of the Colorado*, was considered as sublime and majestic as his *Grand Cañon of the Yellowstone*; Congress purchased it for $10,000 in 1874.

Hayden's teams had just returned from that five-month-long expedition when Jay Cooke & Co. closed its doors.

"The panic of 1873 threw a staggering burden upon the Congress which convened shortly before Christmas," Jackson noted. "It was a new order of things."

The session was long and turbulent, but Congress still found the money to fund another proposed trip to Colorado under Hayden's leadership. The appropriation came so late, however, that they had little time in the field that summer. Stymied still by the lack of railroad transportation and Lakota assertions of sovereignty, Hayden chose to return to Colorado for the next two years.

Geological surveys remained of interest to congressmen intent on mapping the West for settlement and on proving the nation's geological exceptionalism. But the panic and depression of 1873 prompted many politicians to consider how best to streamline these efforts. While Hayden and his team were in Colorado, three additional surveys were out in the field, led by Hayden's rivals Powell, Clarence King, and George Wheeler. Beginning in 1874, Congress began holding hearings about the future of the surveys. Should they be combined into one organization? And should they operate under the direction of the War Department or the Department of the Interior?

Although Hayden understood how valuable the U.S. Army was for provisioning and protecting his expeditions, he still firmly believed that geological surveys should be led by scientists. Men trained in a range of scientific fields, he argued, were best suited to producing knowledge and promoting both resource use and landscape appreciation. He could see the utility of a single U.S. geological survey and felt, of course, that he was the man to lead it. In 1877, after the army intensified its war on Lakotas in their homelands and Sitting Bull began to lead his people to Canada, Hayden returned to the Yellowstone. His expedition's work there was important but not spectacular. And it took Hayden away from a growing fight over the reorganization of the surveys.

It was about this time that Hayden's symptoms began to appear, and he received his syphilis diagnosis. He wrote a defense of his vision of the U.S. geological survey, but it did not have his usual energy, that magnetic prose that convinced Congress to preserve Yellowstone as a national park. He was also distracted, unable to see that Powell and King had come together to campaign against him.

In January 1879, representatives in the House debated the future of government surveys as part of a funding bill. The measure dissolved the four existing surveys and combined them, leaving it to President Rutherford B. Hayes to appoint a director. The U.S. Geological Survey would thereafter focus on scouting for mineral resources, surveying lands for homestead claims, and determining which areas of the West could be developed with irrigation. The federal government would no longer support the production of pure scientific knowledge for the benefit of the American people.

"Ornithology is a delightful and useful study,"

Ohio representative and future president James Garfield said during the debate over the measure. "But would it be wise for Congress to make an appropriation for the advancement of that science?" If anyone mistook his meaning, Garfield added, "In my judgement, manifestly not."

President Hayes appointed Clarence King as the first director of the USGS. Two years later, he resigned, and John Wesley Powell replaced him. Congress kept Hayden on in the position of U.S. geologist, paying him $4,000 a year to help prepare specimens and reports. The money enabled him and Emma to remain living in their house in Philadelphia until his death, from complications of syphilis, in December 1887.

"He represented in science the curiosity, the intelligence, the energy, the practical business talent of the western people," a fellow scientist said of Hayden. "He exactly met the wants of the Great West."

All three of these men—Jay Cooke, Sitting Bull, and Ferdinand Hayden—determined the future of the American West during the Reconstruction era. They were raised in different familial circumstances (Hayden's was the most hardscrabble and Sitting Bull's the most advantageous, born as he was into a family of

Lakota chiefs), but they were all men of ambition. They discovered their talents as young men and worked to establish themselves as leaders in their respective communities.

They also had larger visions for the future of their nations, rooted in their beliefs about who should have rights as citizens and who should control the undulating prairies, jagged mountain peaks, and fertile valleys of the West. Each of them used the political, economic, and cultural power they wielded to try to bring these larger visions into reality. They were not alone in these endeavors. Family members, allies, and community members supported their ideas and helped to realize and publicize them.

Cooke, Sitting Bull, and Hayden knew, or knew of, one another. The actions they took during the 1860s and 1870s affected the others, sometimes directly and sometimes obliquely. They took many paths: through the corridors of the U.S. Capitol, the hallways of the Smithsonian, the business district of Philadelphia, the snow-covered badlands of the Lakota territory. Sometimes their paths crossed, and sometimes they collided.

At the center of so many of these paths was Yellowstone: the Basin, with its geothermal curiosities and its awe-inspiring canyon; and the river valley, connecting the Basin to the Missouri River and crossing through Lakota homelands.

It was a landscape of both darkness and light, an "empire of shadows" that drew Hayden, Sitting Bull, and Cooke into its midst, and reflected so much of what America had become.

EPILOGUE

Wonderland

N athaniel Langford submitted his first report as superintendent of Yellowstone National Park almost a year after his appointment. In the spring of 1872, when Congress notified him of his new position, Langford immediately traveled west to Montana, then joined Ferdinand Hayden's survey team over the summer. Nothing had changed since his first visit to the Basin in 1870.

"The park is at present accessible only by means of saddle and pack trains," he informed Congress. "A few years only can elapse before it will be reached by railroads; but until then it must be accommodated with good wagon-roads, or remain unvisited except by the few who are willing to endure the privation and exposure incident to horseback travel."

Langford made other suggestions in his report regarding the sale of leases to business proprietors catering to the tourist trade and the implementation of Montana laws within the park boundaries. He predicted a surge of visitors for leisure and for scientific exploration, drawn to the unique natural features in the Basin.

"New wonders are continually presenting

themselves," he wrote. "We venture to say that there is not in the world, within the same limit, so many wonderful freaks of physical geography, much to amaze and delight the beholder."

The Forty-Second Congress appreciated Langford's report but did nothing about it. Neither did their successors. Over the next five years, distracted by the financial depression and divisions within their own party, they did almost nothing to provide infrastructure for tourists in the nation's first national park. They did not pay Langford a salary, and he had no funding to build roads or hotels. Most Americans seemed to lose interest as well. The crowds of visitors that Langford, Hayden, and Cooke had imagined did not materialize. Between 1873 and 1883, when the Northern Pacific line was completed, annual visitation averaged between five hundred and one thousand. Most were adventurous world travelers like the Earl of Dunraven, an Irish peer who visited as part of a hunting trip in the Rocky Mountains, and parties of prominent western businessmen, politicians, and their wives.

Yellowstone continued to be a crossroads, however, for the many Indigenous communities living on its edges. They tracked small buffalo herds and hunted elk and deer that gathered in the Basin during the winter, attracted by the warmth of the geothermal region. In their travels through the Basin, Crow, Shoshone, Bannock, and Blackfoot hunters rarely ran into Americans or Europeans. An exception occurred in 1877, when a Nez Perce band in a running fight with the U.S. Army came through the park and took several tourists hostage. After leaving the Basin, they moved down the Yellowstone River into Lakota country, hoping to join Sitting Bull's band in Canada. The U.S. Army caught and finally defeated them forty miles south of the international border. Two of the soldiers involved in the chase were Lieutenant Gustavus Doane and Major Lewis Merrill.

In the wake of these battles, Congress finally committed some money to improving infra-structure in the park. In the summer of 1878, an energetic new superintendent arrived to replace Nathaniel Langford. Michigan resident Philetus Norris, a former frontier trapper, U.S. Army veteran, and real estate developer, did not have much money to spend. The country was just coming out of the depression, and Congress had given him just $10,000. But Norris was frugal and determined. He hired a crew, and together they built a sixty-mile road connecting the White Mountain (now called Mammoth Hot Springs) to the Firehole River using picks, shovels, and axes. By the time the Northern Pacific Railroad began to transport more than five thousand tourists into the park every year, Norris had constructed a series of roads through the northwestern part of the park, a headquarters at Mammoth, and several other buildings.

The Northern Pacific's completion also dramatically increased the white population along the edges of the park. The towns of Livingston and Gardiner, established between the railroad terminus and the northern entrance to Yellowstone, served the needs of tourists and adventurers. They also proved welcoming to poachers, who entered the park and overhunted elk, deer, and buffalo. By 1886 the situation had become so concerning that Congress turned Yellowstone National Park over to the Department of War to monitor and contain these men they saw as vandals. The military's presence was meant to be temporary, but they stayed for thirty years.

Throughout the 1870s and 1880s, Yellowstone remained the nation's only large national park. In 1875 Congress preserved one thousand acres on Mackinac Island in Lake Huron but did not pass legislation to create another national park on a grand scale for another fifteen years. The panic of 1873 continued to reverberate, and wars against Native peoples resisting U.S. reservation policies diverted congressional attention and appropriations to military matters. And after the elections of 1874, Republicans no longer controlled both the Senate and the House of Representatives. Given the Democrats' hostility to taking lands out of production for the purposes of preservation, it was unlikely that any attempt to create national parks would pass until Republicans had control of both houses of Congress once again. They achieved this—and held the presidency—in 1890, and that year Congress created Yosemite, Sequoia, and General Grant National parks in California.

Although politicians had not acted to preserve the wilderness in the 1870s and 1880s, popular momentum for a national park movement had been building. New publications like *Picturesque America* and the magazine *Forest and Stream* described the nation's natural landscape to a general audience of readers. The Appalachian Mountain Club and Theodore Roosevelt's Boone and Crockett Club formed to advocate for preservation (the retention of lands in their "wilderness" state) and conservation (the protection of natural resources through scientific management). In 1890, the U.S. Bureau of the Census published its population statistics and declared that areas with a population density fewer than two persons per square mile no longer existed. The "frontier" was closed. This realization prompted action. Preservation advocates insisted that white Americans needed to have wide open places, "empty" landscapes in which to rejuvenate themselves.

To designate many of these places as national

parks Congress needed to declare them public lands, which meant taking them from Indigenous peoples. The passage of the Dawes Act made that easier, as did the violent repression of the Ghost Dance, the murder of Indigenous leaders like Sitting Bull, and the massacre at Wounded Knee, which also occurred in 1890. That the creation of America's national parks required Native land dispossession is a hard truth, one that does not often appear in popular accounts of this movement.

As the federal government battled Native peoples for control of the West in the 1880s and 1890s, they withdrew their support almost entirely from Black southerners. The Democrats who regained power in state legislatures across the South and in Congress passed restrictive voter registration and election laws, as well as measures that segregated white and Black residents in public places. The Ku Klux Klan reemerged, and racist violence resumed. The federal government did nothing to intervene. Black southerners had to rely on their own communities (as they always had) for protection and survival.

Given all that came afterward, the fact that the Grant administration and the Republican Congress exerted their power to explore and preserve Yellowstone and to protect the civil rights of Black southerners in 1871–72 seems extraordinary. It was a watershed moment in the Reconstruction era, a point at which the federal government acted out of a higher sense of purpose in the West and in the South. That their policies in the West would damage Indigenous communities was of no real concern to them. They did not see it as contradictory that they would oppress Native peoples in the West while simultaneously fighting for the citizenship rights of Black men and women in the South. Republicans in the early 1870s saw both projects as part of a national ideal: to create productive and patriotic American citizens.

Their policies were not uncontested. They provoked violent resistance in the towns and fields of southern states like South Carolina and in the badlands of Lakota territory. They fragmented the Republican Party. In this context, Yellowstone promised to be a place that proved America's greatness by virtue of its natural wonders. But its geysers and mud pots revealed the reality of this strange country: the United States is both beautiful and terrible. It is both fragile and powerful. And that what lies beneath the surface in this nation is always threatening to explode.

Acknowledgments

I t was a Thursday afternoon in March 2020, and I was sitting in the microfilm room at the National Archives in College Park, Maryland. As I was reading through letters sent to the scientist-explorer Ferdinand Hayden in the 1870s, a staff member dropped by my desk.

"The library will be shutting down at 5:00 p.m. on Friday," he whispered, "because of Covid."

I spent the next day dashing from department to department in the archives, pulling maps and sketches from the survey, and taking notes on whatever sources I could get my hands on. Then I flew home to Boston, disappointed that my first archival research trip for *Saving Yellowstone* had been cut short.

The National Archives, along with most other research libraries across the nation, were closed for the foreseeable future. So I researched and wrote 80 percent of a book about travel and exploration from my own living room.

Throughout this terrible year, as the pandemic knocked the publishing industry sideways, Kathy Belden and Heather Schroder were consistent sources of support and encouragement. Kathy and Sally Howe offered insightful comments on the manuscript that have made *Saving Yellowstone* a much better book. Many thanks are also due to the production and design team at Scribner for all their hard work and attention to detail.

I am grateful to the curators and staff at NARA II, who guided me through the collections system during that one magical week of research. Over the past year, several colleagues procured resources for me that I was unable to get ahold of myself: Erin Luckett at Readex, Amy Kohout, Brooks Simpson, Amy Blair, and Dave Thomson. Special thanks to Kerri Clement, who went to the Yellowstone Research Library once they reopened and took photographs of the sources I needed.

To the archivists and others who digitized collections of photographs and newspapers (particularly those at newspapers.com, Wyoming Historical Newspapers, Colorado Historical Newspapers Collection, and the Library of Congress): thank you for making these collections accessible to scholars. I could not have written *Saving Yellowstone* without them. I also appreciate the generosity of Melissa Murphy and Heather Oswald at Baker Library Special Collections, and Mary Wilke and Marie Waltz of the Center for Research Libraries, for scanning documents for me. I also benefited from the hard work of historians who have come before me and collected, edited, and published primary documents related to the Yellowstone and

Northern Pacific Railroad surveys, particularly Marlene Deahl Merrill and M. John Lubetkin.

Joni Kinsey first introduced me to Ferdinand Hayden, along with the gorgeous artwork of William Henry Jackson and Thomas Moran, back in my first semester of graduate school at the University of Iowa. A timely Zoom conversation with her helped me to shape the book's narrative of Moran's *Grand Cañon of the Yellowstone*. Countless #twitterstorians helped with queries regarding 1870s railroad routes, the effects of acidic water on leather, and other nerdy topics.

The many brilliant historians and writers in my writing groups provided vital help on early chapters. Thank you to the members of Book Squad: Liz Covart, Sara Georgini, Heather Cox Richardson, Caitlin DeAngelis, Kevin Levin, Chris Parsons, Joe Adelman, and Karin Wulf; Team Kate: Kate Jewell and Kate Grandjean; and MG Writing Workshop: Carole Emberton and Tammy Ingram.

Bruce Baker and Jameson Sweet read drafts of the entire manuscript and gave me incisive, challenging, and immensely valuable feedback. Jimmy also gave me critical advice regarding Lakota orthography (throughout the book I have used New Lakota Dictionary, version 4.1). I cannot thank him enough.

My Pandemic Survival Squad is large and contains multitudes. I am especially grateful for the friendships of Nancy Serrano-Wu, Jen Medearis Costello, Lindsay Chervinsky, and Tita Chico.

My parents, John and Lynn Fritschel, first took me to Yellowstone in 1982, as one stop on a summer trip into the northern Rockies, and I have been yearning to go back ever since. By the time you read this, I will have seen them *and* Old Faithful again in real life, which will have made me extraordinarily happy.

Dan Nelson has been an ideal partner in these trying times: hilarious, supportive, and happy to binge-watch whatever television or movie series I selected. While this past year has been a journey of a sort, I can't wait to get back out on the road with him and explore new places.

This book is dedicated to Anne Moore and Marlys Ferrill, two of my high school teachers who encouraged my interest in history and literature and challenged me to experiment with my writing style. To them and all the K–12 teachers out there: thank you for the incredible work that you do to inspire and support students, and to bring knowledge into the world.

BIBLIOGRAPHY

MANUSCRIPT SOURCES

Baker Library Special Collections, Harvard Business School, Boston, Massachusetts
Jay Cooke & Co. Records
Jay Cooke Memoir

Library of Congress, Geography and Maps Division, Washington, D.C.
William H. Gamble and Samuel Augustus Mitchell. *Plan of the City of Washington: The Capital of the United States of America.* Philadelphia, 1873.

National Archives and Research Administration, College Park, Maryland
Record Group 57.2.3. Records of the U.S. Geological Survey
Fiscal Records and Ledgers, 1869–1880 (Microfilm 623, Roll 20)
Letters Received, 1866–1872 (Vols. 1–5, Microfilm 623, Rolls 1–2)
Letters Received, 1871–1879 (Microfilm 623, Roll 5)
Letters Received from Government Agencies, 1867–1879 (Microfilm 623, Roll 14)

Miscellaneous Records Relating to the Hayden Survey, 1867–1879 (Microfilm 623, Roll 21)

Record Group 57- HAA, HAB, and HAC. Hayden Survey Artwork, 1869–1872

Record Group 57-Hayden Survey. Cartographic Records

Maps Relating to the Activities of Ferdinand Hayden, 1869–1881
>   Folder: Yellowstone National Park
>   Folder: Wyoming, Idaho, Utah

Yellowstone Research Library, Gardiner, Montana

Thomas Moran Diary, 1871

Diary of Capt. George L. Tyler, 1871 [transcription by David H. Wallace, April 2009]

William Henry Jackson. "With Moran in Yellowstone," in *Famous American Mountain Paintings*, vol. 1, 149–158. Rare Separates Collection.

GOVERNMENT DOCUMENTS

Annual Report of the Board of Regents of the Smithsonian Institution, showing the operations, expenditures, and condition of the Institution for the year 1871. 42nd Congress, 2nd Session. Senate Miscellaneous Document 149.

Appropriations for Sioux Indians. Letter from the Secretary of the Interior, transmitting estimate of appropriations for subsisting Teton and other bands of Sioux Indians, in Montana. January 25, 1872. 42nd Congress, 2nd Session. House Executive Document 102.

Barlow, J. W., and D. P. Heap. *Report of the Reconnaissance in Wyoming and Montana Territories*, December 8, 1871 (April 18, 1872). 42nd Congress, 2nd Session. Senate Executive Document No. 66.

Biographical Directory of the United States Congress, 1774–present. https://bioguideretro.congress.gov/Home/.

Bryce, Sandra A., James M. Omernik, David E. Pater, Michael Ulmer, Jerome Schaar, Jerry Freeouf, Rex Johnson, Pat Kuck, and Sandra H. Azevedo. *Ecoregions of North and South Dakota*. Reston, Va.: U.S. Geological Survey, 1996.

Condition of the Indian Tribes: Report of the Joint Special Committee, March 3, 1865. Washington, D.C.: Government Printing Office, 1867.

Congressional Globe, 1871–72. Washington, D.C.: Washington Office of the Congressional Globe, 1872.

Doane, Gustavus C. *Report of Gustavus C. Doane*, submitted February 24, 1871. 41st Congress, 3rd Session. Senate Executive Document No. 51.

Hayden, Ferdinand V. *Preliminary Report of the United States Geological Survey of Montana and Portions of Adjacent Territories, being a Fifth Annual Report of Progress*. Washington, D.C.: Government Printing Office, 1872.

_____. *Twelfth Annual Report of the United States Geological and Geographical Survey of the Territories*, Part 2. Washington, D.C.: Government Printing Office, 1883.

Journal of the House of Representatives of the United States. 42nd Congress, 2nd Session. Washington, D.C.: Government Printing Office, 1872.

Journal of the Senate of the United States of America. 42nd Congress, 2nd Session. Washington, D.C.: Government Printing Office, 1872.

Langford, Nathaniel Pitt. *Report of the Superintendent of the Yellowstone National Park for the Year 1872*. Washington, D.C.: Government Printing Office, 1873.

Letter from the Secretary of the Interior re: Supplies for Indians of Milk River Agency, December 20, 1871. 42nd Congress, 2nd Session. House Executive Document 23.

McGrath C. L., A. J. Woods, J. M. Omernik, S. A. Bryce, M. Edmondson, J. A. Nesser, J. Shelden, R. C. Crawford, J. A. Comstock, and M. D. Plocher. *Ecoregions of Idaho*. Reston, Va.: U.S. Geological Survey, 2002.

Proceedings in the Ku Klux Trials at Columbia, S.C. in the United States Circuit Court, November Term 1871. 42nd Congress, 1st Session. Columbia, S.C.: Republican Printing Co., 1872.

Report of the Joint Select Committee to Inquire into the Condition of Affairs in the Late Insurrectionary States Made to the Two Houses of Congress, February 19, 1872. 13 volumes. Washington, D.C.: Government Printing Office, 1872.

Report of the Secretary of the Interior; being part of the message and documents communicated to the two Houses of Congress at the beginning of the second session of the Forty-second Congress, 1871. 42nd Congress, 2nd Session. House Executive Document 1, pt. 5, v. 1.

Report of the Secretary of War [. . .] at the beginning of the second session of the Forty-Second Congress, 1871. House Executive Document 1, pt. 2.

Report on the Alleged Outrages in the Southern States. 42nd Congress, 1st Session. Report No. 1. Washington, D.C.: Government Printing Office, 1871.

Report to the President by the Indian Peace Commission, January 7, 1868. 40th Congress, 2nd Session. House Executive Document No. 97.

Reports of Committees of the House of Representatives. 42nd Congress, 2nd Session, 1871–1872. Washington, D.C.: Government Printing Office, 1872.

Testimony Taken by the Joint Select Committee on the Condition of Affairs in the Late Insurrectionary States: South Carolina. Vol. II. Washington, D.C.: Government Printing Office, 1872.

Teton Sioux Indians. Letter from the Secretary of the Interior, relative to the condition, location, &c., of the Teton Sioux. January 15, 1873. 42nd Congress, 3rd Session. House Executive Document No. 96.

United States Geological Survey, Geological Survey Bulletin 1347, *Geologic History of the Yellowstone Region.* https://www.nps.gov/parkhistory/online_books/geology/publications/bul/1347/contents.htm.

U.S. Statutes at Large, 1861–1863. 37th Congress. Washington, D.C. Government Printing Office, 1862–1864.

U.S. Statutes at Large, 1871–1873. 41st–42nd Congress. Washington, D.C.: Government Printing Office, 1872–1874.

U.S. Statutes at Large, 1888–1889. 50th Congress, 2nd Session. Washington, D.C.: Government Printing Office, 1889.

Van Trump, Philadelph. "Ku-Klux Report: South Carolina." *Reports of Committees of* the House of Representatives 2nd Session, 42nd Congress. Vol. 2, No. 22. Washington, D.C.: Government Printing Office, 1872: 509–88.

Woods, Alan J., James M. Omernik, John A. Nesser, J. Shelden, J. A. Comstock, and Sandra H. Azevedo. *Ecoregions of Montana*, 2nd ed. Reston, Va.: United States Geological Survey, 2002.

PRINTED PRIMARY SOURCES

Burke, Edmund. *A Philosophical Inquiry into the Origin of Our Ideas of the Sublime and Beautiful, with an Introductory Discourse Concerning Taste*. 1757; New York: Harper and Brothers, 1844.

Coffin, Charles Carleton. *The Seat of Empire*. Boston: Fields, Osgood, and Co., 1870.

Cole, Cornelius. *Memoirs of Cornelius Cole: Ex-Senator of the United States from California*. New York: McLoughlin Brothers, 1908.

Cole, Thomas. "Essay on American Scenery." *American Monthly Magazine* 1 (January 1836): 1–12.

Cooke, Jay. *Journal of Jay Cooke: Or, The Gibraltar Records, 1865–1905*. Ed. James E. Pollard. Columbus: Ohio State University Press, 1935.

Crofutt, George A. *Crofutt's Transcontinental*

P.R.R.: Tourist's Guide. 3rd rev., vol. 4. New York: George A. Crofutt, 1872.

Everts, Truman C. "Thirty-Seven Days of Peril." *Scribner's Monthly* 3, no. 1 (November 1871): 1–17.

Gilder, Richard Watson. *Letters of Richard Watson Gilder*. Ed. Rosamond Gilder. Boston: Houghton Mifflin Co., 1916.

Grant, Ulysses S. *Papers of Ulysses S. Grant*. 31 vols. Ed. John Y. Simon. Digital Collections, Mississippi State University Libraries. https://cdm16631.contentdm.oclc.org/digital /collection/USG_volume/.

_____. *The Personal Memoirs of Ulysses S. Grant*. Ed. John F. Marszalek. Cambridge, Mass.: Belknap Press of Harvard University Press, 2017.

Hayden, Ferdinand V. "The Wonders of the West II. More about the Yellowstone." *Scribner's Monthly* 3 (February 1872): 388–96.

Jackson, William Henry. *Time Exposure: The Autobiography of William Henry Jackson*. New York: G. P. Putnam's Sons, 1940.

Langford, Nathaniel. "The Wonders of the Yellowstone [Part I]." *Scribner's Monthly* 2, no. 1 (May 1871): 1–17.

_____. "The Wonders of the Yellowstone [Part II]." *Scribner's Monthly* 2, no. 2 (June 1871): 113–28.

LaPointe, Ernie. *Sitting Bull: His Life and*

Legacy. Salt Lake City: Gibbs Smith, 2009.

Lubetkin, M. John, ed. *Before Custer: Surveying the Yellowstone, 1872*. Norman, Okla.: Arthur H. Clark Co., 2015.

_____. *Road to War: The 1871 Yellowstone Surveys*. Norman, Okla.: Arthur H. Clark Co., 2016.

Merrill, Marlene Deahl, ed. *Yellowstone and the Great West: Journals, Letters, and Images from the 1871 Hayden Expedition*. Lincoln: University of Nebraska Press, 1999.

Northern Pacific Railroad. "Alice's Adventures in the New Wonderland," 1885.

Official Guide to the Yellowstone National Park: A Manual for Tourists. St. Paul, Minn.: W. C. Riley, 1890.

O'Sullivan, John. "Annexation." *The United States Magazine and Democratic Review* 17 (New York: 1845): 5–6, 9–10. https://www .americanyawp.com/reader/manifest-destiny /john-osullivan-declares-americas-manifest -destiny-1845/.

Picturesque America; or, The Land We Live In, a Delineation by Pen and Pencil. Vol. 1. New York: D. Appleton & Co., 1872.

Thoreau, Henry David. *Walden* (1854). In *The Writings of Henry David Thoreau*. Ed. J. Lyndon Shandley. 1971; Princeton: Princeton University Press, 2014.

Waggoner, Josephine. *Witness: A Hunkpapa*

Historian's Strong-Heart Song of the Lakotas. Ed. Emily Levine. Lincoln: University of Nebraska Press, 2013.

White, Charles A. *Memoir of Ferdinand Vandeveer Hayden, 1839–1887.* National Academy of Science, 1894.

Whitman, Walt. *Leaves of Grass.* New York: The Modern Library, 2001.

SECONDARY SOURCES

Abeyounis, Andrew. "Before They Were Red Shirts: The Rifle Clubs of Columbia, South Carolina." Master's thesis, University of South Carolina, 2014.

Anderson, Nancy K. "Curious Historical Artistic Data." In *Discovered Lands, Invented Pasts: Transforming Visions of the American West,* ed. Jules Prown et al., 1–36. New Haven: Yale University Press, 1992.

Andrew, Rod, Jr. *Wade Hampton: Confederate Warrior to Southern Redeemer.* Chapel Hill: University of North Carolina Press, 2009.

Arenson, Adam, and Andrew R. Graybill, eds. *Civil War Wests: Testing the Limits of the United States.* Berkeley: University of California Press, 2015.

Baker, Bruce E. "Drovers, Distillers, and Democrats: Economic and Political Change in Northern Greenville County, 1865–1878." In *After Slavery: Race, Labor, and Citizenship in the Reconstruction South*, ed. Bruce E. Baker and Brian Kelly, 159–75. Tallahassee: University Press of Florida, 2013.

———. *This Mob Will Surely Take My Life: Lynchings in the Carolinas, 1871–1947.* London: Continuum, 2008.

Barratt, Carrie Rebora. "Mapping the Venues: New York City Art Exhibitions." In *Art and the Empire City: New York, 1825–1861*, ed. Catherine Hoover Voorsanger and John K. Howat, 47–82. New York: The Metropolitan Museum of Art and Yale University Press, 2000.

Barreyre, Nicholas. "The Politics of Economic Crises: The Panic of 1873, the End of Reconstruction, and the Realignment of American Politics." *Journal of the Gilded Age and Progressive Era* 10, no. 4 (October 2011): 403–23.

Bartlett, Richard A. *Nature's Yellowstone.* Tucson: University of Arizona Press, 1974.

Beaumont, C. L. "The Picture Sales of New York, a Retrospective History." *New York Times Saturday Review of Books and Art* (December 11, 1897): 10–11.

Beckner, Sarah. "More Than a Record: An Analysis of the Stylistic Development in W. H. Jackson's Photography, 1868–1871." Master's thesis, Rochester Institute of Technology, August 1990.

Bell, Griffin B. "The Attorney General: The Federal Government's Chief Lawyer and Chief Litigator, or One Among Many?" In *The John F. Sonnett Memorial Lectures at Fordham University School of Law: A Half Century of Advocacy and Judicial Perspectives*, ed. Dennis J. Kenny and Joel E. Davidson, 119–39. New York: Fordham University Press, 2017.

Bigler, David. "Mormon Missionaries, the Utah War, and the 1858 Bannock Raid on Fort Limhi." *Montana: The Magazine of Western History* 53, no. 3 (Autumn 2003): 30–43.

Black, George. *Empire of Shadows: The Epic Story of Yellowstone*. New York: St. Martin's Griffin, 2012.

Blight, David. *Race and Reunion: The Civil War in American Memory*. Cambridge, Mass.: Belknap Press of Harvard University Press, 2002.

Boag, Peter. "Thomas Moran and Western Landscapes: An Inquiry into an Artist's Environmental Values." *Pacific Historical Review* 67, no. 1 (February 1998): 40–66.

Boner, Bradly J. *Yellowstone National Park: Through the Lens of Time*. Boulder: University Press of Colorado, 2017.

Bowler, Peter J., and Iwan Rhys Morus. *Making Modern Science: A Historical Survey*. Chicago: University of Chicago Press, 2005.

Bradley, Lawrence W. "Dinosaurs and Indians: Fossil Resource Dispossession of Sioux Lands, 1846–1875." *American Indian Culture and Research Journal* 38, no. 3 (2014): 55–84.

Bridges, Hal. *Iron Millionaire: Life of Charlemagne Tower.* Philadelphia: University of Pennsylvania Press, 1952.

Brinkerhoff, Val. "The Symbolism of the Beehive in Latter-day Saint Tradition." *BYU Studies Quarterly* 52, vol. 2 (2013): 141–50.

Burlingame, Michael. *Abraham Lincoln: A Life.* 2 vols. Baltimore: Johns Hopkins University Press, 2009.

Butler, Howard Russell. "Thomas Moran, N.A.—An Appreciation." *The American Magazine of Art* 17, no. 11 (November 1926): 559–60.

Calhoun, Charles W. *The Presidency of Ulysses S. Grant.* Lawrence: University Press of Kansas, 2017.

Casper, Scott E., Jeffery D. Groves, Stephen W. Nissenbaum, and Michael Winship, eds. *A History of the Book in America.* Vol. 3. Chapel Hill: University of North Carolina Press, 2007.

Cassidy, James. G. *Ferdinand V. Hayden: Entrepreneur of Science.* Lincoln: University of Nebraska Press, 2000.

Chappell, Philip E. "A History of the Missouri River." *Collections of the Kansas State Historical Society* 9 (1904): 237–94.

Chernow, Ron. *Grant*. New York: Penguin, 2017.

Chervinsky, Lindsay M. *The Cabinet: George Washington and the Creation of an American Institution*. Cambridge, Mass.: Harvard University Press, 2020.

Chianese, Robert. "Avoidance of the Sublime in Nineteenth-Century American Landscape Art: An Environmental Reading of Depicted Land." *Amerikastudien / American Studies* 43, no. 3 (1998): 437–61.

Chittenden, Hiram M. *The Yellowstone National Park: Historical and Descriptive*. Cincinnati: Robert Clarke Company, 1895.

Chmiel, Louis L. *Ohio: Home of the Wright Brothers, Birthplace of Aviation*. Self-published, 2013.

Clary, David A. *"The Place Where Hell Bubbled Up": A History of the First National Park*. Washington, D.C.: National Park Service, 2009. http://npshistory.com/handbooks/natural/yell/clary/sec3.htm.

Coleman, Jon T. *Here Lies Hugh Glass: A Mountain Man, a Bear, and the Rise of the American Nation*. New York: Hill & Wang, 2012.

Collins, James P. "Native Americans and the Census, 1860–1890." *Prologue Magazine* 38, no. 2 (Summer 2006). https://www.archives.gov/publications/prologue/2006/summer/indian-census.html.

Colon, Sigma. "Watershed Colonialism and Popular Geographies of North American Rivers." *Open Rivers* 8 (Fall 2017). https://editions.lib.umn.edu/openrivers/article/watershed-colonialism/#_ftn1.

Coover, Roderick. "Picturing the Great Unknown: John Wesley Powell and the Divergent Paths of Art and Science in the Representation of the Colorado River and Utah Canyonlands." In *On Writing with Photography*, ed. Karen Beckman and Lilliane Weissberg, 14–40. Minneapolis: University of Minnesota Press, 2013.

"Colter's Hell and Jackson Hole." Yellowstone Association and Grand Teton Natural History Association. Grand Teton National Park, 1962. https://www.nps.gov/parkhistory/online_books/grte1/chap8.htm.

Conniff, Richard. "Mammoths and Mastodons: All American Monsters." *Smithsonian Magazine* (April 2020). https://www.smithsonianmag.com/science-nature/mammoths-and-mastodons-all-american-monsters-8898672/.

Curtis, Kent A. *Gambling on Ore: The Nature of Metal Mining in the United States, 1860–1910*. Boulder: University Press of Colorado, 2013.

Dall, William Healey. *Spencer Fullerton Baird: A Biography*. Philadelphia: J. B. Lippincott, 1915.

Darley, Gillian. *Vesuvius*. Cambridge, Mass.: Harvard University Press, 2011.

Daston, Lorraine, and Katherine Park. *Wonders and the Order of Nature, 1150–1750*. New York: Zone Books, 2001.

Dean, Adam Wesley. *An Agrarian Republic: Farming, Antislavery Politics, and Nature Parks in the Civil War Era*. Chapel Hill: University of North Carolina Press, 2015.

Diamant, Rolf. "Lincoln, Olmsted, and Yosemite: Time for a Closer Look." *The George Wright Forum* 31, no. 1 (2014): 10–16.

Dippie, Brian W. " 'CHOP! CHOP!': Progress in the Presentation of Western Visual History." *The Historian* 66, no. 3 (Fall 2004): 491–500.

Downes, William Howe. "American Painters of the Mountains." *The American Magazine of Art* 25, no. 4 (October 1932): 192–202.

Downs, Gregory P. *After Appomattox: Military Occupation and the Ends of War*. Cambridge, Mass.: Harvard University Press, 2015.

Du Bois, W. E. B. *Black Reconstruction in America, 1860–1880*. New York: Athenaeum, 1962.

Duncan, Dayton. *Seed of the Future: Yosemite and the Evolution of the National Park Idea*. Yosemite National Park: Yosemite Conservancy, 2013.

Dussias, Allison M. "Science, Sovereignty, and Sacred Text: Paleontological Resources and

Native American Rights." *Maryland Law Review* 55, no. 1 (1996): 84–159.

Eelman, Bruce W. "Entrepreneurs in the Southern Upcountry: The Case of Spartanburg, South Carolina, 1815–1880." *Enterprise & Society* 5, no. 1 (March 2004): 77–106.

_____. *Entrepreneurs in the Southern Upcountry: Commercial Culture in Spartanburg, South Carolina, 1845–1880*. Athens: University of Georgia Press, 2008.

Elwell, Craig K. "Brief History of the Gold Standard in the United States." Washington, D.C.: Congressional Research Service, 2011.

Emberton, Carole. "Axes of Empire: Race, Region, and the 'Greater Reconstruction' of Federal Authority after Emancipation." In *Rethinking American Emancipation: Legacies of Slavery and the Quest for Black Freedom*, ed. William A. Link and James J. Broomall, 119–45. New York: Cambridge University Press, 2016.

_____. *Beyond Redemption: Race, Violence, and the American South after the Civil War*. Chicago: University of Chicago Press, 2013.

_____. "Unwriting the Freedom Narrative: A Review Essay." *Journal of Southern History* 82, no. 2 (May 2016): 377–94.

Estes, Nick. *Our History Is the Future: Standing Rock Versus the Dakota Access Pipeline, and the Long Tradition of Indigenous Resistance.* New York: Verso, 2019.

Eubanks, Lila Carpenter. "The Deseret Museum." *Utah Historical Quarterly* 50, no. 4 (Fall 1982): 361–76.

Farrell, Justin. *The Battle for Yellowstone: Morality and the Sacred Roots of Environmental Conflict.* Princeton: Princeton University Press, 2015.

Finger, John R. *The Eastern Band of Cherokees, 1819–1900.* Knoxville: University of Tennessee Press, 1984.

Flanagan, Maureen A. *Seeing with Their Hearts: Chicago Women and the Vision of the Good City, 1871–1933.* Princeton: Princeton University Press, 2002.

Flower, Dean. "Humboldt's New World Landscape." *The Hudson Review* 70, no. 1 (Spring 2017): 9–21.

Foner, Eric. *Reconstruction: America's Unfinished Revolution, 1863–1877.* New York: Harper Perennial, 1989.

_____. *The Second Founding: How the Civil War and Reconstruction Remade the Constitution.* New York: W. W. Norton, 2019.

Forman, Jr., James. "Juries and Race in the Nineteenth Century." *Yale Law Journal* 113 (2004): 895–938.

Foster, Mike. *Strange Genius: The Life of*

Ferdinand Vandeveer Hayden. Niwot, Colo.: Roberts Rinehart, 1994.

Francaviglia, Richard V. *Over the Range: A History of the Promontory Summit Route of the Pacific Railroad.* Boulder: University Press of Colorado, 2008.

Francis, Marilyn G. "Mary Nimmo Moran: Painter-Etcher." *Woman's Art Journal* 4, no. 2 (1983–1984): 14–19.

Frankel, Oz. *States of Inquiry: Social Investigations and Print Culture in Nineteenth-Century Britain and the United States.* Baltimore: Johns Hopkins University Press, 2006.

Gage, Justin. *We Do Not Want the Gates Closed Between Us: Native Networks and the Spread of the Ghost Dance.* Norman: University of Oklahoma Press, 2020.

Genetin-Pilawa, C. Joseph. *Crooked Paths to Allotment: The Fight over Federal Indian Policy after the Civil War.* Chapel Hill: University of North Carolina Press, 2012.

Gilmore, Glenda Elizabeth. *Gender and Jim Crow: Women and the Politics of White Supremacy in North Carolina, 1896–1920.* Chapel Hill: University of North Carolina Press, 1996.

Goetzmann, William H. *Army Exploration and the American West, 1803–1863.* Austin: Texas State Historical Association, 1991.

Goldstein, Malcolm. *Landscape with Figures: A History of Art Dealing in the United States.* New York: Oxford University Press, 2000.

Goode, James M. *Capital Views: Historic Photographs of Washington, D.C., Alexandria and Loudon County, Virginia, and Frederick County, Maryland.* Washington, D.C.: Smithsonian Books, 2012.

Graner, Emma D. "Dangerous Alice: Travel Narrative, Empire, and *Alice's Adventures in Wonderland.*" *CEA Critic* 76, no. 3 (November 2014): 252–58.

Green, Tyler. *Carleton Watkins: Making the West American.* Berkeley: University of California Press, 2018.

Greenwald, Diana Seave. "The Big Picture: Thomas Moran's *The Grand Cañon of the Yellowstone* and the Development of the American West." *Winterthur Portfolio* 49, no. 4 (Winter 2015): 175–210.

Hafen, Thomas K. "City of Saints, City of Sinners: The Development of Salt Lake City as a Tourist Attraction, 1869–1900." *Western Historical Quarterly* 28, no. 3 (Autumn 1997): 342–77.

Hahn, Steven. *A Nation Under Our Feet: Black Political Struggles in the Rural South from Slavery to the Great Migration.* Cambridge, Mass.: Belknap Press of Harvard University Press, 2003.

_____. *A Nation Without Borders: The United States and Its World in an Age of Civil Wars, 1830–1910.* New York: Viking, 2016.

Haines, Aubrey L. *The Yellowstone Story.* 2 vols. Yellowstone, Wyo.: Yellowstone Library and Museum Association, 1977.

_____. *Yellowstone National Park: Its Exploration and Establishment.* https://www.nps.gov/parkhistory/online_books/haines1/iee2e.htm.

Hale, Grace Elizabeth. *Making Whiteness: The Culture of Segregation in the South, 1890–1940.* New York: Pantheon Books, 1998.

Hämäläinen, Pekka. *Lakota America: A New History of Indigenous Power.* New Haven: Yale University Press, 2019.

Hammer, Kenneth M. "Come to God's Country: Promotional Efforts in Dakota Territory, 1861–1889." *South Dakota History* 10, no. 4 (1980): 291–309.

Harrington-Lueker, Donna. *Books for Idle Hours: Nineteenth-Century Publishing and the Rise of Summer Reading.* Amherst: University of Massachusetts Press, 2019.

Hazard, Sharon *Long Branch in the Golden Age: Tales of Fascinating and Famous People.* Charleston, S.C.: The History Press, 2007.

Heacox, Kim. *An American Idea: The Making of the National Parks.* Washington, D.C.: National Geographic, 2009.

Heald, Weldon F. "Thomas Moran: Depicter of Western Grandeur." *Montana: The Magazine of Western History* 15, no. 4 (Autumn 1965): 42–53.

Henderson, Rodger C. "The Piikuni and the U.S. Army's Piegan Expedition: Competing Narratives of the 1870 Massacre on the Marias River." *Montana: The Magazine of Western History* 60, no. 1 (Spring 2018): 48–70, 93–96.

Heyman, Rich. "Locating the Mississippi: Landscape, Nature, and National Territoriality at the Mississippi Headwaters." *American Quarterly* 62, no. 2 (June 2010): 303–33.

Hildebrandt, Hugo John, and Marie Hildebrandt. *Lake Erie's Shores and Islands*. Charleston, S.C.: Arcadia Publishing, 2015.

Holmstrom, Bethany D. "Civil War Memories on the Nineteenth-Century Amateur Stage." *Theatre History Studies* 33 (2014): 4–34.

Howe, Craig, and Abe Katz. "Traditional Lakota Governance." *Rootstalk* 1 (Spring 2015): 35–40.

Howe, Winifred E. *A History of the Metropolitan Museum of Art*. New York: Metropolitan Museum of Art, 1913.

Irwin, Leonard Bertram. *Pacific Railways and Nationalism in the Canadian-American Northwest, 1845–1873*. Philadelphia: University of Pennsylvania Press, 1939.

Jackson, W. Turrentine. "Salt Lake City: Wells Fargo's Transportation Depot during the Stagecoach Era." *Utah Historical Quarterly* 53, no. 1 (Winter 1985): 4–39.

Jacoby, Karl. *Crimes Against Nature: Squatters, Poachers, Thieves, and the Hidden History of American Conservation*. Berkeley: University of California Press, 2001.

John, Gareth. "Image/Text/Geography: Yellowstone and the Spatial Rhetoric of Landscape." In *Observation Points: The Visual Poetics of National Parks*, ed. Thomas Patin, 140–64. Minneapolis: University of Minnesota Press, 2012.

Johnson, Walter. *The Broken Heart of America: St. Louis and the Violent History of the United States*. New York: Basic Books, 2020.

Jones, Karen. *Civilizing Nature: National Parks in Global Historical Perspective*. New York: Berghahn Books, 2015.

Kaczorowski, Robert J. "To Begin the Nation Anew: Congress, Citizenship, and Civil Rights after the Civil War." *The American Historical Review* 92, no. 1 (February 1987): 45–68.

_____. *The Politics of Judicial Interpretation: The Federal Courts, Department of Justice, and Civil Rights, 1866–1876*. New York: Fordham University Press, 2005.

Karuka, Manu. *Empire's Tracks: Indigenous*

Nations, Chinese Workers, and the Trans-continental Railroad. Oakland: University of California Press, 2019.

Kassis, Dimitrios. *Icelandic Utopia in Victorian Travel Literature.* Newcastle upon Tyne: Cambridge Scholars Publishing, 2016.

Keiter, Robert B. *To Conserve Unimpaired: The Evolution of the National Park Idea.* Washington, D.C.: Island Press, 2013.

Key, Sewall. "The Legal Work of the Federal Government." *Virginia Law Review* 25, no. 2 (December 1938): 165–201.

Khan, Yasmin Sabina. *Enlightening the World: The Creation of the Statue of Liberty.* Ithaca: Cornell University Press, 2010.

Kinsey, Joni L. "Shoshone Falls: The Niagara of the West." *SiteLINES: A Journal of Place* 10, no. 2 (Spring 2015): 16–18.

———. *Thomas Moran and the Surveying of the American West*, 2nd ed. Washington, D.C.: Smithsonian Books, 2012.

Knox, Page. "Publishing and Promoting a New York City Art World: *Scribner's Illustrated Monthly*, 1870–1881." In *New York: Art and Cultural Capital of the Gilded Age*, ed. Margaret R. Laster and Chelsea Bruner, 90–104. New York: Routledge, 2018.

Koile, Wendy. *Disasters of Ohio's Lake Erie Islands.* Charleston, S.C.: History Press, 2015.

LaDuke, Winona. *All Our Relations: Native Struggles for Land and Life.* Cambridge, Mass.: South End Press, 1999.

Landrum, J. B. O. *History of Spartanburg County.* Atlanta: Franklin Printing and Publishing Co., 1900.

Lang, Andrew F. "Republicanism, Race, and Reconstruction: The Ethos of Military Occupation in Civil War America." *Journal of the Civil War Era* 4, no. 4 (December 2014): 559–89.

Larson, Henrietta M. *Jay Cooke: Private Banker.* New York: Greenwood Press, 1968.

Lewis, Tom. *Washington: A History of Our National City.* New York: Basic Books, 2015.

Liestman, Daniel. "Utah's Chinatowns: The Development and Decline of Extinct Ethnic Enclaves." *Utah Historical Quarterly* 64, no. 1 (Winter 1996): 70–95.

Litwack, Leon F. *Trouble in Mind: Black Southerners in the Age of Jim Crow.* New York: Alfred A. Knopf, 1998.

Lubetkin, M. John. " 'No Fighting Is to Be Apprehended': Major Eugene Baker, Sitting Bull, the Northern Pacific Railroad's 1872 Western Yellowstone Surveying Expedition." *Montana: The Magazine of Western History* 56, no. 2 (Summer 2006): 28–41.

———. *Jay Cooke's Gamble: The Northern Pacific Railroad, the Sioux, and the Panic of 1873*. Norman: University of Oklahoma Press, 2006.

MacDonald, Douglas H. *Before Yellowstone: Native American Archaeology in the National Park*. Seattle: University of Washington Press, 2018.

Mack, Adam. *Sensing Chicago: Noisemakers, Strikebreakers, and Muckrakers*. Urbana-Champaign: University of Illinois Press, 2015.

Mackintosh, Barry, Janet A. McDonnell, and John H. Sprinkle, Jr. "Shaping the System: Before the National Park Service." *The George Wright Forum* 35, no. 2 (2018): 5–11.

Marsh, Kevin R. "Crossing Divides: An Environmental History of Idaho." In *A New History of the Gem State*, ed. Adam Sowards, 44–72. Seattle: University of Washington Press, 2014.

Martinez, J. Michael. *Carpetbaggers, Cavalry, and the Ku Klux Klan: Exposing the Invisible Empire During Reconstruction*. New York: Rowman & Littlefield, 2007.

Martyn, Henry. "History of the *Century Magazine*." *The Quarterly Illustrator* 1, no. 2 (Spring 1893): 93–96.

Mason, Kathy S. *Natural Museums: U.S. National Parks, 1872–1916*. Lansing: Michigan State University Press, 2004.

McConnell, Roland C. "Isaiah Dorman and the

Custer Expedition." *The Journal of Negro History* 33, no. 3 (July 1948): 344–52.

McCrady, David G. "Living with Strangers: The Nineteenth-Century Sioux and the Canadian-American Borderlands." PhD dissertation, University of Manitoba, 1998.

McFeely, William S. "Amos T. Akerman: The Lawyer and Racial Justice." In *Region, Race, and Reconstruction: Essays in Honor of C. Vann Woodward*, ed. J. Moran Kousser and James M. McPherson, 395–415. New York: Oxford University Press, 1982.

McKenzie, William A. *Dining Car to the Pacific: The 'Famously Good' Food of the Northern Pacific Railway*. Minneapolis: University of Minnesota Press, 1990.

Menard, Andrew. *Sight Unseen: How Frémont's First Expedition Changed the American Landscape*. Lincoln: Bison Books, 2012.

Menig, D. W. "The Mormon Culture Region: Strategies and Patterns in the Geography of the American West, 1847–1964." *Annals of the Association of American Geographers* 55, no. 2 (June 1965): 191–220.

Mercier, Laurie. "Creating a New Community in the North: Mexican Americans of the Yellowstone Valley." In *Montana: A Cultural Medley*, ed. Robert R. Swartout, Jr., 271–99. Helena, Mont.: Farcountry Press, 2015.

Meringolo, Denise D. *Museums, Monuments, and*

National Parks: Toward a New Genealogy of Public History. Amherst: University of Massachusetts Press, 2012.

Miller, Angela. "Everywhere and Nowhere: The Making of the National Landscape." *American Literary History* 4, no. 2 (Summer 1992): 207–29.

Mitchell, Martin. "Gentile Impressions of Salt Lake City, Utah, 1849–1870." *Geographical Review* 87, no. 3 (July 1997): 334–52.

Moran, Ruth B. "Letter." *The American Magazine of Art* (November 9, 1926): 645–46.

Morse, Kathryn. *The Nature of Gold: An Environmental History of the Klondike Gold Rush*. Seattle: University of Washington Press, 2003.

Morton, Frederick W. "Thomas Moran, Painter: Etcher." *Brush and Pencil* 7, no. 1 (October 1900): 1–7, 9–13, 15–16.

Munden, Christopher P. "Jay Cooke: Banks, Railroads, and the Panic of 1873." *Pennsylvania Legacies* 11, no. 1 (May 2011): 3–5.

Myers, Andrew H. "Prelude to Little Bighorn: The Seventh U.S. Cavalry in the South Carolina Upcountry." In *Recovering the Piedmont Past: Unexplored Moments in Nineteenth-Century Upcountry South Carolina History*, ed. Timothy P. Grady and Melissa Walker, 53–86. Columbia: University of South Carolina Press, 2013.

Nabokov, Peter. *American Indians and Yellowstone Park: A Documentary Overview.* Yellowstone National Park: National Park Service, 2002.

Nash, Roderick Frazier. *Wilderness and the American Mind,* 4th ed. New Haven: Yale University Press, 2001.

Naugle, Ronald C., John J. Montag, and James C. Olson. *History of Nebraska,* 4th ed. Lincoln: University of Nebraska Press, 2014.

Nelson, Megan Kate. *The Three-Cornered War: The Union, the Confederacy, and Native Peoples in the Fight for the West.* New York: Scribner, 2020.

Nelson, Scott Reynolds. "Livestock, Boundaries, and Public Space in Spartanburg: African American Men, Elite White Women, and the Spectacle of Conjugal Relations." In *Sex, Love, Race: Crossing Boundaries in North American History,* ed. Martha Hodes, 313–27. New York: New York University Press, 1999.

———. *Iron Confederacies: Southern Railways, Klan Violence, and Reconstruction.* Chapel Hill: University of North Carolina Press, 1999.

Newhall, Beaumont, and Diana Edkins. *William H. Jackson.* Fort Worth: Amon Carter Museum of Western Art and Morgan & Morgan, 1974.

Noonan, Mark J. "Modern Instances: Vanishing Women Writers and the Rise of Realism in *Century Illustrated Monthly Magazine*." *American Literary Realism* 42, no. 3 (Spring 2010): 192–212.

Novak, Barbara. *Nature and Culture: American Landscape and Painting, 1825–1875*, revised ed. New York: Oxford University Press, 1995.

O'Brien, Jean M. *Firsting and Lasting: Writing Indians out of Existence in New England.* Minneapolis: University of Minnesota Press, 2010.

Oberholtzer, Ellis Paxson. *Jay Cooke: Financier of the Civil War.* 2 vols. Philadelphia: George W. Jacobs & Co., 1907.

Ogden, Kate Nearpass. "Sublime Vistas and Scenic Backdrops: Nineteenth-Century Painters and Photographers at Yosemite." *California History* 69, no. 2 (Summer 1990): 134–53.

Oman, Kerry R. "The Beginning of the End: The Indian Peace Commission of 1867–1868." *Great Plains Quarterly* 22 (Winter 2002): 35–51.

Oravec, Christine L. "To Stand Outside Oneself: The Sublime in the Discourse of Natural Scenery." In *The Symbolic Earth: Discourse and the Creation of the Environment*, ed. James G. Cantrill and Christine L. Oravec,

58–75. Lexington: University Press of Kentucky, 1996.

Ostler, Jeffrey. *The Lakotas and the Black Hills: The Struggle for Sacred Ground.* New York: Penguin, 2010.

Ostrowski, Carl. *Books, Maps, and Politics: A Cultural History of the Library of Congress, 1783–1861.* Amherst: University of Massachusetts Press, 2004.

Paddison, Joshua. *American Heathens: Religion, Race, and Reconstruction in California.* Berkeley: University of California Press, 2012.

Painter, Nell Irvin. *The History of White People.* New York: W. W. Norton, 2010.

Parry, Mae. "History, Culture, and Traditions of the Northwestern Shoshone: Early History." In *Coyote Steals Fire: A Shoshone Tale.* Comp. and ed. The Northwestern Band of the Shoshone Nation, np. Logan, Utah: Utah State University Press, 2005.

_____. "The Northwestern Shoshone." In *History of Utah's American Indians*, ed. Forrest S. Cuch, 25–72. Boulder: University Press of Colorado, 2000.

Parsons, Elaine Frantz. *Ku-Klux: The Birth of the Klan during Reconstruction.* Chapel Hill: University of North Carolina Press, 2015.

Pauly, John J. "The Great Chicago Fire as a

National Event." *American Quarterly* 36, no. 5 (Winter 1984): 668–83.

Pearl, Matthew. "K Troop: The Untold Story of the Eradication of the Original Ku Klux Klan." *Slate* (March 4, 2016). http://www.slate.com/articles/news_and_politics/history/2016/03/how_a_detachment_of_u_s_army_soldiers_smoked_out_the_original_ku_klux_klan.html.

Peckham, Harry Houston. *Josiah Gilbert Holland in Relation to His Times*. Philadelphia: University of Pennsylvania Press, 1940.

Penot, Agnes. "The Perils and Perks of Trading Art Overseas: Goupil's New York Branch." *Nineteenth-Century Art Worldwide: A Journal of Nineteenth-Century Visual Culture* 16, no. 1 (Spring 2017). http://www.19thc-artworldwide.org/spring17/penot-on-the-perils-and-perks-of-trading-art-overseas-goupils-new-york-branch.

Platt, Susan. "Paradigms and Paradoxes: Nature, Morality, and Art in America." *Art Journal* 51, no. 2 (Summer 1992): 82–88.

Prince, K. Stephen. *Stories of the South: Race and Reconstruction of Southern Identity, 1865–1915*. Chapel Hill: University of North Carolina Press, 2014.

Proctor, Bradley D. " 'From the Cradle to the Grave': Jim Williams, Black Manhood, and Militia Activism in Reconstruction South

Carolina." *American Nineteenth Century History* 19, no. 1 (2018): 47–79.

Public Lands Foundation. "America's Public Lands: Origin, History, Future." Arlington, Va., December 2014. https://publicland.org /wp-content/uploads/2016/08/150359_Public _Lands_Document_web.pdf.

Pyle, David M. "Visions of Volcanoes." *19: Interdisciplinary Studies in the Long Nineteenth Century* 25 (2017): 1–30.

Richardson, Gary, and Tim Sablik. "Banking Panics of the Gilded Age, 1863–1913." *Federal Reserve History.* https://www.federal reservehistory.org/essays/banking-panics-of -the-gilded-age.

Richardson, Heather Cox. *How the South Won the Civil War.* New York: Oxford University Press, 2020.

———. *West from Appomattox: The Recon- struction of America after the Civil War.* New Haven: Yale University Press, 2007.

———. *Wounded Knee: Party Politics and the Road to an American Massacre.* New York: Basic Books, 2010.

Risch, Barbara. "The Picture Changes: Stylistic Variation in Sitting Bull's Biographies." *Great Plains Quarterly* 20 (Fall 2000): 259– 80.

Rogers, William Warren, Jr. " 'Not Reconstructed by a Long Ways Yet': Southwest Georgia's

Disputed Congressional Election of 1870."
Georgia Historical Quarterly 82, no. 2
(Summer 1998): 257–82.

Ross-Bryant, Lynn. "Sacred Sites: Nature
and Nation in the U.S. National Parks."
*Religion and American Culture: A Journal of
Interpretation* 15, no. 1 (Winter 2005): 31–
62.

Rudwick, Martin J. S. *Bursting the Limits of
Time: The Reconstruction of Geohistory in
the Age of Revolution.* Chicago: University of
Chicago Press, 2007.

Runte, Alfred. "Promoting the Golden West:
Advertising and the Railroad." *California
History* 70, no. 1 (Spring 1991): 62–75.

———. *Trains of Discovery: Railroads and
the Legacy of Our National Parks*, 5th ed.
New York: Roberts Rinehart, 2011.

Rust, Thomas C. *Watching over Yellowstone:
The US Army's Experience in America's
First National Park, 1886–1918.* Lawrence:
University Press of Kansas, 2020.

Rzeczkowski, Frank. "The Crow Indians and the
Bozeman Trail." *Montana: The Magazine of
Western History* 49, no. 4 (Winter 1999): 30–
47.

Sachs, Aaron. *The Humboldt Current:
Nineteenth-Century Exploration and the
Roots of American Environmentalism.* New
York: Oxford University Press, 2007.

Schuyler, David. *Sanctified Landscape: Writers, Artists, and the Hudson River Valley, 1820–1909*. Ithaca: Cornell University Press, 2012.

Scott, Kim Allen. *Yellowstone Denied: The Life of Gustavus Cheyney Doane*. Norman: University of Oklahoma Press, 2015.

Sellars, Richard West. *Preserving Nature in the National Parks: A History*. New Haven: Yale University Press, 1997.

Shapiro, Herbert. "The Ku Klux Klan During Reconstruction: The South Carolina Episode." *The Journal of Negro History* 49, no. 1 (January 1964): 34–55.

Shugerman, Jed Handelsman. "The Creation of the Department of Justice: Professionalization Without Civil Rights or Civil Service." *Stanford Law Review* 66, no. 1 (January 2014): 121–72.

Simkins, Francis B. "The Ku Klux Klan in South Carolina, 1868–1871." *The Journal of Negro History* 12, no. 4 (October 1927): 606–47.

Simpson, Brooks D. *Let Us Have Peace: Ulysses S. Grant and the Politics of War and Reconstruction, 1861–1868*. Chapel Hill: University of North Carolina Press, 1991.

_____. *The Reconstruction Presidents*. Lawrence: University Press of Kansas, 1998.

Slawson, Robert G. "Medical Training in the United States Before the Civil War." *Journal of Evidence-Based Complementary and Alternative Medicine* 17, no. 1 (2012): 11–27.

Smith, Stacey L. *Freedom's Frontier: California and the Struggle over Unfree Labor, Emancipation, and Reconstruction.* Chapel Hill: University of South Carolina Press, 2013.

Sneve, Virginia Driving Hawk. *Sioux Women: Traditionally Sacred.* Pierre: South Dakota Historical Society Press, 2016.

Spaulding, Norman W. "Professional Independence in the Office of the Attorney General." *Stanford Law Review* 60, no. 6 (April 2008): 1931–79.

Spence, Mark David. *Dispossessing the Wilderness: Indian Removal and the Making of the National Parks.* New York: Oxford University Press, 2000.

_____. "Dispossessing the Wilderness: Yosemite Indians and the National Park Ideal, 1864–1930." *Pacific Historical Review* 65, no. 1 (February 1996): 27–59.

Spinney, Robert G. *City of Big Shoulders: A History of Chicago,* 2nd ed. Ithaca: Cornell University Press, 2020.

Standing Bear, Luther. *Land of the Spotted Eagle.* 1933; Lincoln, Neb.: Bison Books, 2006.

Stiles, T. J. *Custer's Trials: A Life on the Frontier of a New America.* New York: Vintage, 2015.

Stockwell, Mary. *Interrupted Odyssey: Ulysses S.*

Grant and the American Indians. Carbondale: Southern Illinois University Press, 2018.

Stoll, Mark. "Milton in Yosemite: 'Paradise Lost' and the National Parks Idea." *Environmental History* 13, no. 2 (April 2008): 237–74.

Sudia, Theodore W. "National Parks and Domestic Affairs." *The George Wright Forum* 4, no. 4 (1986): 19–27.

Summers, Mark Wahlgren. *The Ordeal of Reunion: A New History of Reconstruction.* Chapel Hill: University of North Carolina Press, 2014.

Sweet, Jameson. "Native Suffrage: Race, Citizenship, and Dakota Indians in the Upper Midwest." *Journal of the Early Republic* 39, no. 1 (Spring 2019): 99–109.

The Missouri River Ecosystem: Exploring the Prospects for Recovery. National Academies Press, 2002. https://www.nap.edu/read/10277/chapter/3.

Thomson, David K. " 'Like a Cord through the Whole Country': Union Bonds and Financial Mobilization for Victory." *Journal of the Civil War Era* 6, no. 3 (September 2016): 347–75.

Tichi, Cecilia. "Pittsburgh at Yellowstone: Old Faithful and the Pulse of Industrial America." *American Literary History* 9, no. 3 (Autumn 1997): 522–41.

Tovías, Blanca. "A Blueprint for Massacre: The

United States Army and the 1870 Black-feet Massacre." In *Theatres of Violence: Massacre, Mass Killing, and Atrocity Throughout History*, ed. Philip G. Dwyer and Lyndall Ryan, 126–40. New York: Berghahn Books, 2012.

Trelease, Allen W. *White Terror: The Ku Klux Klan Conspiracy and Southern Reconstruction*. New York: Harper & Row, 1971.

Truettner, William H. " 'Scenes of Majesty and Enduring Interest': Thomas Moran Goes West." *The Art Bulletin* 58, no. 2 (June 1976): 241–59.

Tullidge, Edward William. *History of Salt Lake City*. Salt Lake City: Star Printing Company, 1886.

Urquhart, Frank John. *A History of the City of Newark, New Jersey*. Vol. II. New York: Lewis Historical Publishing Co., 1913.

Utley, Robert M. *Sitting Bull: The Life and Times of an American Patriot*. New York: Henry Holt, 1993.

Valencius, Conevery Bolton. *The Lost History of the New Madrid Earthquakes*. Chicago: University of Chicago Press, 2013.

Vecchio, Diane C. "From Slavery to Freedom: African-American Life in Post-Civil War Spartanburg." In *Recovering the Piedmont Past: Unexplored Moments in Nineteenth-*

Century Upcountry South Carolina History,
ed. Timothy P. Grady and Melissa Walker,
107–34. Columbia: University of South
Carolina Press, 2013.

Vestal, Stanley. *Sitting Bull: Champion of
the Sioux*. 1932; Norman: University of
Oklahoma Press, 1989.

Vetter, Jeremy. *Field Life: Science in the
American West during the Railroad Era*.
Pittsburgh: University of Pittsburgh Press,
2016.

Wagner, Virginia L. "Geological Time in
Nineteenth-Century Landscape Paintings."
Winterthur Portfolio 24, no. 2 (Summer–
Autumn, 1989): 153–63.

Wagoner, Page, Kristina Lanphear, and Edward
Solo. *Historic Architectural Survey of the City
of York: Final Report*. Atlanta: Brockington
and Associates, Inc., November 2008.
http://nationalregister.sc.gov/SurveyReports
/HC46001.pdf.

Waite, Kevin. *West of Slavery: The Southern
Dream of a Transcontinental Empire*. Chapel
Hill: University of North Carolina Press,
2021.

Walker, David. *Railroading Religion: Mormons,
Tourists, and the Corporate Spirit of the West*.
Chapel Hill: University of North Carolina
Press, 2019.

Wallach, Allan. "For a Social History of the

Hudson River School." *American Art* 31, no. 2 (Summer 2017): 43–45.

Waugh, Joan. *U.S. Grant: American Hero, American Myth*. Chapel Hill: University of North Carolina Press, 2009.

West, Elliott. *The Last Indian War: The Nez Perce Story*. New York: Oxford University Press, 2009.

White, Richard. "Information, Markets, and Corruption: Transcontinental Railroads in the Gilded Age." *Journal of American History* 90, no. 1 (June 2003): 19–43.

_____. *Railroaded: The Transcontinentals and the Making of Modern America*. New York: W. W. Norton, 2011.

Whittlesey, Lee H. " 'Everyone Can Understand a Picture': Photographers and the Promotion of Early Yellowstone." *Montana: The Magazine of Western History* 49, no. 2 (Summer 1999): 2–13.

Wilkins, Thurman, and Caroline Lawson Hinkley. *Thomas Moran: Artist of the Mountains*, 2nd ed. Norman: University of Oklahoma Press, 1998.

Williams, Kidada E. *They Left Great Marks on Me: African American Testimonies of Racial Violence from Emancipation to World War I*. New York: New York University Press, 2012.

Williams, Lou Faulkner. *The Great South*

Carolina Ku Klux Klan Trials, 1871–1872. Athens: University of Georgia Press, 1996.

Wilson, Randall K. *America's Public Lands: From Yellowstone to Smokey Bear and Beyond*, 2nd ed. New York: Rowman & Littlefield, 2020.

Wiswall, Mrs. E. A. "Art at the Capitol." *The Aldine* 7, no. 11 (November 1874): 212–13.

Wurst, LouAnn. " 'Human Accumulations': Class and Tourism at Niagara Falls." *International Journal of Historical Archaeology* 15, no. 2 (June 2011): 254–66.

Wyckoff, William. *How to Read the American West: A Field Guide.* Seattle: University of Washington Press, 2014.

Yenne, Bill. *Sitting Bull.* Yardley, Pa.: Westholme Publishing, 2008.

Zuczek, Richard. "The Federal Government's Attack on the Ku Klux Klan: A Reassessment." *The South Carolina Historical Magazine* 97, no. 1 (January 1996): 47–64.

About the Author

Megan Kate Nelson is a writer and historian living in Lincoln, Massachusetts. She has written about the Civil War, U.S. western history, and American culture for the *New York Times*, the *Washington Post*, *Smithsonian* magazine, and *The Atlantic*. Nelson earned her BA in history and literature from Harvard University and her PhD in American studies from the University of Iowa. Nelson is also the author of *The Three-Cornered War*, a finalist for the Pulitzer Prize; *Ruin Nation*; and *Trembling Earth*.

Center Point Large Print
600 Brooks Road / PO Box 1
Thorndike, ME 04986-0001 USA

(207) 568-3717

**US & Canada:
1 800 929-9108**
www.centerpointlargeprint.com